COLONIAL SUNSET, REPUBLICAN DAWN

COLONIAL SUNSET, REPUBLICAN DAWN

ELIZABETH BOSTOCK

Matador
9 Priory Business Park
Kibworth Beauchamp
Leicestershire LE8 0RX, UK
Tel: (+44) 116 279 2299
Fax: (+44) 116 279 2277
Email: books@troubador.co.uk
Web: www.troubador.co.uk/matador

ISBN 978 178462 3142

British Library Cataloguing in Publication Data.
A catalogue record for this book is available from the British Library.

Printed and bound in the UK by TJ International, Padstow, Cornwall
Typeset in 11pt Aldine401 BTRoman by Troubador Publishing Ltd, Leicester, UK

Matador is an imprint of Troubador Publishing Ltd

This book is dedicated to
my family and all my friends worldwide

CONTENTS

FOREWORD

I have always kept diaries, and that is why I have turned the pages back to a date when and where my association with Mark and Lif Bostock began: Tuesday 20th February 1973 in Colombo.

Let me put it in proper context. I was captain of the MCC England cricket team that had just scrapped its way through three-and-a-half exhausting months of the hardest cricket in the toughest land, India. We had lost 2-1 in 5 Test matches, but in those days there were no whistle-stop tours, but rather, the full perambulation, battling against state after state. In Colombo we were to continue the tour by playing matches in Ceylon over ten days, before setting off for another series in Pakistan. Ceylon did not enjoy Test-playing recognition in those days, but everyone knew what fine cricketers they were, graduating from excellent schools. I certainly did, because I had led a minor MCC tour out there three years earlier.

My first meaningful conversation in 1973 was with Mike Denness, my vice-captain. Would he lead the side for ten days so that I could clear my mind by relaxing away from cricket? In retrospect, it worked well, but perhaps better for Mike than for me, because, as I discovered, you would not select Mark Bostock to lead you to a world of peace through quiet contemplation. Here was an all-action Ceylon rugger player, skilled at hockey, golf and shooting, with an inventive turn of mind, which I spotted as we floated gently in a small craft, a few hundred yards from the mainland to a small island resort called Bentota. There were cords sloping back from boat to water that on closer inspection were towing bottles of what he called "a little refreshment".

Thus, on 20th February, I found myself with the rest of the MCC touring team, partying in the sunshine around a Bostock beach bungalow on idyllic sands, sea water for bathing, a fresh water lagoon for waterskiing and a never-ending passage of food and drink from shore into the mouths of England's cricket talent. I never again confused the notion of taking a peaceful break with Mark Bostock with hopes of sober silence and listlessness beneath palm trees. And yet, the sight of Lif waterskiing was the one graceful sensation of the day: a complete contradiction to the muscular efforts of Lancashire batsman Barry Wood, a novice attempting new skills, while half-submerged in water for fifty yards, before sinking. Barry blamed the boat for its lack of throttle.

The Bostocks – and this includes daughters Gillian and Claire – were always wonderful hosts to cricket visitors then and long after and on my frequent returns to Sri Lanka as a writer and broadcaster on cricket, the hospitality was forever generous. My own family, Joan, my wife, daughters Joanna and Anabel, retain wonderful memories of a Christmas spent at Bullers Lane with the Bostocks, or sleeping outdoors under mosquito nets in Chilaw, the beach house at the mouth of the Dedru Oya that Mark made, golf at Royal Colombo where Lif was twice the Ladies' captain as well as up in Nuwara Eliya alongside the Hill Club.

We were joined at one stage by Tim Rice, then of Super Star fame and his wife Jane, with children Eva and Donald plus nanny. Sri Lanka was so attractive and fun, but at the heart of it all were Mark and Lif Bostock and indeed, Mark and I had obvious links. We were both members of Marylebone Cricket Club and of the Royal and Ancient Golf Club of St Andrews. We had also both played decent rugby.

It was in golf that Mark's entrepreneurial zest has built a lasting monument to the Bostock family name. It was when he and Lif were in Wales with us that he told me about the plans he harboured for a super golf course and a resort – the magnificent development of the Victoria Golf and Country Club Resort at Kandy. He asked me about golf architects and I was able to support his instinct for entrusting the work to Donald Steel, an old college friend of mine while we were at Christ's College Cambridge. The inaugural Mark Bostock Memorial Trophy was held at Victoria in 2008.

Lif may not recall me as the most delicate houseguest because after a long evening of family charades up at the Aislaby estate in Bandarawela, it fell to me to act out the title of the John Le Carre book "The Naïve and Sentimental Lover". I cast around in all directions for vital words, revealing images or any action that would give a clue. In frustration, I had to sit down... heavily... on a glass tabletop, smashing it and sending splinters of glass all over the drawing room carpet.

Of such shambles, great friendships are made and it is a pleasure to introduce this book written by Lif, with over-the-shoulder interjections from Gillian, no doubt and urgings from Sydney by Claire.

It has been a pleasure to have played occasional but constant walk-on parts in their lives, and to respond to the touch of a glass in response to Mark's call for "LGT – First of the Day". Lif and Joan were never far behind us, but always with the vaguely disapproving yet ladylike expression of "if we cannot beat them, we may as well join them".

Tony Lewis
Porthcawl
Mid Glamorgan
Wales

ACKNOWLEDGEMENTS

My grateful thanks go to all those, whose input has been so encouraging. Firstly, all members of my immediate family; but also Tony Whitham, Donald Steel, Paul Manickam, Bent Hvidt, Wendy Partridge, JRM (Maurice) Perera, Tony Lewis, Bernard Cribbins, Sir John Nicholas, Errol Johnson and most of all David Llewellyn.

INTRODUCTION

This book had modest beginnings; it was originally intended as a family record of Mark Bostock's and my life, spent mainly in Ceylon/Sri Lanka. It is often said by succeeding generations that they regretted not asking a parent or grandparent about their lives. It was our daughter Gillian, who suggested Mark should write a memoire and introduced him to David Llewellyn, a reporter, to guide and encourage him.

Mark got so far, but finally gave up with a typical remark – "nobody wants to know about a silly old bugger like me!" His subsequent death meant it was my task to complete the manuscript. When I was first enthused by the idea of this biography I had no concept how much work and research would be required of me; it has been challenging, but also good fun.

It is with thanks to my new and now dear friend, David, that this record has been published. He believed that the interest in this memoire would stretch beyond the family, since historically it spanned Colonial rule in Ceylon to independence for Sri Lanka. David came up with the wonderful idea of beginning by separately covering each of our childhoods up until the time we met in Ceylon in 1952 – then chronicling our life together.

The book covers the history and political events that impacted on the Bostock family during a period of more than 100 years on the island country which we all came to love.

Elizabeth Bostock
Crowborough, England 2015

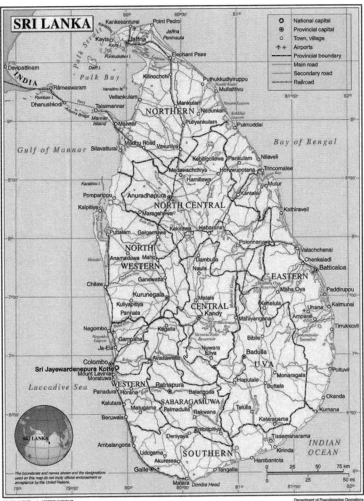

SRI LANKA

⊚	National capital
◉	Provincial capital
○	Town, village
✈ ✈	Airports
——	Provincial boundary
	Main road
	Secondary road
	Railroad

Kankesanturai
Point Pedro
Jaffna Peninsula
Kayts
Kayts I.
Karaitivu I.
Jaffna
Punkudutivu I.
Elephant Pass
Palk Strait

Devipattinam
INDIA
Palk Bay
Kilinochchi
Puthukkudiyiruppu
Mullaittivu

Rámeswaram
Pamban I.
Iranaitivu Is.
Vellankulam
Mankulam
Nedunkeni
Kokkilai Lagoon
Pulmoddai

Dhanushkodi
Talaimannar
Mannar Island
Mannar
Pooneryn
Pullyankulam
NORTHERN
Nanthi Kadal
Nayaru Lagoon

Gulf of Mannar
Silavattural
Madhu Road
Vavuniya
Kebitigollewa
Pankulam
Nilaveli
Bay of Bengal

Medawachchiya
Horuwupotana
Trincomalee
Koddiyar Bay

Karaitivu I.
Pomparippu
Anuradhapura
Hamilewa
Mutur

Kalpitiya
Maragahewa
NORTH CENTRAL
Kantalai
Kathiraveli

Puttalam
Galgamuwa
Kakirawa
Habarane
Polonnaruwa
Valachchenai

NORTH WESTERN
Anamaduwa
Maho
Dambulla
Naula
Minneriya Tank
Chenkaladi
Batticaloa

Chilaw
Ganewatta
EASTERN
Maha Oya
Paddiruppu

Kuliyapitiya
Kurunegala
Matale
Kehelula
Uhana
Kalmunai

Pannala
CENTRAL
Kandy
Mahiyangana
Amparai
Tirrukkovil

Negombo
Gampaha
Kegalla
Victoria Falls Reservoir
Bibile
Senanayake Samudra

Ja-Ela
Nuwara Eliya
Badulla

Colombo
Avissawella
UVA
Pottuvil

Sri Jayewardenepura Kotte
Mount Lavinia
Moratuwa
Haputale
Monaragala

Laccadive Sea
WESTERN
Ratnapura
Buttala

Panadura
Horana
Balangoda
Okanda

Kalutara
Matugama
SABARAGAMUWA
Pelmadulla
Rakwana
Tellula
Kumana

Beruwala
Deniyaya
Embilipitiya
Kataragama

Ambalangoda
Udugama
Tissamaharama
INDIAN OCEAN

Akuressa
SOUTHERN
Kirinda

Galle
Tangalla
Hambantota

Matara
Dondra Head

| 0 | 25 | 50 | 75 km |
| 0 | 25 | 50 ml | |

SRI LANKA

Map No. 4172 Rev. 1   UNITED NATIONS
January 2004

Department of Peacekeeping Operations
Cartographic Section

1

VIKINGS AND PIRATES

By the time Mark Bostock gave up smoking, at the age of 11, he had already begun the chronicle of his life and his adventures along the way. True to his Viking roots however, the young Bostock employed the 20th Century equivalent of a *'skald'* or Norse poet-cum-scribe, to commit the adventures of his childhood to paper.

Apparently, while at his prep school Mark would narrate his version of a 'Book at Bedtime' for his fellow pupils in his dormitory. A surprisingly lengthy manuscript, carefully typed by a loyal friend, whose name – illegibly scrawled on one page of the typescript – appears to be John Kay, has survived from those days. It is entitled 'M Bostock's Jungle Life in Ceylon'.

In his preface the assiduous typist states: 'When M C Bostock first told his … stories in the school dormitory, they proved so interesting that I thereupon resolved to make a book, or, at least a story or two about his jungle life.'

The third tale in Kay's book details a whimsical account of Mark's birth. It is early morning in the Bostock household in Ceylon and Mr Bostock, who has been snoring, wakes up suddenly: 'Mr Bostock started up in bed, put on his bedroom slippers and ran along to Eve's [his daughter] bedroom where there was a cot and when he got to the cot a Baby lay in it! Mr Bostock rejoiced. He skipped (not ran for he was too joyous) along to Mrs Bostock's bedroom where she lay, eating roast potatoes. ... "... come and see," panted Mr Bostock. ... "I can't, I must finish my roast potatoes." "That doesn't matter, just come along, because MARK IS BORN!'"

It is a delightful interpretation of birth, the mysterious, miraculous appearance of the baby Mark in a cot in his sister's bedroom, and an enduring image of his mother's languid not to say utterly relaxed state at such a momentous time, apparently reading a book and reluctant to go to the cot because she has a hole in her slippers. The fevered imagination of a pre-pubescent boy, fired by the bible and divine conception. Mark was clearly happy with this concept of conception and the description of the birth of his second sister, Ruth, follows a similar pattern, the only difference on this occasion that the cot in which she is discovered is in Mark's bedroom, rather than Eve's.

Mark then led his school chums through his Christening, at which he lists a number of guests and accompanies it with what is captioned as a 'squared' map of Ceylon. This ceremony is followed by 'Mark's First Ceylonese Adventure' which involves a lion (not a creature generally found there, but given its size and ferocity, it was the minimum requirement to satisfy the appetite for excitement of the eager listeners, who, in any event would have been ignorant of the wildlife of Ceylon) and the front stairs and back stairs of the Bostock family home; the flights of stairs themselves are turned into props for moments of high farce with Mark's parents falling down them and tripping over each other's bodies at the bottom.

The leonine tale was clearly such a success that Mark included a tree leopard in his next story which has him visiting an Up-Country bungalow. The second part of the story sees Mark shooting and killing an elephant.

Given the gene pool from which he sprang, perhaps it is little surprise that he had such a zest for adventure and story-telling from such an early age.

The actual facts surrounding his birth are a trifle more mundane and a little less dramatic than the version recorded by his faithful *skald*. Mark Bostock was born in Sri Lanka, which was then known, in 1926, as Ceylon, the second child of Norman Sandeman Bostock and Elizabeth Bostock (née Pyman), and sadly there was no grand proclamation of his arrival, although his mother was most certainly not reading a book at the time of the event.

It was quite a family into which he was born, one which could trace its roots back to the Vikings, something to which Mark later proudly referred in a letter to a distant relative, Edward Bostock – a member of the Burma Bostocks, as opposed to the Ceylon Bostocks. Mark wrote: 'We Bostocks are Vikings – bloody pirates!' It clearly captured his imagination.

He went on to explain to Edward: 'The first record of our lineage commences with the Viking de Bötha, who sailed from, I think, Esbjerg on the West Coast of Denmark, commanding three long boats. They rounded the North Cape and sailed down the West Coast of Scotland, pillaging as they went. I can't imagine that they picked up anything worthwhile in 850AD down that coast, but I suppose they might have had a bit of fun in Glasgow! The three Viking boats sailed further south before turning in at the Mersey and proceeding up a small river, now called The Dane, for obvious reasons.

'They grounded at the first foot and cattle crossing and de Bötha and his clansmen set up his stockade. This was then called de Bötha's Stockade, which eventually became Botestock and finally, Bostock. Gradually they became integrated into the countryside. In 1066 Sir Ralph de Bostock was involved in a skirmish near Hastings and I think he was on the winning side, which probably accounted for his knighthood. They then became the Bostocks of Bostock Green on the river Dane in the County of Cheshire.'

As it turned out William the Conqueror gave the Bostock land to a fellow Norman who took his name from the place whence he came in Normandy, the village of Vernon. According to the Domesday Book the Bostock land at that time was owned by a Saxon named Osmer, although it is far more likely that the landowner would have been of Danish stock.

Mark was extremely enthusiastic about his family history and chronicled their progress into the modern day, although it was his father's cousin Francis 'Fronnie' Bostock, a resident of Cape Town, who did the hard graft. He delved into the past in a truly thorough manner, digging deeply to unearth the family's roots and produce an impressive family tree, which reveals a direct bloodline that can be traced all the way back to King Edward III, embracing Jane Seymour, third wife of Henry VIII, and the Percy family – the Earls of Northumberland, Hotspur and all that – and the Earls of Egremont along the way. Understandably Mark, ever hungry for evidence of his family's roots, wrote longingly at one point: 'I wish I could lay my hands on the scrolls of parchment in Cousin Fronnie's hand, because he had found that the Bostocks were linked to the monarchy in the 13th and 14th Centuries – not that that was possibly a sterling reputation.' Fortunately those 'scrolls' were eventually unearthed.

As the Elizabethan era drew to a close Fronnie's diligent research revealed that the Bostocks "... spread themselves over Cheshire and other parts of England as minor gentry and yeoman farmers, with one branch ending up in Chevening in Kent. That was Mark's seventh Great Grandfather Samuel Bostock. An important London branch of the family was based in Dartford and there is a brass effigy on the floor by the Chancel steps in Dartford Church of Captain Arthur Bostock and his wife and children, all kneeling. Interestingly Arthur was the son of Charles Bostock, Master of the Scrivener's Company and his secretary was John Milton, father of the poet also John Milton.

Mark revealed the origin of the family Coat of Arms. 'Somerset House records show that it was about that time [the mid-17th Century] that we were granted our coat of arms and the family motto – *Frangas Non Flectes* [Tr: You may break me, but you shall not bend me]. Lionel Bostock, who was the youngest Brevet Colonel at that time in the First World War, went on to administer Southern Sudan, while my Grandfather and father were in South Africa – all of them old colonials. It was Lionel who commented that for a colonial our motto was damned silly and inappropriate, as all the people we dealt with were bamboos who swayed with the wind, not oak trees, which would never yield to the elements. Lionel used to say of our motto: "A Bostock is often broke but he is never caught bending"!

"A bastard line of Bostocks settled in the Norfolk area but they were only entitled to wear a part of our rather complicated coat of arms. I am the male end of our true lineage, but there is a distant cousin of the same line living in New Zealand."

Moving forward a couple of centuries and it can be revealed that the latterday 'Viking' who travelled as far as Ceylon in the 19th Century was Mark's Grandfather John Henry Bostock, a civil engineer, who, while working for the eminent 19th Century civil engineer Sir John Coode, had been responsible, among other things, for the construction of Dover Harbour. Civil engineering was something of a family speciality in those far-off days, because J H Bostock's father, John Stileman Bostock, was also an engineer.

In 1894, journeying a little further than his Scandinavian forebears, J H Bostock was appointed by the Ceylon Government to be the Resident Engineer of the harbour works in Colombo.

In the 16 years that he held the post J H Bostock was responsible for building the extension to the South West breakwater in Colombo Harbour, from the junction at the Pilot's Station to the lighthouse end, as well as overseeing the building of the Island Breakwater. In addition John Henry Bostock was also responsible for the construction of a graving dock 700 feet in length, coaling jetties (of which more in a moment), reclamation and a patent, or marine railway, slipway capable of taking vessels of 1,200 tons weight.

John Henry Bostock lived in a magnificent mansion below the Cathedral, Church of Christ, Mutwal. In those days Mutwal was a select residential district of Colombo, and therefore *the* place to live. There were five acres of garden and a very spacious bungalow, but the Bostocks did have the odd problem with the setting. For example, for the duration of the South-West monsoon the bungalow would fill with coal dust. This was because just below the bungalow were situated the aforementioned coaling jetties (engineer for these one J H Bostock), and during discharge the monsoon winds would pluck up the coal dust and cover the whole of that area including the church, with an unsightly and unwelcome black coating.

J H Bostock's son Norman, Mark's father, had been born in Horsham, West Sussex and having attended Marlborough

College, did not settle permanently in Ceylon until he had finished his schooling in 1910. Sadly his father had died in this same year, on April 12th, aged 63, from dengue fever and was buried in Kanatte Cemetery.

An obituary in the journal of the Institution of Civil Engineers, to which he had been elected as a member in May 1878, described J H Bostock as: "A man of high character," adding, "Mr Bostock was greatly respected in Ceylon. Although a strict disciplinarian on the works, he possessed singular qualities when dealing with labour and its troubles and was beloved by his staff and by the [labour]."

On his arrival in Colombo in 1910 Norman Bostock joined Hayley and Kenny, an import/export company, where he worked until 1914 and the outbreak of the First World War; at which point he returned to England and joined the South Staffordshire Regiment, and had a distinguished service. That Norman survived the war is remarkable, since he was twice decorated for bravery, winning the Military Cross and bar, as well as being mentioned in despatches three times. Acts of bravery accorded such accolades had every chance of being recognised posthumously, but Norman survived life-threatening situations on every occasion. He attained the rank of Major and on demobilisation in 1920, he returned to Ceylon, where he briefly picked up his career with Hayley and Kenny.

Not long after that though he moved to Aitken Spence where he was a senior assistant in the shipping department.

It was around this time that Norman met his wife-to-be, Elizabeth Pyman. Mark has recorded an anecdote of his father's pursuit of Elizabeth, a chase around the globe which further underlined the resourcefulness of his father, one of the many attributes of his character, which must therefore have been inherited by his son.

According to Mark it was "... a rather amusing story ...", but actually it had a broad vein of romanticism running through it, but perhaps that was not Mark's style to recognise the romantic in his father. Romantic or humorous it certainly bears telling, and, for the most part, in Mark's words:

"There were two well known, middle-aged bachelors in Colombo in those days," he began. "They were Oswin Wickwar, who was in Harrisons and Crosfield, and A. J. Wickwar, who was the Surveyor General. They hailed from West Hartlepool in County Durham in England; and Elizabeth Pyman's father, Frederick Haigh Pyman, was a ship-owner and a ship-builder, and whose business was based in West Hartlepool, although his home was over the border in North Yorkshire.

"Frederick Pyman decided to send his two daughters, Ruth and Elizabeth, on a round-the-world tour after World War One, as a gesture of gratitude for their war-time service, which they spent helping to nurse the disabled soldiers in the mansion of one of his relatives, in the Marches of Wales. Incidentally, my mother, Elizabeth Pyman, was awarded the MBE for her nursing service.

"My grandfather on my maternal side told his two old friends the Wickwars to look after his two daughters on their arrival in Ceylon, and so they were taken on numerous jungle, shooting and exploratory expeditions, where they were joined frequently by my father.

"When they returned to England Norman decided to follow them and hopped on to the next Bibby Line boat and chased the two sisters up to Yorkshire, to old man Pyman's family home Dunsley Hall near Whitby."

Despite Mark seeing the funny side of it, that must have been a daunting journey for the young Norman, travelling so far to ask for the hand of the daughter of an eminent man he had never met before. The Pyman shipping business had been founded by Frederick's father George, who had had Dunsley Hall built for his son in the very early 1900s – these days it is a privately run country house hotel.

Mark continued: "At the time no one in the Bostock family had a clue which of the two sisters my father wished to marry. In the end though it turned out to be Elizabeth Pyman, whose hand he had sought, and my father proposed to her in the garden of a country vicarage in a village called Aislaby, in Co. Durham, not far from the Pyman home."

Aislaby has an entry in the Domesday Book, the lands were apparently owned by the Count of Mortain, and the survey was ordered by William I in 1085. The translated entry reads: "In Aislaby (near Whitby) are 3 carucates to the geld, and there could be two ploughs. Uhtraed had 1 manor there. Now Richard Sordeval has it of the count. There are six acres of meadow, (and) pasture 1 league long and 1 broad. TRE (it was worth) 10s.8p [53p] now it is waste."

A carucate was notionally the land that could support one family. It consisted of 120 acres, ie an amount that could be tilled by an eight-ox plough team. The geld was a tax value. A league is approximately 1½ miles, while TRE means 'in the time of King Edward', which was accepted for the purpose of the survey as being January 1066 and 'now' refers to the time of the survey in 1086. The reference to 'waste' is believed to mean that a great drop in value had taken place due to a catastrophic fall in population and economic resources.

Aislaby, pronounced 'azelbee' in Yorkshire (the tea estate is pronounced 'aze-labee' by the Bostock family), is a long village of stone buildings set on a hill overlooking the River Esk. At the time that the courageous Norman Bostock was getting down on one knee in the garden of the vicarage to propose to his future wife in the very early 1920s, the church of St Margaret was barely in its twenties, having been rebuilt in 1897 to replace an earlier chapel that had been constructed in the late 18th Century. However, the newness of the church could not detract from the overall attraction of the village and so taken were Norman and Elizabeth with Aislaby, that they were to name a tea estate after it, as a lasting memorial to the start of their romance.

2

BOUNDARIES
AND
BOARDERS

Norman Bostock married Elizabeth Pyman at St Michael's, Polwatte, an area of Colombo, on March 18th 1922. The wedding reception was held at the prestigious Prince's Club (as it was then known) on the Racecourse, although it very nearly didn't. Norman had to submit a comprehensive guest list, which included two people of mixed race, known in Ceylon as 'Burghers'. These were half Dutch, half Singhalese. One of these people of mixed race was an eminent King's Counsel, Noel Gratiaen. On seeing these two 'burghers' the committee members felt that their inclusion crossed the social boundaries and so they informed Norman that they had to be taken off the guest list, because the Prince's Club policy was not to admit people of mixed race.

Being an enlightened man, Norman put his foot down and threatened not only to resign his membership but would make public the reason for such a stance. Reason prevailed and they were able to celebrate their wedding in style in the Prince's club with *all* of their close friends and relatives.

The honeymoon was spent at the Railway bungalow, courtesy of Norman's aunt Miriam, John Henry Bostock's eldest daughter, who had married Geoffrey Philip Greene, who by then had become the General Manager of the

Railways (GMR). The Railway Bungalow was up-country in Pattipola, and it was the scene of a rather distressing incident for the young honeymooners, although yet again the bravery of Norman Bostock was once more in evidence.

According to Mark there was a very tame sambhur, a large deer, which used to frequent the garden. Mark explained: "It was considered a pet by my grandfather. The Bogawantalawa planters, who were a rough, tough old lot used to hunt pig and sambhur with a motley pack of hounds, and having drawn the Elk Plains with no success they remembered this pet sambhur at Pattipola and so they set these hounds on to this luckless animal.

'When finally exhausted after the chase, this fine animal came back to the safety of the Pattipola bungalow and actually entered the house and stood its ground in a bathroom. My father confronted this mob of planters and told them that it was private property and ordered them out, whereupon they told him that if they weren't allowed to do their worst they would set their pack of pariahs on him if he didn't clear out. During the altercation some of the hounds managed to get into the bathroom and the poor sambhur was dragged down and killed."

The honeymooning couple soon got over the incident and according to Mark had great fun doing the shopping for food. The bungalow was in a remote place and difficult to access by road but was quite close to the railway, Mark wrote: "My parents had enormous fun provisioning themselves. There was a 'bogey' which consisted of a flat timber platform on four wheels with a handbrake. My father and mother used to push this bogey on to the incline just a hundred yards or so from the Pattipola station – the highest point on the railway line, after which it was all downhill to Colombo – and then, once on the downhill railtrack, which went all the way to Bandarawela, they used to roll along, adjusting the speed of their vehicle by judicious application of the handbrake.

"Once in Bandarawela they would free-wheel into a siding, before jumping off the bogey and heading off to do their shopping. On their return in the afternoon they would pile their purchases onto the bogey's flatbed, then they would latch the contrivance on to the end of the night mail train to Colombo, which would then tow them all the way back to Pattipola where they unhitched in the evening."

There was little doubt that Mark's father was something of a 'man-of-action'. Norman Bostock had not long been married when the following incident took place.

"My father was on duty for Aitken Spence on a pontoon out in the harbour during the South-West Monsoon when the sea was rough. Passengers were climbing the gangway from the pontoon, one of these, an elderly lady, suddenly slipped, and fell between the pontoon and ship's side. Without considering his personal safety my father jumped on this old lady's head and swam her out, underneath the pontoon to safety, just before the pontoon smashed against the ship's side, which would certainly have been the end for the old girl.

"For his trouble Norman Bostock never received a word of thanks from the old lady whose life he had saved, and the gold cigarette case which was his wedding present from his wife slipped out of his pocket and is still somewhere on the bottom of Colombo Harbour."

The year following his marriage saw Norman leave Aitken Spence, to join the broking firm of Keell and Waldock. Norman was a keen sportsman and played rugby, at centre, and hockey, where he was a centre half. The two partners of Keell and Waldock, Watty Keell and Harold Waldock had formed the halfback combination for Colombo Hockey and

Football Club's Rugby First XV for a decade or so in their youth, and they were therefore always ready to recruit keen sportsmen for their company. In those early days in the 1920s the office of Keell & Waldock was housed in the modest setting of the Millers Building in the Fort area. It was only later that the firm moved into more spacious accommodation in Ceylinco House, before finally settling in Glennie Street.

Watty Keell was, by all accounts, quite a character, and apparently he used to appear regularly dressed in a very military style. Later, when Mark joined the firm after demobilisation, Watty was to prove an able teacher and an invaluable mentor as the young man began his education in the tea industry in earnest.

By the mid-1920s Norman had become a father with the birth of his first child Eve, then along came Mark Cresswell Bostock. He emerged into an unsuspecting world on September 21st 1926, in the rented family home of Sweden Bank, Alexandra Place, Colombo 7. Another sister, Ruth, followed on October 18th 1928, there was then a slightly longer gap before the emergence of Hugh, a younger brother for Mark, on June 22nd 1931. Tragically, when he was just 18 months old Hugh succumbed to dengue fever, just as his grandfather had done almost two decades earlier and was buried alongside John Henry Bostock in Kanatte Cemetery.

Hugh's death made enough of an impression on Mark to warrant a brief tale, as told to John Kay. 'Now it happened that Mark slept in the same bedroom as Hugh to keep him company. ... one night a wild cat came in through the window and by the noise as it broke the glass of the window, it woke Hugh out of his peaceful dream. Through Hugh's shouting he woke up Mark, who, hearing the shouts and seeing a ghostly figure crawling about the floor, shot, hit and killed it. He turned on the electric light so that he might see his victim ... Mark rushed to the bed where Hugh was. The bed bars were broken. Hugh died afterwards though.' It is almost as if Mark felt he was somehow involved, if not partially to blame for Hugh's death, and it forms a sad little footnote to the tragic death of the youngest Bostock.

Had it not been for the swift response of Norman there could well have been more deaths in the family, he decided it would be prudent to move the remainder of the family up-country, out of the danger area of this mosquito borne disease also known as breakbone fever.

In the early years Mark and his two sisters were looked after by an English Nanny, who was married at that time to a soldier called Buckle. Nan, as she was fondly called, remained in the family's service long after the three children had grown up, although by the time Mark had children of his own she had given up 'nannying' and instead performed other domestic duties for the next generation of the family.

Nanny Buckle was quite a character, there was one famous occasion when Norman entered the servants' sitting room and spied Nan filling in her coupon for the 'Pools'. "What are you doing wasting your money on that kind of gambling?" he remarked. To which Nan replied: "And what about that pink newspaper that you study every week?" This was a reference to Norman's copy of the Financial Times, where he followed closely his investments in stocks and shares, and since this was, in its own way, as much of a gamble as the 'pools' Norman, wisely, made no response to Nan's riposte.

It was during the 1920s that Norman began purchasing land. According to Mark, his father: "... started by buying land three miles out, north of Bandarawela, combining forces with A.J. Wickwar, but while AJ bought his land on the right-hand side of the then Gansabawa path running from Bandarawela to Attampitiya, my father bought land on the left-hand side. AJ's property was known as Malwatte and Norman called his estate Aislaby after the village in Yorkshire where he had proposed to my mother.

"My father used to supervise the planting at Aislaby at weekends. He used to climb aboard his Rudge-Whitworth motorcycle after the office had closed at 1 o'clock on Saturdays and drive through Ratnapura and on up the Haputale Pass on this strange machine, which was driven by a rubber belt from the engine to the rear wheel.

"In monsoon weather, with the rain pouring down, the belt used to slip frequently on the Haputale Pass, thus bringing the motorbike to an unscheduled halt, and Norman would be forced to dismount and shove his machine up the road until the gradient slackened enough so that he was able to mount again and continue at a slightly faster pace astride his machine.

"On a Sunday night after supervising the planting of Aislaby and the building of the factory, he would motor-bike into Bandarawela, and put the Rudge-Whitworth on to the train, having left only a thimbleful of petrol in the tank, which was a privilege allowed him by his brother-in-law, Geoffrey Greene, the General Manager of the Railways, because no vehicle was meant to be taken on to a train with any combustible fuel in it. Then, early on the Monday morning, when the train pulled into Maradana station, father, in his office whites, would push his motorbike out of the station and make his way into the office in Australia Building in the Fort. They were tough pioneers in those days."

The young Mark showed an interest in sport from a very early age. He was especially fascinated by cricket, and until a garden coolie sawed off a convenient branch, which overlooked the Sinhalese Sports Club Ground's cricket pitch, while sitting at the wrong side of it, Mark had the perfect seat from which to watch matches unfold and many happy hours were spent on this lofty perch.

He was very much his father's boy, and was apparently so devastated to be leaving his father that when the time came for him aged six to head for prep school in England, he tried to squeeze himself through the porthole of his cabin and jump ship on to the tender from which his father was waving him goodbye. Of course he did not succeed in this endeavour. According to the 'Chronicle' as written by his fellow prep school pupil, Mark's sister Ruth was also upset at her brother having to go away to boarding school.

The school that Mark Bostock was sent to in 1933 was Heathfield School, in Keston on the outskirts of Bromley in Kent.

His first letter home, in response to one from his sister Ruth was so short that one of his teachers, Miss Garvey, had to write a PS to it in which she apologised for its brevity.

John Kay recorded a conversation he had with Mark in the early days of the young Bostock's boarding school life in which Mark asks: 'I suppose you know I'm Ceylonese?' When the answer is received in the affirmative, according John Kay Mark then asked: 'Shall I tell stories ... in the dormitory?'

It was this same John Kay who wrote out a list of the daily routine in order to help Mark settle in. The list begins: '1 Maid comes in. 2 You get up. 3 You wash. 4 You dress – at this point Mark interrupts with an optimistic 'then you have breakfast'. 'No' comes the answer. And Kay continues: 5 You go downstairs to the schoolroom. 6 Mr Hallam says prayers. 7 *Then* breakfast.' The timetable continues in similar vein until bedtime, 45th instruction on the list.

Kay refers to himself as Mark's 'one friend out of all his schoolboy enemies' a possible veiled implication, taken in conjunction with reference to the fact that he was Ceylonese, that the six-year-old Mark was being bullied because of his newness and/or his nationality. It is doubtful that he was bullied for long however, because, new boy or not, Ceylonese or not, Mark Cresswell Bostock was a natural sportsman, and prowess on the games field is one of the quickest ways to win friends and convert enemies.

The pupils were apparently only based in Keston for Mark's first term, before, Mr Hallam, the headmaster, moved the establishment lock, stock and pupils some 30 miles to the south, to Hurst Green in East Sussex, at Boarzell. It was here that Mark's sporting prowess came to the fore. He excelled at high hurdles and rugby and captained the school's First XV as well as playing for the school's cricket First XI. He was also a keen shot and was in the shooting VIII.

In these formative years Mark spent many school holidays with his cousins. For the main part his uncles were all fortunate enough to own large homes, chiefly in Northumberland. Slaley Hall was the home of his Uncle Lindsay and Aunty Ruth. All the cousins spent the most wonderful holidays there, sometimes there were so many children that they were even able to form their own family ice hockey team, and they regularly used to challenge the youthful occupants of neighbouring homes to matches. But it was not all play for the children on these holidays. On one occasion the boys were all put to work on the land, which included digging their swimming pool, and once it was finished, keeping it clean.

The other home that proved a great base for holidaying was Dunsley Hall, residence of Uncle Cress and Auntie Gwen 'Pinsie' The cousins on the Pyman family were June (nicknamed Tickle), Mike, who was blessed with a number of nicknames among them 'Wiggy' and 'Ats Boy'. Mark's sobriquet was 'Omar' as in Omar Khayyam 'Oh Mark I am'. The author of all these nicknames was Uncle Cress, who was also responsible for Eve, Mark's older sister being dubbed Sue – a relic of the days when she was toddler in Ceylon and Uncle Cress had overheard her Nanny encouraging her to use the potty by saying 'soo, soo'.

It was during these times that Mark was first introduced to shooting and had drilled into him the discipline of owning and carrying a shotgun. Safety first was the order of the day and he was made to carry his unloaded piece in the company of the gamekeeper and to go through the drill of breaking the gun and unloading it when going through gates and over stiles and fences, then re-loading once the obstacle had been cleared. He developed into a very good shot, so much so that when he was a little older one of his uncles even called on Mark's skill with a rifle by asking him to help with the culling of deer on his estate.

Mark was also introduced to fly-fishing during these family get-togethers. He took it up in 1941, following in his father's footsteps, and he was to enjoy many a happy day on the River Kennett and, later in life in Ireland when he would be accompanied by his brother-in-law Mike Thornton where they spent their holidays fishing on the river Eriff. The Eriff was famous for the Asleigh falls which was a well-known salmon leap.

Inevitably it was during the family holidays that Mark had his brief flirtation with another product of the British colonies – tobacco. He used to recount, with a mischievous glint in his eye, how he and his cousin Mike Pyman would head off to the moors to collect heather and various other weeds that caught their fancy. These they would take back home and mix them, together with a few strands of real pipe tobacco filched from their fathers' pouches, and then the pair would roll their own cigarettes.

The smoking habit did not last long, however, and one day they felt really sick. The fathers quickly realised what was amiss and insisted that after dinner the two boys join the men in the billiard room to be scorers for the evening. The air was made thick with the smoke of pipes and cigars and after an hour or so in this fug the boys felt even worse. Which is when the 11-year-old Mark for one, gave up the habit. A decision that was just as well, because had he persisted in smoking it is doubtful whether, in later years, Mark would have become one of the finest tea tasters of his generation in Ceylon, since a 'clean' palate is a prerequisite for tea-tasters.

From Boarzell Mark went on to Marlborough College, where he was in Littlefield House. Early on it emerged that he had a remarkably good singing voice, so the choir master tried to persuade Mark to join the choir, but that meant having to choose between the choir and cricket and that was no contest as far as Mark was concerned. He actually featured in most team sports while at Marlborough and for many years he held the high hurdles record for the school. But it was not all play at Marlborough and Mark's academic ability saw him acquire six credits in his seven School Certificate examinations. An amusing incident occurred many years later as a direct result of Mark's prowess at high hurdles. Mark was seated in one of the leading hotel in Colombo with his back to the entrance when he heard a voice saying "Bostock – it is Mark Bostock, isn't it? Mark turned round and was confronted by a chap he did not immediately recognize who explained that he always used to come second behind Mark in the high hurdles at Marlborough and that he recognized Mark by the back of his ears! Mark had quite protruding ears at the time which, according to his elder daughter, Gillian, 'he grew into" in older age.

In the sixth form Mark found himself sharing a study with two other pupils, Ken Atkin and Michael Sparkes. The former eventually became a House Prefect, which gave him the authority to punish junior boys, including applying the cane. Ken, who was a left-hander, did not have a particularly good aim with the cane, so he practised his strokes on the luckless Mark, invariably leaving his 'practice target' black and blue everywhere except where the cane was supposed to land. The genial Michael Sparkes was a tall, gangly fellow and throughout his schooldays found himself the butt of innumerable public school pranks, but the uncomplaining victim took all of it in good part. Coincidentally all three study companions would be reunited in Ceylon in adulthood. Ken went to work for Keell and Waldock, thanks to Norman Bostock, while Michael ended up as a tea planter in Ceylon.

3

GETTING A
TASTE FOR LIFE ...
AND TEA

Mark departed Marlborough in 1944, with the country still deeply involved in the Second World War. Young men were ever keen to volunteer. Many of his school friends were a year older than Mark and were therefore 18 when they stepped up to volunteer for the military and serve their country, but Mark did not want to be left out and although he was still only 17 when he left school he decided he would follow them.

His height helped him and he was able to 'fudge', or lie about, his age. He initially joined the Royal Naval Volunteer Reserve (RNVR), which apparently did not sit well with the family, since historically the Army was where the males of the family had traditionally headed when moved to serve their country.

This was confirmed when, a few years before his death, Mark wrote: 'I was a disappointment to the family. I 'fudged' my age and joined the Naval Air Branch, or Fleet Air Arm. The male Bostocks thought this was outrageous as all Bostocks in history, whenever there was a conflict, had joined the Army. As I had quite serious knee problems and wanted to fly it was logical to join the FAA and be taken to the war and not have to square-bash, or march, endlessly.'

On entering the Senior Service his father Norman had just two pieces of advice for his son. "Darling Boy (his usual form of address to his son), Never go into whorehouses, and never get tattooed." By all accounts Mark adhered to the advice thereafter.

Mark was in the Exmouth Division, HMS Raleigh, before attending Edinburgh University, courtesy of the Royal Navy, from October 1944 to March 1945; after which he went to HMS King Alfred for officer training. It was there that Mark made an exceptional friend called Para Bennett whose father was the first Maori Bishop in New Zealand and a special Bishopric had to be created for him as his appointment had set a precedent. Although he did train for the Fleet Air Arm this branch was over subscribed and so Mark had stoically to settle into other duties which included minesweeping.

Before the outbreak of war Mark's father Norman had risen to a position in Keell and Waldock where he was virtually running the firm between 1933 and 1940. Geoffrey Greene's son Neville had also joined the firm, and was eventually to become the senior partner, but pre-war it was Norman's show. Although Watty Keell was still a working partner, he had very little to do with the day-to-day running of affairs, not since his partner Harold Waldock had died.

Mark takes up the story: "My father officially retired in 1940, when he caught an Imperial Airways plane to England in order to try to join up with his old regiment again. I recall him telling me that this Hannibal Biplane took six days for the journey from Colombo to England. To his intense annoyance and regret he was turned down by the Army for active service, but was offered a sedentary assignment with his old rank of Major, which he declined. He finished the war as an assistant to Lord Beaverbrook, an old chum, at the Ministry of Aircraft Production in

London, becoming 'The Beaver's' right hand man, in charge of co-ordinating all the repairs to damaged bombers and getting them back into service again.

'Norman returned to Ceylon in 1945 for 18 months, in order to allow those members of Keell and Waldock who had stayed on, to go on leave. I met my father there in 1945, when I was changing aircraft carriers because my ship, The Indefatigable, was going on to Australia and I was destined for the Pacific in a frightful American Liberty flat-top, which I joined in Trincomalee.

'During the short time with my father in Colombo we purchased another small tea estate adjoining Aislaby at Bandarawela, and we also purchased 350 acres of land in South India, near Trivandrum which was to become Greenham Estate and which is now the highest yielding rubber estate in India.'

Norman had also planted some Brazil nut trees on Greenham Estate. The monkeys revealed their intelligence after gathering the nuts, by hurling them to the ground in order to crack them open, actions which posed a considerable threat to the rubber tappers and anyone else within range, for that matter.

Having served in the Pacific, Mark was demobbed in Trincomalee in 1947 and almost immediately set about his apprenticeship in the tea trade, basing himself initially at the family estate, Aislaby.

The tea plant Camellia Sinensis was, as its name suggests, a native of China, a country which was the only one in the world in the 18th and 19th centuries which cultivated tea. There are reports that a tea plant grew wild in Ceylon, however it was not until 1824 that a tea plant was brought to Ceylon by the British from China. Until then Ceylon was known for its cinnamon crops and later for its coffee production.

The first tea bushes were planted in the Royal Botanical Gardens in Peradeniya. Further plants were imported from India a decade or so later, but it was not until Queen Victoria had been on the throne for thirty years that the plant was first grown on a commercial scale. The person credited with this big step is James Taylor, who set up a tea plantation on the Loolecondera Estate in Kandy in 1867. The initial size of the estate was 19 acres. Within five years Taylor has established a tea processing plant at Loolecondera and that same year, 1872, saw the first sale of tea at Kandy. Twelve months later the first shipment of Ceylon tea, a modest 23lb, found its way to the global market in London. Within twenty years Ceylon tea set a world record price of £36.15s per pound at the London Tea Auctions in Mincing Lane.

In the early days of tea planting in Ceylon, the China *jat* (variety) of tea was widely grown and with good results. The China *jat* was very hardy, but it had very small leaves which contributed to low yields and difficult harvesting. There were initial doubts as to whether the larger leaved Assam *jat* would suit the local conditions, but when it was introduced it was soon realised that this variety was indeed suitable. It was more vigorous than China *jat* and gave higher yields.

The early planters faced difficulty obtaining adequate supplies of seed, which at that time was very expensive. A few enterprising planters made money growing tea for seed. The tea plant will reach a height of thirty feet or more and bears seed in large quantities. However, in commercial production the bush is pruned every two to four years to keep it at a maneagable height for picking and it is not allowed to run to seed. Pruning also encourages fresh vigorous shoot growth, hence higher yields.

The industry no longer relies on seedling tea. Much higher yields are obtained through vegetatively propagated (VP) tea. Mother bushes for VP are selected for high yields and disease resistance. New plants are raised from single leaf cuttings taken from the selected mother bush. These single leaf cuttings are grown under shade in polythene sleeves in the estate 'nursery'. In the case of Aislaby, Mark used to insist that the polythene bags were deeper than those normally used, and he would not allow the plants to be transplanted out into the field until the root structure balanced the upper growth.

The vast majority of the workforce on a plantation is employed in harvesting, or plucking. This is labour intensive as the mature shoots, consisting of two leaves and a bud are selectively harvested, leaving a single leaf above a small round leaf known as a "fish leaf" which encourages further growth of the flush. The immature shoots are not touched, but allowed to develop for the next round of harvesting in a week to ten days. The pluckers head out into the fields in the early morning moving at lightening speed among the plants, an experienced picker will selectively pick ten to twenty suitable shoots in both hands while leaving the rest undamaged. The picker will also discard course leaves and hard stalks. The flush being the only elements of the plant which possess the flavour and the aroma of the tea. The pluckers' pick is weighed three times a day, at 9am , noon and 4.00 pm.

The timetable for harvesting varies from estate to estate and according to the weather. At Aislaby they aimed for a seven-day round, which meant that each tea bush was picked four times a month. Since Aislaby had around four million tea bushes this entailed tight organisation and the employment of more than a thousand pluckers but the return in terms of yield and quality were rewarding. (There is also a nasty spore which can attack the leaves in misty and damp weather. This is known as 'blister blight'. A practised tea taster can detect tea which has been affected. It also limits the 'flush'.)

After weighing, the fresh tea leaves are placed in open weaved coir sacks and collected by the estate lorry, thence transported down to the factory immediately. Each of the pluckers receives a note of the amount they have individually plucked and any poundage above a set daily norm is paid to them as an incentive over and above their daily wage.

When the leaf arrives at the factory it is weighed and then is spread out on nylon or hessian "tats" for the withering process. In the old days, hessian tats were used in the withering loft and these were wired to wooden posts with about 4in spacing between tats. The leaves used to be spread out by one of the factory workers using a stick. Later on 'trough withering' was introduced. This allows the leaves to be spread out at a greater depth and a draft of air passed over and through them by fans which can also be reversed. This has greatly reduced the time taken for this part of the process. Essentially, the withering process reduces the moisture content of the leaf to prepare it for rolling.

Once the leaves are sufficiently withered they are sent down a chute to the rollers which, at Aislaby, were positioned on the ground floor of the factory. A roller comprises a large cylindrical drum, with a cone on the bottom that gives the leaf a twist and avoids turning everything into a mush. The drum rotates in a circular motion over a table, and imparts a twist to the leaf. The roller mimics the traditional method of rolling tea leaves between the palms of the hands. After 30 minutes of rolling the "fines" as they are known, are then removed by a "roll-breaker" and the residue is rolled again until all of it has been reduced to the required size.

The fines, called *dhools*, are placed on fermenting tables until they are judged to be ready for firing. At this stage they have changed to a coppery colour and the aroma of tea becomes apparent. The fermentation process is stopped as soon as the tea arrives in the drier.

There are different processes for different types of tea. Black tea, which is the chief product of the Sri Lankan tea industry, requires 100 per cent oxidation, whereby the chlorophyll is gradually broken down and tannins are released. It takes a couple of hours in high humidity, and after the fermentation process is complete the leaves are then fired to help them dry and bring out the best of their qualities.

Once the leaves have been fully 'fired', they go into the grading machine. One of the many innovations introduced by Mark, as he became more experienced, was the introduction of a novel idea whereby different *dhools* could be blended before being cooled and then transferred to the tea chests for Auction or export. Tea chests were made of plywood and lined with aluminium foil and tissue paper, which kept the tea from "greying"

There are four main varieties of tea, the most popular of which is black tea. Green tea is made from autoxidised (ie unfermented tea leaves), which have been rolled to release their flavour; white tea, which is the world's rarest, since it can only be harvested for a handful of weeks in any year, is grown chiefly in Fujian Province in China, and the processing methods are kept secret by the Chinese; but in fact it has also actually been grown in Sri Lanka on Handunugoda Estate, in the region of Ahangama.

There is also Oolong tea, and this too is grown chiefly in China and Taiwan. It is a semi-fermented tea, a cross between green and black teas. Many people are under the misapprehension that the names 'Pekoe', 'Broken Orange Pekoe', 'Fannings' etc. represent different types of tea, whereas they are purely different grades of leaf size. For the Middle East market the dust is very popular as a small amount of dust tea makes a strong cup of tea. Much of the Continent prefers bigger size of leaf tea which makes a light cup.

If it sounds as if there was a lot to learn, then there certainly was. But Mark set about his apprenticeship with a will. With a view to his future in John Keells, he knew he needed a thorough knowledge of tea in all its aspects; from planting and nurturing, to cultivating and harvesting and finally the process of turning the plants into the money-spinning product that sells worldwide, so he threw himself into his tea education with a will. Initially Mark worked on his father's estate Aislaby at Bandarawela, spending six months as a 'creeper' or trainee assistant, during which time he learned a great deal about the planting and growing of tea. Without this formal, on-site training Mark would not have been able to ask the labour force to do anything; and he also had to know what each job entailed so that he would understand and appreciate when tasks were not being carried out correctly. During his time as a creeper on Aislaby, Mark learned to prune the tea bushes, he dug trenches between the tea plants and the roadways, and he carried out spraying and weeding as well as learning to pluck. On one occasion he came across a cobra and the other labourers told him not to kill it as it was a good snake which guarded their temple.

However, despite being the son of the owner, he was not allowed into the factory during his traineeship, and consequently had to rely on his planter friends on neighbouring estates to let him into their factories in order for him to learn the essentials about tea-making, another vital skill for a tea broker.

Having completed his six months on the estate, Mark was sent off to London to learn tea tasting and evaluating. He spent the whole of his leave with WJ & H Thompson, tea importers who were based in Mincing Lane, which in those days was the hub of the world tea trade. Here Mark was expected to learn the basics of tea-tasting, which had been one of the conditions laid down by Fred Waldock, the senior partner, when offering Mark a job with Keell and Waldock.

So once more he found himself at the bottom of the heap, this time not as a labourer, but rather as a glorified 'office boy'. His duties initially entailed boiling the kettle, measuring out, precisely, the tea to be put into the tasting cups and washing up afterwards. All this was to ensure that by the time he joined Keell and Waldock he would have a good working knowledge of all aspects of tea.

Later on, as he reached the top of the tea trade, Mark's CV would always impress any youngsters who came under his wing for training in the industry, because it showed that he had mastered pretty well every aspect of the tea industry. Not only that, but his technical bent meant that he was forever dreaming up ways to improve production at various stages. Like his father before him Aislaby was always a passion with Mark and he determined from the outset of his involvement that it should become the best tea estate, not only in the Uva region, but throughout the Island. Consequently he was forever looking for potential innovations and improvements to existing methods and machinery. Indeed one of his inventions for blending teas in the factory, which he pioneered at Aislaby, has since become standard in many factories in Sri Lanka and in parts of India, when he eventually became a consultant to a large group of tea estates on the Sub-Continent.

The London tea-tasting lessons over, Mark returned to Ceylon at the end of 1948 and was appointed an assistant in the tea department of Keell and Waldock. By this time Norman Bostock had stepped down from the company, retiring to England in 1946.

All was not well on his return however, Mark had somehow or other contracted hepatitis. 'When I had finished my education of tasting teas from all over the world in Mincing Lane, I arrived out in Colombo just before Christmas, bright yellow with jaundice, to be told I was going to go and live as a paying guest (PG) with André and Babs Willis, who had a very nice house opposite the Police Ground.

André had been at Keell and Waldock before the Second World War. During the conflict he was captured when in the desert and had an unpleasant experience as a POW in Italy, although he did manage to escape once and live with partisans up in the mountains where he learned Italian and became quite fluent in the language. But he was then recaptured when the Germans retreated.'

Mark was subsequently responsible for saving Andre's son, Graham, from all but certain death when he almost swallowed his tongue and the nanny had no idea what to do. Mark acted promptly and stuck his fingers into Graham's mouth and pulled his tongue out.

Mark's education continued with Watty Keell, the head of the company. By all accounts he had a grand time as he picked Watty's brains about pretty well every aspect of tea production.

'Initially I came under the tutelage of the No 1 of the firm – a lovely old boy called Watty Keell – a Welshman,' explained Mark. 'He was in his eighties then, but he was a magnificent tea man and most interested in the manufacture of tea. He had taken me under his wing because I had done my planting time, which was an innovation in Colombo, and it was extremely advantageous for the tea brokers to have a person who was trained in planting as well as tasting, working in the broking house.

'So dear little Watty would tell me to come round to his hotel – The Grand Oriental Hotel (GOH) in the Fort at 12.30 on a Saturday, and we would shoot off in his chauffeur-driven car to visit a particular estate for the weekend. It was a wonderful grooming because he knew his tea intimately. He wasn't a planter but he was able to translate his tasting ability into altering manufacture so as to make something which was appreciably more saleable and through him I learned an enormous amount.

'But it was also a very tiring experience, because the old boy, despite being an octogenarian, (he invariably slept in the car during these weekend rounds) was out in the factory after an early morning cup of tea, and he would be there until 8 or 9 pm. Then it would be back for supper, before, depending on the season, we would go out again immediately after dinner, until about midnight or 1.00am, in order to check on night manufacture.

'He was an absolute expert and it was amazing to see the changes that he recommended being put into effect, and the following day we would taste the result of his endeavours and invariably there was a profound improvement in the liquors and leaf appearance.

'We would spend the Sunday in that planting district, possibly visiting one or two other estates just briefly, or go and tell them that we were coming up again the following weekend. Then I would get back to Colombo at about 7.00 or 8.00pm that night.'

Watty was something of an eccentric by all accounts; apparently one of his little foibles was to collect cocoa beans from samples in the office. His sport was to aim a catapult at the crows who had the nerve to perch on his balcony at the Grand Oriental Hotel. He did not miss many either.

Routine was the key to the industry it would appear and Mark embraced it wholeheartedly, although it was non-stop hard work, and, as time went on and the tutorials with Watty Keell finally ended, hard play took over on Saturday afternoons, still Mark loved the life.

'I fairly quickly fell into the routine of a Tea Broker's life,' he said. 'We had the tea sales on Mondays and Tuesdays, and then immediately after that we started tasting for the next tea sale, that would go on through Wednesday and even into Thursday. Then we would taste all the other teas which were coming up for the next week's auction, and these then had to be compared with similar estates in our catalogue.

'That was followed by us having to go round all the buyers who were based in 'The Fort', an area of Colombo which was the hub of the city's business, by rickshaw, with our catalogue, in order to check up on what they thought of the teas that were coming up for sale the following week. If they thought that we were miles out, or had got a tea wrongly tasted, we had to go back and have another look at it and, likewise for our part, if we felt that they had missed out on a "goodie", they would put it on again and taste it.

'On Friday again we went round the sellers – the big Agency Houses and Proprietary Planters – and told them what we thought their teas were worth, and what they should fetch the following week. They would give us instructions as to the price at which they were prepared to sell.

'On Saturday, working till 12.30, planters used to come down and taste their teas in our office, and there we might advise them to alter the grading, or to do this and that with the manufacture so as to get a liquor that suited the buyers. We generally finished up by having a beer with the planters, and then, at 12.30 it was a bit of a scramble because as often as not we were dashing back to our digs or "chummery", loading up our rugger or hockey kit, golf clubs, black tie and dinner jacket before shooting off Up-Country for a game of rugger or hockey at one or other of the Up-Country clubs such as Radella, Darrawella, Badulla or Dimbulla.'

There were the occasional breaks with routine though. Mark spent the first 12 months in the tea department, before moving over to freight. However, he had not left tea broking behind for ever, as he discovered.

Mark wrote: 'A huge jovial chap – Arthur Lintott – was supposed to stand-in as director in case anybody fell ill so at any one time he could step in to being a rubber broker, a broker on the Stock Exchange or a tea broker. But he hated tea and, if there was anybody he could pass the onus of being the spare tea man on to, Tottie would, because he was quite slow and when you are auctioning tea you have got to move at an enormously fast pace. And dear old Tot just wasn't up to that.

'On one occasion I came back from a rugger weekend and found a note in the bungalow to say that I had got to report to Tottie. I didn't get back till about 10 or 11pm but I still gave him a ring. I got a blast for waking him up, but then he said: "Oh yes, by the way, you are selling tea tomorrow as Maurice has had to go off to England for a knee operation".

'Now this was an awful responsibility because I had been shifted into the freight department and I hadn't done tea for a couple of years and suddenly I was being asked to sell the catalogue on the Monday morning, having not seen the teas. And, of course, some of the buyers in the Auction Room had changed, and I wasn't aware of their names; and there were all sorts of other difficulties.

'On top of all this I had had a nasty cold which I couldn't shake off and in fact I thought it had turned into a sinus problem. But, anyway, I stepped into the breach on the Monday and I sold the catalogue. But the work did not stop there, because I then had to taste the following week's tea, because Tottie flatly refused to do anything except dabble in the finance side of it, and so, before the week was out, I was in an awful state, because this sinus problem hadn't eased up, and you can't taste tea if you are bunged up with a cold and sinus.

'It was a very annoying problem to find myself suddenly stuck back in tea, and what is more, it turned out that I had to continue in this department for about three or four months until Maurice returned, so inevitably during that time my allergies became worse and worse.'

As irritating as it was to Mark to find himself involved with tea, just when he was beginning to establish himself in the freight department, there was a great deal of practical common sense in the way the brokers at Keell & Waldock operated, as he himself realised: 'In K & W we very rightly had to be grounded in all departments so that if somebody went off sick or on leave, we could slip into their job and take it over with no notice at all.'

There was a rigid routine to life in the freight department, as Mark discovered. 'We would go round all the shippers with a daily sheet which we had printed the names of all the ships and their subsequent destinations. This allowed the broking houses to book cargo space for their tea shipments"

It was during this daily round that Mark found himself climbing the stairs to the offices of Sandy Mathewson one day in early 1952. As usual Sandy was at his desk when Mark opened the glass door to let himself in.

Mathewson rose and walked around his desk to greet Mark, a fellow sportsman in the Colombo Hockey and Football Club, where he himself was chairman (Sandy was also chairman of the Ceylon Rugby Union), while Mark was the CH&FC secretary.

Sandy then turned to indicate a young woman seated at a desk nearby. 'Mark, allow me to introduce you to my new secretary, in fact my first personal secretary, Elizabeth Mills. You're going to have to get along with her, because you will be seeing a lot of her, since she will also be doing a great deal of sports club committee work.'

Mark turned to watch as the tall, elegant young woman left her desk to shake hands with him.

4

DEPARTURES
AND
ARRIVALS

Ceylon may have had its rebels in 1951, but with the arrival of Ronald Mills, newly-appointed Captain in Charge, Trincomalee Naval base, there was added one more, his daughter Elizabeth, who had accompanied her mother, under protest, to this far-flung outpost of the British Empire.

The reason for such sentiments was not too difficult to establish. Elizabeth had given her heart (so she believed) to a dashing young Scottish medic, who had been seconded to the British Embassy in Warsaw, which had been her father's previous posting. But at 20 Lif, as she was known to the family, was still obliged to toe the parental line, and she was therefore obliged to accompany her mother in the footsteps of her father, travelling some 5,000 miles east, leaving behind the man she felt was the love of her life, to end up somewhere which, as far as she could see, held no future for her.

Up to that point her life had been peripatetic to say the least, with her father Captain Ronnie Mills rarely spending too long in the same place as he was moved from one Naval posting to another. Elizabeth was born on May 5th 1931 at her parents' home, a modest bungalow called 'Chesil Mist' in Weymouth, which featured prominently in the Mills family. Ronnie and Sylvia had been married there, her brother Ken's future wife Jane was born there, and Elizabeth was to give birth to her first child in the town's former workhouse a quarter of a century or so later.

Elizabeth was the second child of Lieutenant (as he was then) Ronald George Mills and Sylvia, née Gurney. Lif remembered: 'My mother's comment when my brother Ken was born two years earlier had been: "Well, I hope he doesn't pick his nose like his father" As far as I know, she did not make any particular comment at my birth.' Father and daughter were destined not to meet up for a further 18 months, since Ronnie was on the China Station at the time, and when they did finally get together Lif recalled: 'Apparently, I ran away to the corner of the room when he appeared, which upset him, but my mother's response was, "You should be pleased, since it shows she is not used to strange men".'

It was Ken who coined the name 'Lif', because his attempts to get his two-year-old tongue around Elizabeth resulted in the rather briefer 'Lifluf', and the nickname stuck. There was more confusion for Ken at his sister's christening, because for the first time he discovered that there were two grannies. Lif explained: 'Previously, he had only met them one at a time and, despite their being completely different in appearance, he thought of them as one person.

'So, when confronted by the two of them, he decided they each needed a special name in order to make them different. He named my mother's mother 'Little Granny' as she was very little and our paternal grandmother who was wearing a blue dress on that particular day was given the name of 'Blue Granny'.'

Ken was a source of more amusement when, at the age of eight, he was asked by the incoming headmistress of his primary school Westerhall House in Weymouth, what he was going to be when he grew up.

His prompt response was: 'I'm going to be the father of Elizabeth's babies'. The stunned silence can only be imagined. Lif herself recalled an equally ingenuous announcement a few years later, when she declared that if she were not married by the time she was 22, then she would have an illegitimate child before going on to become a missionary. 'Fortunately,' Lif explained, 'I was married at 22 so Ken's services were not required.'

Lif's recollections of her early days are hazy. But I do remember attending a dancing class where we learned the polka and had little bowls and spoons for dancing Little Miss Muffet. We caught the bus to go to the class, and on the opposite side of the road was a church where the clock moved a minute at a time, much to my amazement.'

Her travels began when she was five years old. Her father by that time was on his third appointment in the China Station, in command of HM Submarine Regent. Lif recalled the voyage with her parents. 'We travelled on a Blue Funnel liner – the SS Antenor. Also on board was a couple, Sandy and Maisie Matthewson, who were travelling out to Ceylon after home leave.

'My father was an excellent caricaturist and had drawn a cartoon of Maisie Matthewson playing deck quoits in a pair of trousers, which was quite unusual for a woman in those days. The caption to the caricature, which was subsequently posted on the ship's notice board, read "And who wears the trousers now?" This did not particularly endear my father to Maisie. However, almost 20 years later, Sandy was to become my boss in Colombo.'

Once in Hong Kong, Ronnie Mills' artistic ability was to present him with a useful sideline. Lif recounted: 'my father was commissioned by Tiger Beer to do an advertisement for them, in his free time, on the theme "A for 'orses, but Tiger Beer for you'. When it came to Y for girlfriend, for some reason he wanted a picture of a girl climbing up a hill – probably the Peak. However he just couldn't get it right, so my poor, long-suffering mother had to stand for hours with one foot on a chair.

'My father also illustrated a book with comic pictures of China, accompanied by rather basic poems. It was called "Nothing to Laugh At." One of his pictures, entitled "The Captain's Chair" was subsequently included in the centenary brochure of the Royal Hong Kong Golf Club.'

One episode involving Lif on the voyage that she was able to recall appeared to have repercussions once they arrived at their destination. 'On the boat going out to China there was no fresh milk so my mother made me whisk up powdered Cow and Gate milk with water. On arrival at Hong Kong, and having breakfast at the very smart Peninsular Hotel, I was presented with a wonderful glass of ice cold milk, which I drank with much glee, only to bring it up a few seconds later all over the beautiful white linen table cloth.'

There was one major blemish to this early adventure for Lif. The trip had to be made without her brother Ken. Lif remembered: 'He was then seven years old and the Admiralty in their wisdom reckoned the climate in Hong Kong was unsuitable for children over 7. I missed Ken terribly and often used to dream he was with me and awoke in great disappointment to find it was just a dream.'

She was to spend two happy years in Hong Kong, and recalled: 'Few memories survive of those years in China, but I can still picture the flat in Kowloon in Lunar Building where we lived, up 97 stairs and no lift. We had a lovely cook call A Yow and my much loved amah, A Sung Je. Lif's mother was somewhat surprised when A Yow presented her young daughter with a Chinese God of plenty at Chinese New Year and she still has it to this day.

'A Sung used to accompany me to Laloma Kindergarten by rickshaw each morning and to the park in the afternoons. When I was playing with the other children, I couldunderstand a certain amount of what the Amahs were chatting about, although I would not have been able to translate it.

'Family lore has it that I would be able instantly to summon a rickshaw when my parents wanted to go out for the evening – no doubt including some pretty fruity language not usually used by a five-year-old. Our cook and A Sung used to speak to each other in pidgin English as neither could understand the other's dialect. On my return to England I was invited to a children's party and decided to go in my Chinese outfit and resolved only to speak in Chinese. In all probability my "fluent" Chinese was made up of a few phrases which were repeated and had no particular meaning but it was sufficient for one little boy to excitedly report to his mother that there had been a little Chinese girl at the party.

'During those years, the only contact with Hong Kong Island was via the ferry. Whenever we went over on the ferry I used to 'entertain' or annoy the other passengers by singing "Do you know the sampan man who lives in Wey Hai Wey?" while I danced back and forth. The response was "Yes I know the sampan man," the singer was then supposed to join me in a long line. Being mainly a solo act, I used to sing the response as well.

The fleet and families used to go up to Wey Hai Wey in the summer months, and I can remember living in a long line of flats and attending a children's party where we were all presented with Japanese dolls which didn't appeal to me at all but I had to pretend I liked it.'

By late 1938 the first serious rumblings of a possible Second World War were gathering momentum and all the naval families were evacuated from the mainland to Hong Kong Island on a battleship and thence to England by boat. The seven-year-old Lif was just recovering from a bout of malaria. She said: 'On the voyage all the children were taken on a tour of the ship, which included a visit to the 'galley' where the dough for the bread was being churned around in a huge sort of vat. This was about the last straw for me.'

On arrival in the United Kingdom the family moved into rented accommodation. 'A lovely house in Fareham, with an acre of garden," said Lif. This was Checkfield, in Park Lane, and Lif's brother Ken enlarged on the description: 'This was a lovely large house which we had taken on a lease unfurnished. 'By the time our mother had finished furnishing it, she had £18 remaining; with which she purchased a car for £13 and a Singer sewing machine for £5.'

Ken recalled the car fondly: 'It was an old Morris Cowley with a 'dickie' – an extra seat incorporated into the boot of the car – the registration number of which was OU 7064. Ken and Lif loved travelling in the dickie – health and safety would certainly not have allowed it, or at least not without crash helmets, safety harness and possibly even a parachute. The dear old car, which we had called "Richard Rattlebang", met a sad end when it failed to take a bend and ended up in the ditch in Holyhead."

Initially Lif attended Fareham Court School before switching after a short time to a convent-run establishment in the town. There she recalled her mother taking a nun to task over the amount of homework that was being handed out to her daughter; this was not the only time that Sylvia was to confront her daughter's teachers. Lif remembered the consequences of her mother's outburst: 'I had the embarrassment, when homework was being doled out, of being given fewer verses of the Bible to learn or fewer pages of a book to read than the others in my class, the homework announcement was always prefaced with the words "...and for Elizabeth Mills, verses..., pages..."

'Despite this, I was very happy and learned to sew and embroider most meticulously and also increase my ability to memorise verses of the Bible and, subsequently, poems and plays when learning elocution later on.'

The winter of 1939, the first one of the Second World War saw the Mills family on the move again, this time to the frozen north, at 92, Rating Lane, Barrow-in-Furness. Their father and mother were already in situ, the children followed by train, having been placed in the charge of the guard. When they reached their destination their mother suggested she give the guard a tip for his services, but Ken instantly said: 'No, give it to the nice man in our carriage, who played noughts and crosses with us.'

The reason the family was there was because their father had been given command of HM Submarine Tetrarch, and the vessel was being constructed in Vickers Armstrong's shipyard. It was launched, controversially, by their mother on November 14th 1939, the Admiralty had not wanted to make a fuss, but Vickers had other ideas and invited Sylvia to do the honours. Afterwards she was presented with a beautiful, ivory cigarette box, for which she thanked the Vickers management most profusely. Their reaction was to ask her to "open the box"; on doing so Sylvia found a naval crown brooch with the sails set with diamonds, rubies, emeralds and sapphires.

The family shivered throughout Christmas in Rating Lane. Ken said: 'It was an extremely cold winter and fuel was in very short supply. We had to make a sledge out of an old orange box and tramped down to the railway siding to collect half a hundredweight of coal.' While Lif recalled: 'There was four feet of snow. Bread was also in very short supply, and the only shop where it could be purchased was the Co-op. When our mother reached the head of the queue to pay for her loaf she was asked for her Co-op number. Of course she had never had one, and there was much muttering from those behind her. The next time she went there she made up a number to avoid any further embarrassment.'

After the holidays Ken returned to his prep school and the rest of the family repaired to Fareham and their rented house "Checkfield". As for HM Submarine Tetrarch, Ronnie was out on patrol in it in 1940, and enjoyed a distinguished career in her, ending the year by being promoted to Commander. Sadly, shortly after Ronnie Mills had left her, the submarine was sunk with all hands on board. The story of the crew's harrowing ordeal when the submarine had to dive deeper than she was built for and remained there for 48 hours can be found in the Imperial War Museum.

The Mills were at Checkfield throughout the Battle of Britain, an anxious time for everyone, yet oddly, an exhilarating time for children at least. Lif remembered: 'Of course it was an anxious time for our mother as our father was at sea in his submarine for a lot of the time, and out of communication. And with Fareham being just outside Portsmouth we were in a potentially dangerous area, since it was targeted by the German bombers. Despite all that we thought it was all rather exciting, and enjoyed looking out of the window to see all the barrage balloons going up in flames. I remember we used to re-make candles from the drips of the spent ones, and our mother used to encourage us to wear our gas masks while we were playing football in the garden.'

There was one rather more dramatic thing that the two Mills children learned to do during these troubled months of the war. Lif again: 'When we were out for a cycle ride together my mother taught Ken and me how to throw ourselves off our bikes. She would shout "Messerschmitts overhead!"' We then had to throw ourselves into the nearest ditch. It was just a game for us, but it had its serious side since the German planes used to fly low enough to have fired on people at random as they got rid of any surplus ammunition, not to mention any remaining bombs on board, in order to make their planes lighter and therefore more fuel efficient as well as faster, which allowed them to evade their pursuers more easily.'

Shortly before the D Day landings, the Mills family were somewhat surprised to find a whole line of army vehicles parked opposite their home. These vehicles were nicknamed "Priests" but were in fact self-propelled guns (similar to today's tanks) and used for artillery purposes. Sylvia in her usual way made friends with the soldiers and invited them in to tea. Ken and Lif wanted to make the soldiers a mascot but could not have made one in the form of a priest as, according to Naval tradition, it was unlucky to have a priest on board a submarine and they were worried the same might be true with these vehicles. A mascot of some sort was duly made and given to the soldiers, just in time as they disappeared as quickly as they had arrived and were obviously part of the strategic invasion of France.

5

SCHOOLDAYS

Lif's schooling was somewhat unsettled, to say the least. At some point shortly after returning from Barrow-in-Furness to Fareham, Lif found herself in yet another educational establishment, having to make yet more friends. She was sent to stay with an aunt and two cousins in Grayshott and attended that village's Primary School.

She said: 'One of my memories of that time is that we were called either Light Keepers or Lighthouse Keepers, I don't remember which, and we knitted scarves and Balaclava helmets for the Navy. I also had to give a talk on 'Buoys'. One thing that my cousins and I did not enjoy was when my aunt decided to grow potatoes in her garden in response to the national 'Dig for Victory' campaign. Our job was to clear the patch of all its stones.

'As cousins we had a good time together and one of them, Barbara became a good friend, but I am afraid we were rather cruel to Ann – the older daughter. We were allowed to climb trees in those days and there was one marvellous huge fir tree in the garden – ideal climbing.

The appointment of Lif's father to Commander of Submarines based on HMS Forth, the depot ship, which was moored in the Holy Loch off the Firth of Clyde, meant yet another move for the family, and yet another school for Lif. Thus it was that in 1942 the Mills found themselves in digs at Woodend, Hunters Quay, a house owned by the three McLean sisters of that parish.

Lif did not enjoy the little adventure when the family paid their first visit to Woodend to inspect their new lodgings. Ken recalled: 'When we first went to check it out, we couldn't get anybody to answer the bell so our mother went round to the side of the house and noticed a small window open and very naughtily she proceeded to post Lif through it. She found the door locked and then heard footsteps coming down the stairs and panicked, but managed to scramble out again before being discovered.'

During their sojourn in Scotland the family experienced a little bit of the glamour and glitz of the film world, as Ken explained: 'One memory stands out from that time, and that was the filming of 'We dive at dawn', alongside HMS Forth. John Mills was the hero of the film, which was about a submarine that had been disabled in the Baltic Sea. At some stage the producers gave our father the script they intended to use for the diving scene to see if it was appropriate. They had used some of the most awful phrases such as 'Start up the donkey'. Our father proceeded to write an entirely new script, and when he and Mother attended the film studio to watch the finished film they realized the producers had taken Father's script word-for-word with no acknowledgement having been made of his contribution.'

Lif was enrolled at Sandbank village school where she recalled: 'I had the dubious distinction of being the only Sassenach. My friend, Doreen Brown, whose parents owned a small hotel in Dunoon, was less than popular when she proposed the name of the Rose Patrol in our newly-formed Girl Guide troop. However, it was always a source of amusement to my Mother that I was chosen to dance the Petronella – a Scottish country dance – on Parents' Day.

'This school concentrated primarily on The Three Rs, with one afternoon per week being dedicated to either history, ranging from 1066 to the modern day, or, probably, world geography with particular emphasis on Scotland. Our history lesson was usually a list of dates on the blackboard with our teacher Mr. Wallace pointedly looking at me and saying '…and this is where the Scots beat the English'.

'We all lived in dread of Mr. Wallace, particularly if he was in a bad mood as he carried a curled-up leather strap in his pocket which he administered to one's hand for any minor crime. However, the mental arithmetic which occupied the first half hour of every morning has stood me in good stead ever since, and I can still recite my tables better than my children or grandchildren and add a column of figures in my head much faster than I can with a calculator!

'Mr. Wallace used to give us weekly tests on each Friday afternoon, at the conclusion of which we all had to gather up our books and come to the front of the class. The lucky child who had top marks was allowed to sit in the furthest corner of the class and thence in descending order of merit, until the unfortunate and less bright pupils inevitably found themselves in the front row, sitting right under his nose.'

Life at Woodend was clearly a happy time for the Mills family. The children had their own adventure playground on their doorstep. Lif said: 'We used to make camps in the woods behind the house. And I remember that we also fashioned a home-made billiard table using a cotton under-blanket laid out on the dining-room table. It had tree branches inserted into old stockings to act as the 'cushions', while the feet of other stockings were turned into the 'pockets'.

'One day Ken and I were painting, and eating oranges while doing so, and we decided to put the paint water in front of the gas stove and add the orange peel. This was our first experiment in making marmalade! There was one thing which I never enjoyed doing, and that was going to a nearby tenement building and knocking on all the doors of the flats and collecting the 'Penny-a-Week envelopes, a regular collection made to help the local war effort. In fact I was pretty frightened about it all.'

The two years in Scotland passed fairly uneventfully for Lif and her brother, then their father was posted back to Portsmouth. This meant the family could return to Fareham and they anticipated being able to take up residence in Checkfield, however, unfortunately for them it had been sub-let, so they had to kick their heels. Ken by now had won a scholarship to Dartmouth, intending to follow in the wake of his naval officer father, and that first summer back in the South saw the children spending most of it in the village of Stanton in the Cotswolds as the guests of a family called Studd.

Lif described this period of the children's lives: 'The Studds had generously welcomed us in and looked after us really well. They had two daughters older than us, but who nevertheless joined in with our games and the building a camp up in the hills behind the house. The Studds also had some lovely collie dogs. It was my first holiday from boarding school and I disgraced myself by wetting my bed, much to my mother's intense embarrassment.'

That first boarding school to which the 12-year-old Elizabeth Mills was sent was The Chilterns, a private establishment near Monks Risborough in Buckinghamshire. It was owned and run by a daunting woman, a Mrs Moore, whose chief aides were her hen-pecked husband and her daughter. Lif said: 'Quite how or why my parents chose this school is still a mystery.'

The school was managed on very old-fashioned lines, and according to Lif: 'At the age of 12 we still went to bed at

7.00pm, even during the summer, when the clocks were put forward two hours for daylight saving during the war, yet they still expected us to go to sleep while the sun was still shining.'

Memories of the meals are not good either. Lif recalled: 'The food was terrible at The Chilterns. The porridge was lumpy and we were allowed no milk or sugar with it, but it all had to be eaten. When bacon was on the menu it would appear floating in a pool of oil or fat. Mrs Moore used to sweep down the dining room in her imperious way and, if no-one got up to open the dining room door to let her out, she would say, "I'm waiting, girls.'

But if there was austerity and a degree of misery to life in The Chilterns, there was also lots of fun, and there are echoes of well known girls' boarding school stories that were all the rage throughout much of the first half of the 20th Century, in Lif's time under Mrs Moore's harsh, Spartan regime. In fact some of her anecdotes could have been taken from books such as Elinor M Brent-Dyer's Chalet School stories or Elsie J Oxenham's series, known as The Abbey Girls, coincidentally this latter series was set in Buckinghamshire, as well as Enid Blyton's schoolgirl tales.

'We got up to all sorts of high jinks,' confessed Lif, 'and we were frequently caught by the vindictive matron – Miss Murdoch – who used to test all the floorboards along the corridors so that she knew which ones squeaked.

'As luck would have it, my first dormitory had a tradition of peeing out of the window. This was initially born out of necessity, since we were not supposed to leave the room from 7.00pm to 7.00am, but then it developed into a bit of a game. Inevitably, I had to be initiated.

'This practice was brought to a rapid close when my great friend, Margaret Scott, had her bottom hanging out over the window bars and very nearly peed on the hapless geography mistress, who was doing her rounds below. With the teacher's words "Margaret, whatever ARE you doing?" ringing in her ears, my friend bolted back to her bed. I leave the repercussions to your imagination.

'One of our favourite games was known as Round the World and entailed trying to circumnavigate the dormitory, without putting your feet on the ground, by means of beds, cubicle rails, chairs, et cetera. The punishment which was meted out when we were caught usually included a lecture by Mrs. Moore, which used to culminate in tears. We would subsequently have to write out endless lines.

'My mother was so incensed when one of my letters home was merely 100 lines of "I am deceitful, despicable, dishonest..." that she tackled Mrs. Moore on Sports Day and, much to the delight of my friends, was seen pacing up and down the field with my enraged mother, and clearly coming off worse. Most of the other parents were far too frightened to speak up and fight for their children in this way.'

There were other extra-curricular activities which did not earn the wrath of Mrs Moore or the School Matron. 'I remember doing Shakespeare's *The Tempest*. Originally, I had been chosen by our elocution teacher Mrs Pirie to play Miranda, the daughter of Prospero. It wasn't to be however, because a rather rich and influential parent insisted that his daughter be given the part.'

Never mind, there was always sport and among the sports that Lif enjoyed at school was netball. 'Being tall it suited me,' she said. 'I was in attack, a shooter. But fixtures against other schools were difficult to organise, home or away. It was the war years, so interschool sports were not that easy to arrange because of travelling in the blackout and of course there was also petrol rationing, which restricted where we could go.'

Naturally various versions of the facts of life were an inevitable topic of conversation among the girls in school and Lif recalled one particular pupil who managed to put the facts across in a way that distressed the young Lif. 'We had a girl in our dormitory who was a doctor's daughter and she had read all the books that she wasn't supposed to read. So she was quite explicit about sex and took it upon herself to educate the rest of the dorm.

'I remember being terribly upset and burying my head under the bedclothes and trying not to listen. Then when I came home for my first holidays, I challenged my mother and asked her why *she* had never told me as then it would have been all right. She made excuses and ended up by saying that I would find out when it came to be my turn to being a mother. I thereupon resolved that if ever I had a daughter going to boarding school that I would tell her *before* she went.

'And in due course, I became a mother, and when I was faced with my eight year-old daughter Gillian going to the Hill School I remained true to my resolve. Many of my friends wished I had instructed *their* daughters as well. I told them that imparting such facts of life to their daughters was their job.'

'Despite these incidents and having to learn the piano and practise for half an hour each day on a tinny instrument in a hot and dusty hall, and despite having to eat lumpy porridge for breakfast with no milk or sugar, and despite having to force down bacon that was swimming in an ocean of fat, I was actually quite happy at The Chilterns. And it was there that I developed my enjoyment of elocution and acting under the wonderfully enthusiastic Miss Pirie.'

In all Lif was to spend two years at The Chilterns, and it was during this time that the family was finally able to move back in to their beloved Checkfield. It had everything they could want, including a well-provisioned garden.

Lif recalled life back in Checkfield. 'We had a large garden to play in, and there was also a large vegetable garden and some fruit trees which provided 'extras' to our rations. My mother managed the household particularly well and worked hard in the garden. She even found it possible to keep some chickens, something which she did not really enjoy, since she actually hated what she called "fluttery things", and she used to find it hard when she had to pick up a broody hen.

'My mother was also a marvellous shopper and quickly endeared herself to Mr. Bradford who ran the grocer's shop – Crofts – in Fareham. Mr. Bradford frequently added the knuckle end of a leg of ham to what we were officially allowed on our 'points'. Mr. and Mrs. Ward the fishmongers were also a very jolly couple and typical of fishmongers in those days. Mr. Burt was the butcher but went no further than doling out the meagre ration of meat, which was, at one time, a shilling's worth that included two pennysworth (1p) of corned beef per ration book. Horse meat was meant for people to use for their pets, but I remember that it had to be painted green in order to discourage people from eating it themselves. We also used to buy triangular water ices for a penny.

'One holiday we were disappointed with the town fair and so Ken and I decided to stage a fair of our own. We had sideshows such as trying to cover a shilling coin in a bucket of water with a penny piece; bobbing for apples; eating buns which were dangling from a string; a coconut shy; and hoop-la.

'We invited all our friends along and they were allowed a free go on each of the sideshows, but they had to pay a penny if they wanted to have a second chance on anything. We bought all the prizes at Woolworths for a penny each. My mother arrived at the fair heavily disguised. She was introduced as Lady Snodgrass and presented the prizes with hardly any of the children recognizing her. A good time was had by all and it was great fun in the making.'

Sylvia also did her bit for the war and used to go out 'fire watching' for incendiary bombs and, Lif said: 'Because no protective headgear was offered to the volunteers, my mother used to put on her pixie hood and topped it off with the dustbin lid, by which means she hoped she would be able to fend off any shrapnel which might fall.'

The Checkfield household was augmented during the war years by two other family members. This inevitably called for a couple of adjustments to the sleeping and eating arrangements, as Lif explained: 'We had our aunt and "Little Granny" staying with us. We had no air-raid shelter, but mine and Ken's bedroom were transferred to the dining room, and as a result, meals were eaten in the hall.

'One night there were some guests for supper and Ken was desperate for a pee, but he was too embarrassed to leave the bedroom and cross the hall in front of the visitors, so made use of the enamel chamber pot. Of course, this made a great rattling noise and one of the guests sat up in their chair and said 'Hark, hand-rattles'. These were used to alert the population in case of a poisoned gas attack.'

The presence of the two lodgers, especially members of the family, meant the children's mother could be freed up to head for Portsmouth, or wherever and whenever the children's father was ashore, even if it was only for a couple of days. But Lif said: 'I hated her being away; she always left me with a list of jobs to do. I particularly remember washing and ironing the net curtains.'

In 1945 Lif left The Chilterns and was enrolled at her final school. 'It was a few days after VE Day,' she said. 'I went to St. Swithun's, in Winchester.' She was not the only member of the Mills family on the move, her father had been handed yet another posting, this one at Gosport, HMS Siskin – a Royal Naval Air Station – he took over from an RAF commanding officer. Lif observed wryly: "It was typical of the Admiralty that they should appoint a submariner to command an air station."

However, the family enjoyed a great time there and lived in quite the most beautiful house they had ever known, although that did not come about without a fight. The Commanding Officer's rightful house at HMS Siskin was Moat House, but this had been requisitioned for use as the Air Force commander's office, consequently the Mills family were expected to move into the modest Red House. However thanks to Sylvia, who, true to type, rebelled against living there, the Mills were switched to the far superior Moat House. The first working day following their arrival one poor unfortunate young RAF officer got an awful shock when he walked into what he had always known as an office to find himself in a lady's bedroom.

One summer holiday Ken and Lif spent their time devising and creating the treasure hunt to end all treasure hunts. It was in fact a murder hunt and so a lot of bodies had to be made. They filled boiler suits for the bodies and made papier maché faces and the hair used was known as crepe hair. The invitation went out from Sherlock Holmes (Ronnie) Hercule Poirot (Sylvia), Lord Peter Wimsey (Ken) and Father Brown (Lif) – all popular heroes of detective books – to help them solve a murder mystery. The hunt led the competitors all over the air station to find the clues – from the headless body of Lord Peter Wimsey's butler; to the bicycle of Dr. Watson, with an attached label addressed to No.1 Baker Street and thence to a shed where the butler's head was hanging, then across the airport to find the body of Irma La Douce crouched over the controls in the cockpit of an aircraft. The clue was a micro film of the next location, concealed in the fag ends of lipstick stained cigarettes. Across the airfield again to a pillbox and finally back to Moat House. The whole hunt had started with Sherlock Holmes arriving by helicopter to distribute the first clue and ended with Lord Peter Wimsey having arrested the murderer.

There was one comic incident which occurred when one of the local constabulary discovered the rather gory body of the headless butler and went and reported it to the local Police Station. A very wry comment came from a member of the official airfield police –'Pity he didn't tell us, we could have told him where the 'ead was!' There must have been many other memories but these only paled into insignificance in the light and excitement of the murder hunt.

The new school was also a source of pleasurable experience for Lif, who was enrolled along with about 100 other new girls. The main school buildings had been used as an American Hospital during the war and the Summer Term of 1945 was the first term it had re-opened as a school.

'I could hardly believe my good fortune," she recollected. 'There was a wonderfully free feeling there, wholesome food and a lovely, caring housemistress whose name was Miss Brown, and an overall general air of happiness. We were in what was known as an *out-house* called "Hillcroft" and had about 20 minutes' walk to school each morning, until we were allowed bikes in the sixth form, but we reckoned we were infinitely superior to those who were in in-houses up at school.'

If it sounds too perfect, then it was. For the 14-year-old Elizabeth Mills there was one major flaw in this paradise.

Lif said: 'The downside of joining with 100 other new girls was lacrosse. We were endlessly assigned to a beginners' circle, which was thoroughly boring, while we tried to master the various skills needed to play the game. I was also not too keen on having to play cricket in the summer as I reckoned the ball was far too hard.'

When Lif first went to St Swithun's the games mistress was the former England women's vice captain, opening bat and wicketkeeper, Betty Snowball. As it happened she was also a personal friend of Sir Leary Constantine (later Lord Constantine of Maraval and Nelson), the West Indies cricketer, who that summer had captained the Dominions team that defeated England at Lord's. Sir Leary would occasionally visit St Swithun's to lend a hand with the coaching of the school's First XI. Betty Snowball played in a total of ten tests for England, averaging more than 40 runs, and her top score of 189, which was made against New Zealand in 1935, was a world record in women's tests for many years, before falling in 1986, two years before her death.

While St Swithun's catered to a privileged sector of society, the girls were made aware of the fact that they had certain social responsibilities. Lif explained: 'In the summer term we used to invite a group of deprived children from the East End of London to come down to the school. They would only be there for the day, and they would be presented with bunches of bought flowers, although what they really wanted to do was to pick the wild flowers from the hedgerows and the meadows.'

For all the freedoms at St Swithun's there were still one or two restrictions which echoed The Chilterns. 'We could only bath a maximum of three times per week at St Swithun's,' said Lif. 'There was a red line around the inside of the bath, which was the maximum amount of water you were allowed to use. As I recall the water was consequently about four inches deep. So there was no wallowing in the bath, because the water would get cold quite quickly, and it had probably not been particularly hot in the first place. We had 20 minutes each in the bath, but that included the time allowed for getting dried and then dressed.'

Rationing was nationwide, and each person was allowed just two ounces of butter per week, so the girls used to eke out this meagre portion, in order to make the luxury item last a little longer. Lif again: 'Some of us used to cut the butter portion up into 'days', they were reduced to thin slivers as a result. There was an old enamel bread bin which was kept down a passage in the pantry of our school 'house', it was filled with cut bread and on a Saturday we would go through a solemn ritual of eating it all up, bearing in mind there was very little butter left by the end of the week, in order to get down to the fresh bread.'

In all Lif spent what she described as 'three very happy years' at St. Swithun's. She left the school in 1948, when she was in the Lower Sixth, without taking her Higher Certificate – 'That was because I was not destined for University,' she said – however she did gain seven credits in her School Certificate, the equivalent of the modern-day GCSEs, which was no mean feat.

6

MEANTIME,
IN GREENWICH
AND WARSAW ...

Lif not only left school, the whole Mills family also had to leave Hampshire, because Ronnie was handed a new posting, Commander of Greenwich Naval College. That marked quite a change in living accommodation for the family, as Lif noted: 'From living in quite one of the loveliest houses we had enjoyed, Moat House, we went to live in a flat in the College buildings.' Mind you, the Greenwich flat had its advantages. Lif conceded: 'We did have everything we needed and we were waited on by a Wren steward, who brought in all our meals too.

'My mother was not one who could sit idly by and do nothing, so she was given a role at the Maritime Museum, which is situated in Greenwich Park, to study and decipher Lady Hamilton's letters to Admiral Lord Nelson. She became completely engrossed in this work, which was later to put her in favour with Queen Mary, the Queen Mother when Her Royal Highness was on a visit to the Museum, taking tea at the College afterwards.

'Queen Mary was a pretty fierce old lady and if she felt that the person sitting beside her had nothing to say, she had no hesitation in demanding that another person should sit beside her, to ensure that she would be entertained. Thus Sylvia, having worked at the National

Maritime Museum, was brought in to fill the breach and converse with Her Majesty.

'On Queen Mary's arrival at the College, the Admiral's wife, who was a very timid lady, became extremely agitated, since she felt that Her Majesty, who was after all getting on in years, *must* be in need of a 'comfort stop', however, it appears that one should not make such a suggestion to royalty. The Admiral's wife however, unaware of the niceties of royal protocol plucked up the courage to pose the question. Queen Mary responded with a wry: "Well, what do you think?"' The Admiral's wife was left exceedingly red-faced.

It was during the family's time at Greenwich that Lif entered a tertiary education establishment. She enrolled on a nine-month shorthand and typing course in the Queen's Secretarial College for Gentlewomen in Kensington, quite a haul from her new home. It entailed commuting daily from New Cross station in South East London, right across the capital.

It was clearly a place which fostered snobbery, and Lif highlighted one amusing moment, which happened during the selection procedure: 'Miss Simmonds, the principal, used to interview all prospective parents and when my mother had had enough of the inquisition, which she reckoned was to ascertain whether we all ate peas off our knives, she decided to start name-dropping.

'At the time Prince Philip was attending the Staff Course at Greenwich Naval College, where my father was the Commander and this proved the deciding factor in my eligibility.'

While Lif was attending secretarial college her brother Ken was completing his sub Lieutenant's course at Greenwich, and his influence was quickly experienced by Lif as he introduced her into some of the rituals of Royal Naval behaviour. 'I was initiated into beer drinking, with the stern warning that "No naval officer will take you out unless you can drink beer" whereupon Ken and some of his friends handed me a mug of beer and said they were going to time me. I think I did a fair job of downing it and it was certainly the best way to start drinking beer since it can be pretty revolting if one sips it for the first time.'

There was a further royal visit to Greenwich Naval College during the Mills family's time there. 'On another occasion Queen Elizabeth (later The Queen Mother) visited the College with Princess Margaret, who had rather reluctantly accompanied her mother standing in for her father because King George VI was not well. They were due to open a portrait gallery of all the Admirals who had been Presidents at the College.

'A wonderful old man, Mr. Angel, who was in charge of the college silver came to my mother and asked if she had a special silver teapot from which he could serve Indian tea to her Majesty. He already had one for China tea in the college silver vaults, but he needed another. As it so happened my mother had the loveliest of Queen Anne teapots, which delighted Mr. Angel, so he polished it both inside and out, and the Queen chose Indian tea! I am now the proud possessor of said teapot.'

But in general the young Lif Mills was not overly impressed with royalty; witness her reaction to meeting the young naval officer Philip Mountbatten, later Prince Philip, the Duke of Edinburgh.

'A play entitled "She Married The Master" was staged at the college by various members of staff or naval officers doing courses at the college. Ken and his mates had designed and painted the scenery in their spare time. I think I had a small walk-on part, or perhaps it was as a member of the chorus. Whatever, I was deeply jealous of the girl who 'married The Master' as I had a bit of a 'crush' on the Master – a very good looking Sub Lieutenant in Ken's year. In fact, when I was later introduced to Prince Philip, I was far more thrilled with having spoken with Pete Stanford (the Master).'

Life at Greenwich College was most certainly privileged, adhering in many ways, as it did, to high society. There were "balls" rather than "dances" and Lif attended the nearest thing to a debutante's ball in her time there. 'I had a sort of 'Coming Out' dance at the College. My cousin, Barbara Russell, joined me. My mother made me the most lovely white satin ball gown and, as far as I can remember, it was a great occasion. At most Naval parties we all went together as a group and mixed up, so nobody was left out. My official 'escort' was rather a short chap, but at least he enjoyed dancing, and The Naval College certainly provided a marvellous venue for my 'coming out' ball.'

'This particular ball contrasted radically to a rather grand dance to which I was invited by a friend at secretarial college, who rejoiced in the name of Caroline Whittington Moë. It was all very posh, but really rather boring and, apart from taking the floor a few times with Caroline's father, I hardly danced at all. I had been looking forward to it so much, but was bitterly disappointed, so much so, that when I got home from it and my mother asked me how it had gone, I burst into tears.

Meanwhile back at The Queen's Secretarial College for Gentlewomen Lif was getting on rather well with her studies. 'I was one of a curious breed who loved shorthand although I was not so adept with the old typewriters, which required quite strong and dextrous fingers, and it has since taken me a long time to adapt to the modern electronic kind.'

Even so, on those old manual machines Lif achieved the minimum required speed of 60 words per minute. And she also shone with her shorthand, reaching 140 words per minute, a standard which was twenty words more than that required in order to be awarded the diploma.

She had barely completed her formal education when Lif applied for, and was appointed to the Admiralty, fortuitously as a clerk to her father in his new posting – Naval Attaché to the British Embassy in Warsaw, his first appointment as a Post Captain. In fact her father had initially been offered the job of head of the Indian Navy, which would have seen him being based in New Delhi. However, taking advantage of a tradition that a newly promoted Post Captain is allowed the privilege of turning down the first job offered to him, he had requested a posting a little nearer the sea, hence Warsaw!

Lif was taken on by the Admiralty as what was called a "locally employed" secretary; she was then able to work for her father at the British Embassy in Warsaw for the next two years, before undertaking the most important journey of her life.

Life in the British Embassy in Warsaw was not all work for Lif, though, as she explained: 'In the Naval Attaché's office we were not overburdened with work and so on many an afternoon we would close the office door and motor out to the Diplomatic Country Club a few miles out of town. There we started to fashion a basic nine-hole golf course along the banks of the Vistula (Wisla), the longest (651 miles) river in Poland.

'We had sand "greens" – the sand being bound together with old sump oil – and all was going well until we realized we needed a ninth hole to bring us back to the Club House. A kind lady farmer offered us the use of her field which fitted our requirements perfectly. However, when we returned a few days later, she had ploughed up her field! The next setback we had was when the Vistula overflowed its banks. However, the project was somehow completed and the American Ambassador hit the first ball off the first tee and a bottle of champagne was cracked.

'Thereafter, the course became the favoured place for diplomats to take their evening strolls. Oblivious of golf games in progress, the Italian Ambassador's wife in particular was apt to come up just as one was facing a tricky putt and kiss one on both cheeks and start a long conversation. There were many such diversions. Anyway, it kept my Dad and me busy.'

Those were interesting days in Poland, which was under communist control and Lif was a fascinated observer of activities behind this Iron Curtain: 'In those days, the Communists were very much in control of Poland and Konstanty Rokossowski was appointed as Marshal, being hailed as a 'son of the soil' when actually he had been responsible for holding back the Russian army from entering Warsaw until the Germans had had ample time to virtually annihilate the city. Warsaw was over 70 per cent destroyed. During our time there, buildings were being reconstructed from old bricks. Many Poles longed for another war as they felt that was the best hope for their future.

'One year a Peace Convention was held and the flag for the occasion was blue with a dove of peace emblazoned on it. Soldiers were marched to church and the only remaining hotel was requisitioned and furnished with furniture and carpets 'acquired' from private homes, all intended, of course, to give a good impression to visiting delegates.'

Of course in those paranoid times the host Eastern Bloc country would deny Service Attachés access to any and all military installations, so Ronnie Mills and his friend and colleague Charles Lockett, the Air Attaché, would go off on under-cover 'spying' trips. Naturally they would be followed everywhere by the Urzad Bezpieczenstwa or UB, the Polish Secret Police, and so they used to devise all sorts of dodges to evade their 'escorts'. Lif remembered a couple of ruses in particular. 'They would duck under a level crossing barrier just as it was coming down, leaving their escort car stranded the wrong side of it and therefore unable to sneak under and continue the surveillance.

'In Poland when visiting a café or restaurant it was obligatory to leave caps and coats in the vestibule so another favourite was to leave their coats in the car with the driver and go into a bar and order a coffee. Their pursuers were required to leave *their* coats in the cloakroom and as soon as they were settled with coffee on the table, the two military attachés would go out, and be well on their way before their pursuers had retrieved their coats.'

The Mills family appeared to take a rather malicious pleasure in outwitting, frustrating and generally confusing the members of the Polish Secret Police, who were always on duty. Even innocent family outings were monitored by them, but the Mills had another little trick up their sleeves. 'There were always three men in the secret police cars so, being a family of three, we used to go off on a walk in the woods, each going in a different direction, much to the confusion of our followers because they always had to have one of them remaining in the car. It must have created a taxing dilemma for them as they tried to decide who to follow.'

But the watchers were everywhere, even in their home. In their first residence some 20km to the south of Warsaw Lif recalled: 'We were living in the lovely little village of Konstancin-Jeziorna. There we had a wonderful Polish butler by the name of Matthew. He ran our large household, with his wife as our cook. Matthew was always so smartly dressed for dinner parties that many times he would be mistaken for one of the guests. Being of an economical turn of mind, when the dancing started Matthew used to go round the room and empty half-drunk glasses into a jug and re-serve them as new drinks. We reckoned that Matthew had been commissioned to report on us to the UB.

There was a distinct impression of being imprisoned in the country; there was a definite lack of freedom of movement, indeed of freedom itself, in post war Poland, to the extent that embassy staff members were prohibited from fraternising with locals, which meant that socially it was a limited world and Lif clearly found it frustrating. 'Sadly, we were allowed no access to ordinary Polish citizens and so our social world was confined to the international diplomatic crowd.'

Still they did their best. 'We had many good times and parties.' Although one of the first they hosted was perhaps not the greatest of them. 'When my parents had newly arrived they had no idea how diplomatic parties were run so my father decided that their first dinner party would be on Trafalgar Day. Unfortunately, he made a real diplomatic gaffe by inviting the French Ambassador. To compound the error he had drawn a picture of HMS Victory on the menu card.'

The language barrier had to be overcome, in particular by the various attachés and Lif remembered that her father did his best to master Polish, taking regular lessons, but Sylvia was not so assiduous. 'My mother felt she only needed a few words for communicating with our cook. Her most memorable phrase was used to describe mince pies at Christmas. Roughly translated it was "cakes with a carpet on top for Christmas". Fortunately the cook seemed to comprehend and made great allowances for the butchering of her language. Meanwhile, the live turkeys were fattened up in the cellar. There always had to be two of them or else they pined.'

Despite all the restrictions and the secret police, Lif was still able to do a bit of international travel. 'Early on in our time in Warsaw my father had to go over to Berlin to meet up with a naval colleague, who was part of the occupying hierarchy. As soon as this colleague, Gerald Tuck, heard that there was a Mills' daughter in Warsaw, he said "Send her over here quickly. My daughter, Diana is playing 'fast and loose' with all the young army subalterns and there is only one other English girl here!"

'Much to my delight, I was sent off to Berlin for a month. On the day of my arrival there was to be a Black Watch ball and so I had to be rehearsed in the intricacies of Scottish reels. Diana and I sat on the floor and, with the aid of various objects, such as cigarette boxes, books, mugs and a host of other things; we went through the moves of an Eightsome reel, Hamilton House, Strip the Willow and many more. We had a wonderful time.'

But Lif was no Goody-Two-Shoes and she confessed: 'On one occasion we went to the Opera House in East Germany and I am ashamed to say that we spotted a very white marble head. We reckoned she needed livening up and proceeded to add lipstick and a touch of rouge for her cheeks. We incurred the wrath of Rhona Tuck and had to return the next day to clean it all off. Rhona rather regarded me as a bad influence on her daughter, but I think it was six of one and half a dozen of the other. Anyway, we all remained friends for many years.'

Berlin proved to be a lively place for the young Elizabeth Mills, despite her having to do some unspecified studying in the mornings together with Diana. 'Otherwise we had the most tremendous time, going out with a different young man each evening, and riding at quite a speed through the Grunewald. So much so that we had to wipe down the horses before we returned them to the stables. Diana eventually became engaged to, then married, one of those young army escorts, who turned out to be George Younger (Viscount Younger of Leckie), who went on to become the MP for Ayr and joined Margaret Thatcher's cabinet as Scottish Secretary, although at the time I met him he was a charming, but very shy young officer in the Argyll and Sutherland Highlanders.'

Berlin was a magical place to be in those heady post war days and Lif said: 'It was amazing to see how alive and buzzing Berlin was so soon after the war. All the main streets were lit up at night and the main shopping street – the Kurfurstendamm – was thriving and lined with shops full of goods. I made the first and only purchase of my life on hire purchase there, a lovely leather handbag that I had fallen for, but I felt extremely guilty when I walked out of the shop with something on which I had only paid a deposit.'

Lif was to receive a proposal of marriage, although not in Berlin. This request for her hand came when she was on a family holiday from Warsaw. 'It was in Norway,' she said, 'where we were staying at a little skiing village called Gausdal. However, it was springtime, so there was no skiing, but it was still exceedingly beautiful, all the fields were carpeted in wild flowers. Our hotel was excellent and the meals were wonderful, particularly the breakfasts when every imaginable sort of food was laid out on a buffet table – every type of cereal, bread, cold cooked meats, smoked fish, cheeses and wonderful jugs of frothy creamy milk. No lunch was available, but then, after a breakfast like that we did not really need it.

'As for the proposal, that actually came via my mother. This rather odd little Norwegian approached her and said how much he admired me and how he would like to marry me. There was no interest from my side, I may say, I just treated the whole episode as a great joke, but I did make a bit of a mistake when I wore the same dress which he had commented on earlier, so he probably thought he was in with a chance.'

It was back in Warsaw that Lif learned ballroom dancing, something which she grew to love. The lessons began after they had moved to a flat in Warsaw, which was within walking distance of the British Embassy. She was joined in the class by her father.

'The classes were conducted by a glamorous American Marine called Gerry," she recalled. 'Having been trained in the Arthur Murray School of Dance, he was supremely well qualified, and able, to teach us such wonderful dances as the tango, rumba, and samba – to say nothing of the fox trot, waltz, and quick step. It was always very exciting to be called up to demonstrate a new step with Gerry. His great instruction to the ladies was to put their hand firmly on their partner's shoulder and 'resist'. On one occasion the very shy and rather prim Ambassador's secretary was called up and when Gerry said 'Isabel, you're not resisting', she looked up at him coyly and replied "I'm not *used* to resisting" which brought the house down.

'Some of the diplomatic parties were buffet suppers, followed by dancing to gramophone records. There were many continentals, who were superb dancers, and my mother and I used to compare notes when we got home as to whom we had danced with and, even, how many times.'

Warsaw held another attraction for Lif. A man. 'It was during our two years in Warsaw that I really fell in love for the first time. A most attractive doctor arrived at the Embassy, his name was Jock Rushforth. We attended many parties together, invariably staying on into the early hours of the following morning, and he always delivered me home safely.

'The two of us endeavoured to instruct people in the art of Scottish dancing. We often held different ideas as to the way they should be performed, which further confused our multi-national audiences, but it was all great fun. The evenings often ended up with a massive fry-up of eggs and such-like. I was very jealous of Jock because he was able to cook at least three eggs at once and they all turned out superbly. I could only manage one at a time.

'We used to do one rather wicked thing when we were returning late after a party. This would often be at a time when lots of farmers were dozing in their carts as they brought their produce in to town. The farmers used to leave the navigation up to the horses, who clearly knew the way. So what we used to do was to turn the lead horse around, getting it to face the direction from which it had come, and, of course, the other horses would all follow its lead.'

Sadly for Lif, her time in Warsaw ran out. Dr Rushforth had to be left behind, because Captain Mills was needed in another part of the British Empire – Ceylon.

7

SERENDIPITY

For most sea-goers, their first view of the magical island of Ceylon or Sri Lanka – known variously and at different times as the Pearl of the Orient, Paradise Island and Serendip – was of a hazy, half seen, emerald green hump on the horizon. This was most definitely not the case for Elizabeth Mills. Ceylon was anything but a green and pleasant island to her jaundiced eye – an impression which was to endure for some time, despite the efforts of many people around her to persuade her otherwise.

She emerged on deck just as the Marseilles-based André Le Bon, an ancient vessel of the Messagerie Maritimes line that had been commandeered as a troop-ship ferrying French forces to the war in Indo China, was dropping anchor in Colombo harbour. There was no facility for ships of this size to berth alongside the old passenger jetty, so those civilian passengers disembarking had to be ferried ashore. Disembarkation marked the end of a colourful month-long voyage for the two English women.

They had boarded ship in Marseilles in mid-November, in the company not only of France's brave soldiers, but also of a number of female 'camp followers', deemed vital to the needs of the army. In fact mother and daughter, having established themselves in their three-berth cabin, had returned on deck in order to scrutinise very closely the sea of faces of those still to board, in an effort to ascertain which of the women would be joining them for the next few weeks or so in their cabin.

They saw her at almost the same time, very definitely a French tart, a brassy blonde, wearing a fur coat, leopard-skin possibly, fake definitely. The unnatural hair colour and thick layer of make-up was in keeping with the rest of the false image she was trying to project. She was an 'army girl' all right. In unison they remarked: "I bet that's her!" Giggling like schoolgirls when their supposition was confirmed.

As things turned out the *'femme fatale'*, whose name they never actually discovered, proved to be something of an absentee companion, since, on the very first night, as Lif and her mother tucked themselves into their bunks, so the French lady, dressed in her negligee, took herself off, not to reappear until the following morning; when she re-entered the cabin, ruffled her bedding and dented her pillow, seemingly to make it appear that she had slept in it, before turning to the two English women and greeting them with a cheery, *"Bonjour, vous avez bien dormi, mes amies?"*

This was to be the routine for the rest of their brief time together, with just one break, when a stomach ache, *"mal à l'estomac"*, as she put it, confined *'Madame'* to their cabin for a couple of nights, before she was able to resume her nocturnal 'wanderings'. This mysterious behaviour was soon explained when Lif and her mother learned that the woman was in fact the captain's mistress.

It was Sylvia's strongly held belief that their 'cabin-mate' made a distinctly unsuitable and far from ideal travelling companion for her young daughter. In those far-off days 20-year-old women were more naïve, far less worldly wise certainly, than are their 21st Century counterparts, and legally did not reach their 'majority' until they were 21.

Thus it was then, that within a couple of days of boarding the André Le Bon, Sylvia had presented herself at the

Purser's office, to explain her misgivings about her young daughter having to share the same cabin with a lady of dubious virtue. The reaction was not what she had expected, nor indeed, what she had wanted.

No sooner had she mentioned the cabin number, 16A, than a knowing smile spread over the face of the Purser, then, with a shake of his head, he compounded the anxious mother's misery with the words: "Oh, we know *that* cabin," perhaps suggesting to Sylvia that the Purser regarded mother and daughter as being no different to their unwelcome cabin-mate. That was something she could not, and would not, tolerate. Unfortunately the Purser then followed up his revelations about the cabin-mate with the news that, sadly, there was apparently no alternative accommodation, at least not until the ship docked in Djibouti – the one and only stop on the voyage.

Mercifully the problem was solved before Djibouti hove into view, however. Within days, or perhaps that should be nights, the 'lady' abandoned the cabin with its two English roses, and moved herself and all her goods and chattels, to the Captain's quarters, where she perhaps should have been ensconced even before they had weighed anchor in Marseilles.

At this point seasoned travellers might well wonder why Marseilles should have been the starting point for a voyage to Ceylon for an English family. The reason, however, was simple. The women had originally travelled out to Malta, where Elizabeth's brother Ken was based with the Third Flotilla in HM Submarine 'Trenchant', in order to see him before they headed on to a new life in Ceylon.

They had covered the first leg of their epic voyage east in a Royal Fleet Auxiliary vessel, whose cargo consisted chiefly of supplies. However, since the families of Navy personnel were entitled to relatively cheap fares, the ship's manifest revealed the odd parcel of human cargo among its regular ordinance.

The accommodation on board was certainly very far from being luxurious by modern standards, indeed there were no *en suite* bathroom or toilet facilities. These were to be found across the corridor and had to be shared with other passengers.

One of their fellow passengers was a young naval officer called Matt. He was travelling out to Malta with two polo ponies, and proved to be a very entertaining companion. In conversation, he mentioned that he did not like washing his socks every day and so he had a system of rotating them.

The voyage to Malta had entailed crossing the Bay of Biscay, notorious for its inclement, not to say, unpleasant weather. True to form, the sea became distinctly choppy, and extremely rough, consequently many passengers fell ill. They found it difficult to summon up the will even to leave their bunks in order to get on deck where the fresh air would help to dissipate the waves of nausea; the experience left many of Lif and Sylvia's fellow passengers feeling somewhat pathetic, the only food and drink their seasickness allowed them to ingest being a cup of Bovril (the traditional liquid panacea for sea sickness) and some plain water biscuits.

This stormy passage across the Bay of Biscay also became a source of serious concern for Matt, the young naval officer, who explained that horses and ponies cannot be sick in the way that humans are, so he was anxious about the welfare of his equine charges.

Fortunately all the passengers, humans and horses, survived the ordeal and they were very soon able to enjoy the second leg of the journey, which, being on the

Mediterranean Sea, was relatively calm and peaceful and everyone was able to appreciate the contrasting tranquillity of the Med for a couple of days, before the ship docked in Valetta, Malta.

The two women spent a pleasant time on the island, but as enjoyable as those few weeks in Malta were, Lif discovered there was a major drawback to sharing some time with her brother, and that was the brackish water on the island; in those far-off days there was no such thing as desalination, thus the water was barely drinkable and had to be choked down, in fact it was almost impossible to swallow a glass of water without the addition of some cordial.

Eventually it was time to leave Malta, and Lif and her mother were flown to Marseilles, where they boarded the good ship the André Le Bon to continue their longer voyage to Ceylon, arriving in Colombo harbour just before Christmas 1951.

Organised entertainment on board the André Le Bon was minimal, to say the least. However, Sylvia quickly found her niche. Being an accomplished bridge player, she soon joined a table with members of the ship's crew and some army officers. Although Sylvia was proficient in bridge generally, she had never before experienced playing in French. The first time around when the bidding became fast and furious with *'un trèfle'*, *'un coeur'* being declared in quick succession, it came to her turn to bid and, being rather flustered she said *'un moment'*, causing puzzled looks at first, followed by understanding smiles, when it was realised she was not actually making a bid in 'moments', but rather was just gathering her thoughts and searching for the right response in French.

Sylvia laid no claim to being a linguist; however, she was always ready to 'have a go'. As regards speaking French she used to say *"Je parle français comme une vache Espagnol"*.

While her mother was playing bridge, daughter enjoyed herself on the dance floor with some of the French army officers. One young man in particular took rather a fancy to her and asked Elizabeth whether she had a boyfriend. He was, possibly, a bit surprised when she answered 'No', and so he took his chance to ask if she would be interested in forming their own *'entente cordiale'* by taking him on as her French boyfriend.

Being rather uncertain as to what having a French boyfriend might entail, Lif responded by telling him that he could just be a friend. Despite this slight rebuff he continued to woo her and they spent many an evening out on deck, enjoying the romantic scene of the moon on the water and the stars above. Elizabeth was always convinced that it was her rather deep-cut evening dress that he admired. She did continue to wear it from time to time, which was probably an unintentional encouragement.

Ronnie was overjoyed when he saw the ship approaching the passenger jetty in Colombo, bringing his wife and daughter back to him after several weeks on his own in Trincomalee. He had written home rather tragically describing himself as being the last man in to bat while the rest of the team had all gone home. Pellew House, the official residence of the Senior British Naval Officer had an extra long verandah, reminding him of a cricket pavilion.

Colombo was a busy place. The harbour was in the Fort area of the city where trams rumbled through and brokers travelled around to offices by rickshaw; bullock carts were a common sight. The majority of the mercantile offices were to be found in this area of predominantly colonial style buildings, and the quarter also housed the main shopping stores, including the likes of Cargills, Millers and Whiteway Laidlaw, all selling a vast range of imported goods. The place buzzed with activity.

The reluctant new resident was given an opportunity to savour her new surroundings because the Mills family did not head up for Trincomalee immediately, but rather stayed for a couple of days in Colombo, a stay which turned out to be fortuitous. Lif's parents were invited to lunch with the British High Commissioner Sir Cecil Syers and there they became reacquainted with Sandy and Maisie Matthewson, whom they had originally met on board the SS Antenor on their way out to Hong Kong in 1936.

In the course of their conversation Sylvia mentioned to Sandy, a leading buyer and shipper of tea in Colombo, that Lif was hoping to return to the capital from Trincomalee to look for a job as a secretary. According to Lif, Sandy's reaction was to say: "Oh, dear, I've missed out again. I am really looking for a private secretary, but we daren't pinch another from the High Commissioner's office." In those days it was expected that daughters of expatriates would go to work at the High Commission. These secretaries were paid an extremely poor wage, which in the case of the Mills would mean subsidising Lif to work in Colombo.

Finally it was time for Lif and her mother to be taken to their new home and the three of them set off for Trincomalee, where Ronnie was the Senior British Naval Officer and Captain in charge of the dockyard. They were to live in some style as well. 'We lived in Pellew House, a wonderful old Dutch bungalow, which had a verandah that was big enough to accommodate (and did) two deck quoits pitches. There was a panoramic view of Trincomalee harbour, known to submariners as Scapa Flow in technicolour.'

But as idyllic as the setting was, Lif was not happy there she wanted to live and work in Colombo and was determined to contact Sandy Matthewson, who had said he could give Lif an introduction to potential commercial employers in the capital.

Lif duly turned up for what turned out to be an informal job interview. The Matthewsons lived in an extremely well-appointed bungalow in Queen's Road, and when the door was opened to Lif she found herself confronted by a rather large, jolly gentleman, who immediately asked her if she would like a fifty-fifty. Lif accepted the offer of the drink, but she had not a clue as to what a fifty-fifty was, and was slightly worried that it might be a hefty measure of gin and tonic, whisky and soda, or brandy and ginger, or some other very alcoholic cocktail. Her reaction, therefore, when she discovered it was a fruit juice, was one of immense relief.

Things just grew better and better thereafter and after a relatively brief chat with Sandy he said: 'OK, you can start on Monday and my driver will call to collect you at 8.30am.'

Heath and Company, of which Sandy was one of two partners, was one of the major tea buyers at the Colombo auctions, and he numbered Joe Lyons, Tetley's, Twinings and several Middle Eastern firms among his clients. His partner Stan Campbell was in charge of the buying for Australia, which at the time was handled chiefly by the Australian Tea Board.

Lif enjoyed a great working relationship with Sandy, who had not hitherto had the luxury of a personal and private secretary. Her duties included writing his personal letters, as well as those to the various tea companies for whom he bought tea.

Lif recalled: 'Sometimes I had to write letters to his son Alec at prep school and even signed the 'Daddy' on occasion. I also had to run the odd errand for him, such as picking up his prescription cough medicine. And in a few instances I had to sign various shipping invoices, which was a very boring occupation.'

Generally though the Heath and Company work had to be dovetailed with other duties and Lif found herself doing as much secretarial work for the Colombo Hockey and Football Club, of which Sandy was chairman, as well as for the Ceylon Rugby Union, where he was also chairman, as she did for the company.

However Lif discovered that her new employer could be a little protective of his new employee, taking exception, for example, when she was taken out to the cinema on a date with a young trainee from Joe Lyons called David Theobald – but perhaps Sandy's disapproval stemmed from the fact that Lif had been at her new job for barely a week and he didn't want to lose her too quickly.

Naturally the socialising between the Matthewsons and the Mills became a feature of life in the1950s Ceylon and Lif remembered one occasion when, with the prospect of a weekend at her parents' home, she and Sandy travelled up to Trincomalee after work and on the way enjoyed a sumptuous lunch of roast pheasant at the Kurunegalle Rest House. As they walked out to the car following the lunch Sandy decided, much to the consternation of his driver, Richard, that he would take over the driving for the rest of the journey. They had hardly gone any distance when Sandy failed to control the vehicle and the car hit a culvert stone. Sandy hurt a wrist in the collision and then to add insult to that injury, had to telephone the Mills family and ask them to send a car to get them up to Trincomalee. Sandy ended the day with his wrist encased in a plaster cast, and on his return to Colombo suffered any amount of teasing and ribbing from his colleagues and friends when they heard how he had sustained the injury, and on a weekend away with his secretary.

During these early days of her working life in Colombo Lif was a paying guest of Gary and Jocelyn Shattock, at their home in Jawatte Avenue. She was to become extremely friendly with the family. Her social life in those days was centred on the Naval crowd, since ships of the Far East and Persian Gulf fleets frequently stopped off at Colombo, so Sunday supper and the on-board cinema were regular features. 'Girls were not exactly plentiful in Ceylon so those who were able to socialise with the naval officers had a whale of a time. I had lots of boyfriends and enjoyed good times with them but no real sentimental attachment,' she said.

Lif also took part in other activities. 'I joined the Colombo Amateur Dramatic Society, played tennis at the Garden Club and golf at the Royal Colombo Golf Club – courtesy of my father being a member – a privilege accorded to the RN Officers when in Colombo and Trincomalee.

One morning, a few weeks into her job, Lif was sitting at her desk when the glass door to the office was opened by a tall, athletic-looking man. She glanced up at him, saw the shipping list in his hand and realised he must be a freight broker and so she returned to her work.

Meanwhile Sandy rose and walked around his desk to greet the newcomer and exchange a few pleasantries. That done he turned towards his secretary and said: 'Mark Bostock, allow me to introduce you to my new secretary, in fact my first *personal* secretary, Elizabeth Mills. You're going to have to get along with her, because you will be seeing a lot of her, since she will also be doing a great deal of sports club committee work.'

Lif rose and walked around her desk to shake hands with her future husband.

8

WILD PARTIES
AND
A PROPOSAL

It was not love at first sight. After shaking hands, Lif simply returned to her desk and got on with her work, while Sandy and his young visitor launched into the business of the day. As things turned out however there were to be ample opportunities for them to meet thereafter.

A few months after Mark had joined Keell and Waldock, but a while before he was introduced to Lif, he had left his lodgings with André and Babs Willis and had set up house with some other young bachelors in what was known as a 'Chummery'. He described the set-up: 'A chummery was a lovely and remarkable institution. It was an all-male assembly of bachelors. The group of you would take over a bungalow or similar building; then each member of the chummery would be assigned certain specific roles within the group; one would be appointed to do the cook's book, another chap would be put in charge of arranging entertainment et cetera, you were all expected to take on these sort of responsibilities. So I joined up with Mike Thornton who had been in the Indian Army during the war with the Lancers and, who was ultimately to become my brother-in-law; the third member of our household was a lovely, curly-headed madman called Cliff Shaw.

"Mike was up in the top echelon of Ceylon amateur golf, he actually beat Pin Fernando in one final and got into the second or third round of the British Open Amateur at St Andrews and played off scratch. I was a keen golfer in those days. So we had a wonderful chummery, it was called Leura Annexe and was on the Galle Road, just behind the Galle Face Hotel, and was opposite the George Stuart bungalows near St Andrew's, the Scots Kirk. In those days no building along the coast line of Colombo was permitted to be more than one storey high, which was eminently sensible since it permitted the sea breezes to blow through the city and thus they had a wonderful cooling effect throughout the city. Sadly, high-rise buildings inevitably came with 'modernisation'. Leura Annexe was a mouldy little place, but down towards the sea it was lovely, and in any case it was a wonderful place to start off one's bachelor life in Colombo.'

Unfortunately for Mark, this particular group did not last long together, because for a couple of the members their bachelor days were numbered. Mark recounted how it all ended: 'I think it was in the first winter of our chummery that my parents paid us a visit, accompanied by my younger sister Ruth. Mike married my sister, and Cliff shortly thereafter also decided to get married so that was the end of our chummery.

'Mike was Cliff's best man and I remember rehearsing Mike's speech. He had to write it down because in those early days he had quite a pronounced stutter and we couldn't let him have any sentence beginning with "P" for Peter because it was ppppppp and there were quite a few SSSSSSs. So we had to go and plan his speech; he would be marching up and down in the old chummery repeating the lines, while we were giggling at this and that and making changes and correcting it, saying for example, you can't have a sentence beginning with "P". That wedding was a memorable occasion in Kandy, but sadly it meant that we had to split up the Leura Annexe trio.'

But Mark adored the way of life in a chummery, so much so that he decided to start one of his own. He recalled: 'One of my clients, a lovely little man called Dr C O Perera, lived in the Balangoda area, Agar's Land, which I used to visit. He was the doctor in charge of the psychiatry in a nearby hospital. But he also had a big house close to the Welawatte canal, just off the Havelock Road and one day, on hearing about my intention to set up my own chummery, he suggested: "Why don't you take it over because I am not going to live there?"

'He'd only just recently built it for his retirement and it was a very spacious bungalow, but rather unusually it had been built around a rose garden, which was consequently something of a feature in the centre of the building, albeit open to the skies. So I gathered some bachelor chums, Terence Allen from A F Jones, Alan Bayly from Aitken Spence, Richard Pyman, who was a cousin of mine and who also worked for Keells in rubber, then there was Dicky Luff, who was a tea taster and working in Leechmans. So we had four rooms, which at a pinch we could turn into five. It was absolutely splendid.'

But it was not so splendid that the inhabitants of Everard Lodge, as this bungalow was called, did not feel that it could not be improved. Mark said: 'Terence was a brilliant organiser and pretty well from the outset he said we just couldn't have a bloody rose garden, so we all got down to it with *momaties* one weekend – a *momaty* is a sort of Portuguese hoe, used in paddy fields. So we dug out this rose garden and then we got some mason or bricklayer to make a swimming pool for us. In those days we were so poor that we were all living off the smell of an oily rag, even so Terence said we must have some underwater lights in our pool, so a pane of glass was built into the wall of this pool with just some putty around it and a light was installed behind the glass; of course, it was thoroughly unsafe, because the cavity with the power and the light would fill up with water and consequently when this happened any swimmers would receive an electric shock. That apart, it was a wonderful feature, and we had really the greatest chummery in Colombo at that time, and one of the most popular.

'Whenever one of us went on leave we would always open up the room of the chap who was on leave and somebody else would come in and take it on, as a result we had a fairly regular through-put of chaps, who were looking for a bed and consequently there was a lot of movement of people and friends.'

Among this to-ing and fro-ing of bachelors at Everard Lodge was a certain Ken Atkin, the very same former study companion of Mark Bostock when they had been pupils at Marlborough College a few years previously. By coincidence Lif had just started being escorted out by Ken.

As Mark explained: 'In those glorious days we had girlfriends, and girlfriends were passed on to somebody else, so unlike this modern generation, we could go and have a girlfriend, and she wasn't someone you were going to marry, and she wasn't desperate for you to go and put a ring on her finger. There was a lot of fluctuation and the girlfriends came in and joined in the chummery life. We would all go shooting together and head off to piss-ups and rugger matches. It was a lifestyle that simply doesn't exist nowadays, as far as I am aware. They weren't people that you just took out once or twice and then they were yours, in our day everyone was asked out together, as a group or gang. I reckon we had easily the happiest chummery in Colombo in those days.'

Lif certainly had fond memories of the happy times spent there, although Mark was away on leave when she was first introduced to Everard Lodge. 'The bungalow was the venue of many wild parties,' she recalled.

One of the events which occurred annually on Independence Day 4th February, was a soft ball cricket match between the rival rugby clubs – Colombo Hockey and Football Club and the Ceylon Rugby & Football Club. Each club visited the other in alternate years and it was the duty of the visiting team to arrive in a procession of some sort, usually portraying a topical event.

Lif remembered one occasion when the Colombo Hockey and Football Club arrived, dressed up as the Queen's *durbar* or hunting party – Her Majesty and Prince Philip had recently visited India, and the Duke of Edinburgh had taken part in a tiger hunt. For this particular celebration the Colombo Hockey and Football Club had somehow managed to hire an elephant from somewhere and it had 'Prince Philip' (John Burrows) and 'The Queen' (Ann Sawdy) seated on its back. They were also attended by four horses, which were ridden by members of the CH&FC, who were dressed in military attire and carrying pennants; these were followed by a motley collection of other well known characters, ranging from Ghandi, in his white cotton robe and sitting at his spinning wheel, to someone equipped with a wheelbarrow and a shovel to pick up the elephant's droppings. There were dancing girls and others playing an assortment of musical instruments.

Lif said: 'We processed down one of the main roads in Colombo and nobody seemed surprised. However, the current High Commissioner thought we were insulting the Ceylonese, for reasons best known to himself he had completely missed the point. The Ceylon Rugby & Football Club (CR) was exclusively for the Ceylonese and, likewise, the Colombo Hockey and Football (CH) was exclusively for the ex-pats, both Clubs enjoyed a friendly rivalry. A game of soft ball cricket took place, followed by an excellent curry lunch. The return visit of the Ceylon Rugby & Football Club saw them stage a Muslim funeral with all the traditional trappings, including all the members dressed in white with much chanting and laying down of a white cloth over which the coffin was carried by the pall bearers. The only problem was that the 'corpse' in the coffin (the eminent Ceylonese Legal Draftsman, Percy de Silva) became extremely hot and in need of a bit of fresh air so he lifted the lid and sat up, much to the consternation of some travellers in the top deck of a passing bus who all rushed to the side where the funeral cortege was processing almost causing the bus to topple over.'

As an ardent Royalist, Lif had actually made a point of catching a glimpse of The Queen and Prince Philip when they had visited Ceylon in early 1953. Her determination to see the Royal party took her, a non-racing enthusiast, to the race course, where the Queen and Prince Philip were guests. André Willis had managed to get himself a press pass, since he wanted to record as much of the royal visit as possible on his 8mm cine camera. On this occasion they were blessed by being outside the grandstand and standing on the pavement, where they were practically the sole bystanders. Lif reckoned they got their own special wave. 'Sadly, for André,' said Lif, 'his whole reel of film came back blank.'

Around this time a party, organised by the chummery gang, was held at the Queen's Club. The theme was 'Seafarers through the Ages'. Lif was at a bit of a loss as to how she would appear, but eventually decided to be a mermaid. She made an elaborate fish's tail out of bright green satin and wired at the end. This and the green satin top were adorned with shells and her long tresses were made out of crepe hair. Her escort at the time was Ken Atkin and when it came to fitting in his very small car, the tail caused considerable difficulty but, luckily, the car had a sunshine roof so Lif was able to stand up for the short journey.

Other chummery parties embraced some pretty bizarre, not to say naughty, themes. 'One of those was "The thing one would least like to be" and according to Lif that resulted in some extremely outlandish and rather graphic outfits, including the one worn by Terence. 'He turned up dressed as a 'wet fart' with a diaphanous, sort of balloon-like garment around his lower half,' Lif recalled with a certain distaste, 'and he had a seemingly endless supply of stink bombs, which he would let off at inappropriate moments, much to everyone's amusement and discomfort.

'Then there was a mourning party when we were all supposed to wear black, but a few of us decided to break ranks and we dressed ourselves up as "good time girls".'

Everard Lodge was certainly a great source of fun. Mark remembered another such collection of single young men in Colombo whose individual members were not quite as happy and at ease with life. 'There was another chummery I remember that was down in Horton Place. A wild young fellow, also in a broking firm and one of his chummery mates snored like hell, and he used to come in with his popsy late at night and wake up the whole household. It was a one storey, very spacious house and this idiot of a fellow got so sick of this other chap disturbing him at night, that after a monumental thrash, while this chap was snoring on the floor, they lead a cow into the bungalow and persuaded it to lie down beside the snoring body. The unfortunate victim of this prank was considerably non-plussed when he awoke to find a cow lying beside him. Well we didn't have any nasty episodes like that. Ours was a very friendly chummery.'

One occasion Mark remembered very clearly, concerned the chummery cook and the level of the sherry bottle which kept mysteriously going down. Terence and he decided to catch the cook out as they were certain he had been imbibing the sherry on the quiet. So they peed into the bottle, put the cork in and upturned the bottle before putting a discrete pencil mark on the label to mark the level. Over the next few days they watched as the level of the "sherry" went down and then decided to confront the cook with the evidence. Cookie was duly summoned and the accusation with the supporting bottle levels put before him, to which he replied "no no, every night in masters' soup, little little sherry putting". A case of "hoist with one's own petard" or pee!

Lif couldn't actually remember when she and Mark eventually started going out together, but she said: 'It was probably to have Chinese Chow at the Hirmani Gardens Chinese restaurant.' However she did recall that it was around the time that she dressed up as a mermaid that she began to be more aware of Mark, and she started to pay a great deal more attention to him, she even felt a pang of jealousy when she thought he appeared to be rather close to a great friend of his sister, Ruth. Fortunately for Lif that interest was not all-consuming, and Isobel Meredith subsequently married one of Mark's cousins on the Hunting side. In due course, Mike and Ruth and Mark and Lif used to enjoy eating chapattis down at an eating house called Pilawoos in the Pettah. Diners would sit in small cubicles with an overhead fan. One of the games was to see if a chapatti could be thrown up into the fan so that it landed in the next cubicle. Pilawoos still has a mention in "Taste Colombo"

It would appear that the romance between Lif and Ken had been doomed from the first dance. 'I knew I could never get serious about Ken, delightful though he was, because he was the most awkward and appalling dancer,' said Lif.

Mark was particularly light on his feet, something which had not escaped Lif's notice. Through her growing interest in him she gradually became aware that he was beginning to show signs of interest in her. Gentleman that he was, (not to mention sensitive), the Old Marlburian Ken Atkin stepped aside the moment he realised something was afoot between the two and made way for Mark; although the Atkins (Ken did eventually marry) and the Bostocks were to remain great friends thereafter.

So Lif was able to continue her links with the chummery. In the early days of her courtship with Mark the pair was invariably among a group of young people, comprising chiefly the quartet of Everard Lodge Chummery chaps and three or four single young women. Lif described the times thus: 'Many a happy weekend was spent as a chummery girlfriend. Mark played hockey and rugby and these Up-Country rugger and hockey matches were invariably followed by a buffet supper, or the occasional dinner and then a dance at the sports club. These were of a more formal nature, hence evening dress was *de rigueur*, so after the match was over we would all go and change, the girls into gowns, the men into dinner jackets and black ties.'

These weekend trips inevitably involved overnight stops and Lif recalled: 'We invariably stayed with a lovely planter friend, Johnny Johnson, who became extremely embarrassed if ever there was a weekend when it was just the two of us staying, since by then we were regarded as a couple, and there was no other female around to perform the role of chaperone. Johnny was one of the very first people to be told of our engagement, at which news he breathed a huge sigh of relief, since he told us that his reputation among his fellow planters was becoming increasingly precarious because of his broadminded approach to our situation when we were his guests.'

A tradition developed at these Saturday night dinner-dances, which saw the revellers return to Johnny Johnson's bungalow where a thermos of soup would be left out on the table for the party-goers. This taking of soup was not without incident. 'Noel Gratiaen was with us on one such occasion and was distinctly the worse for wear. Indeed when we were following Johnny's car back to his home, he found his passenger a real handful. Noel kept toppling over sideways and almost knocking our host out of the driver's seat.

'Eventually we all arrived at our destination and after manoeuvring the drunken Noel, in to his seat at the table, Johnny, our host, poured out his soup. Johnny then advised Noel to hold on to the stopper of the chilli sherry bottle when adding the contents of the bottle to his soup. Noel however was too drunk for the instruction to register, so, needless to say, the top of the shaker flew off and all the chillies fell into his bowl of soup. However, with the exception of the shaker top itself, which Johnny was able to prevent Noel from spooning into his mouth, he swallowed the lot, and did not seem to notice the fiery chillies as they were ingested.'

After the enormous expenditure of energy the previous day and night, Sundays were, almost of necessity, more leisurely. 'The Sunday programme in those days was pretty regular,' said Lif. 'It would start off with a visit to Beach Road for a swim and some time on the beach. In those early days very few Ceylonese were to be seen on the beach and there were certainly no little boys touting for business as they do in modern days.

'Following the swim, there was usually a massive curry lunch either back at the chummery or occasionally out at Mount Lavinia Hotel just half a mile down the coast. In the evening the routine would usually incorporate a visit to the cinema, with everyone finishing up having a drink at Queens Club with other friends.'

Interspersed among these fun weekends were visits to Aislaby, and whenever they went up to the estate Mark would proudly point out where the factory was situated as they topped the Haputale Pass. Lif was frequently unsure of what she was looking for, but always nodded.

There was one period of alarm for the young couple – the danger being sensed more by Mark than by Lif. There was some sort of unspecified civil unrest in Colombo, and Gary and Jocelyn Shattock's house, where Lif was lodging, was very close to the building which housed Radio Ceylon. Mark's fear was that the insurgents might try to take over Radio Ceylon, and in so doing Lif's lodgings, and more importantly her safety, might be compromised as a consequence. The situation was further exacerbated by the fact that there were just two women, Lif and Jocelyn, left in the house to fight off any attempted invasion of the property because Gary Shattock, who was beset by health problems throughout his life, was in hospital at that time.

The solution was fairly straightforward to Mark's mind. It was his responsibility to provide the two women with some form of protection, so he presented them with his shotgun, not that Lif thought it would do either of the women any good since she was certain that she would have both eyes closed if she had to pull the trigger, thus endangering everyone around her, since if she had no idea where the shot would finish up, no one else could possibly know either. Thankfully the insurgency fizzled out, so Radio Ceylon and Lif and Jocelyn were never troubled, and therefore Lif did not have to use the shotgun.

Mark shared Lif's love of dancing, which quickly became another key feature of their courtship. They soon took to making regular appearances at the dances which were staged at the Galle Face Ballroom – no local 'palais' this, but rather a swish and sophisticated setting. There was a live band, and these evenings also featured a 'cabaret' of sorts; this took place when members of the hotel staff formed a line and swept the dance floor from time to time during the evening. Everything about the Galle Face Ballroom spoke of class. One evening Lif decided to try out a friend's pipe. She was barely a puff or two into it when she was presented with a silver salver, upon which rested a polite note written on the establishment's headed notepaper, which informed her that pipe smoking was not allowed in the hotel ballroom.

These evenings of dance were not confined solely to the young of Ceylon; however, Mark's parents Norman and Elizabeth also enjoyed themselves on the dance floor. And on one occasion when Mark's older sister Eve had joined them for the evening her father danced her around the room declaring proudly: "You'd never think she was a mother of four would you?"

The manager of the hotel Gene Hollo became a good friend of the Bostocks and the best suite was always reserved for visiting members of the family when they came out at Christmas.

When there was no rugby or hockey to distract them they would turn to sport of a different nature – shooting.

Mark and Lif often went on shooting trips with 'the gang' and these trips contained their moments of high jinks and practical jokes. Lif recalled an occasion when she was enthroned on the 'thunder box' preparatory to heading off at an early hour to the snipe fields. Suddenly there was a loud bang right behind her, which caused her to leap off the toilet thinking she had been shot. She hadn't though. It turned out that Ken Atkin had poked his shotgun through a hole in the loo wall and had discharged a blank cartridge. But blank cartridge or not, it certainly scared the proverbial out of Lif.

It was on one of these shooting trips on the North East coast, in April 1953 that Lif and Mark actually became engaged, although it was hardly the most romantic of moments. Lif's long-suffering hosts, with whom she was a paying guest, had been pressed to come along as chaperones for the young couple, especially for Lif, since on this occasion Jocelyn Shattock was the only other female on this particular trip.

They were all staying at a remote rest house near the village of Mulaitivu. The setting was just about as romantic as one could imagine when the young couple went out to the beach hand in hand. The setting certainly lent itself to romance, a remote beach fringed by palm trees which swayed gently in the cool breeze, the sea lapped softly on the shore and a glorious full moon shone overhead. Mark though was not a typical romantic. If anything he was borderline awkward. The pair of them were also being bitten to death by sand flies. Initially the subject of the engagement just cropped up in conversation, with Mark saying that he might one day ask Lif to marry him.

Lif remembered: 'I think I rather pressed him, at that point, since I was certainly very keen to marry him. So eventually Mark announced: "And that is supposed to be a proposal."'

9

A
WEDDING
OR TWO

The deed done, Mark's proposal accepted, the couple then hastened back to the little rest house to get out of the way of the sand flies.

Mark wanted to do everything properly, so he insisted that the engagement could not be made public until he had asked Lif's father's permission to marry her.

Meanwhile when Lif told her Mother that she was hoping to marry Mark, Sylvia's retort was "Well, Darling, he is no oil painting, is he? And another thing, his legs aren't a pair!" That, according to Lif, was so typical of Sylvia's direct approach. Norman Bostock's wise advice to newly-weds or those engaged to be married on the secret of a long and happy marriage was "Always get into your wife's bathwater – done it all my life".

The weekend the engagement became official came when Lif travelled up to Trincomalee by the night mail. She was seen off on the train by her boss Sandy Matthewson, who was delighted with the engagement. Mark was already up in Trincomalee, having just finished making his RNVR contribution to the Joint Naval Exercises, which took place every year when the Indian, Pakistani, British and Ceylonese Navies had exercises together.

Mark duly asked Captain Mills for his daughter's hand in marriage. Lif's father's response was: "Oh, Mark, what a surprise", before promptly heading off for the fridge from which he produced a perfectly chilled bottle of champagne, to give the lie to the "surprise". In addition an inadvertent spelling error turned what should have been a straightforward piece of reporting in the Daily News that weekend into a slightly risqué article which stated that: "Full back Mark Bostock will not be playing for the Colombo Hockey & Football Club Rugby XV as he is up in Trincomalee on navel [sic] manoeuvres."

When it came time to buy their engagement ring, the newly engaged couple went down to Main Street, Pettah, to visit the Central Jewellery Store, owned by a Mr. Harid, who had been the Bostock Family's chosen jeweller for many years. He was also the recommended jeweller to visiting Royal Navy personnel. As soon as Mr. Harid discovered that Elizabeth Mills was about to be part of the Bostock family, he immediately offered to change the sapphires in the pendant that he had previously sold to Ronnie Mills.

There was a lot of affectionate leg-pulling and practical joking among the members of the Everard Lodge chummery. One evening when Mark and Lif had been out together, Mark was delivering Lif home and she noticed a tear in his corduroy trousers so she suggested he leave them with her and she would mend them for him. Thus he went home in his underpants.

The following morning Lif received a phone call just after arriving at the office. The person at the end of the line purported to be the Chief Inspector of the Cinnamon Gardens Police Station.

According to Lif the conversation ran thus: "Is that Miss Mills?" a question to which Lif responded in the affirmative.

The 'chief inspector' then asked if she had been out the previous evening with "one Mark Bostock". Again she replied in the affirmative. The 'police officer' then made the shocking announcement that the aforementioned Mark Bostock had been had up for 'indecent exposure'.

Naturally Lif was distressed by the news and as soon as she had put down the phone on the 'Chief Inspector', she rang Mark in great consternation and asked if he was in trouble.

The conversation went on for a while until the boys at the other end of the phone could contain their laughter no longer and finally admitted that it was a spoof.

For the record the trousers did get mended and were duly returned to their rightful owner.

Mark and Lif's wedding was set for October 3rd 1953, but Lif used to tease Mark that he would never have proposed if his great friend, Terence Allan, hadn't done it a few weeks earlier. She felt that Mark did not want to be held responsible for the break-up of the chummery at Everard Lodge, and that instead he had waited for one of the others to make the first move, then he knew it would be OK for him to follow suit.

Mark's version of the break-up of the Everard Lodge chummery certainly supported Lif's view. 'We broke up, inevitably, because Terence had got a steady, absolutely lovely girl Mary, or Maria, who had come out with her old uncle, I'm not sure on what pretext. Terence suddenly came in and over a whisky said, "Look old chap, I'm afraid I'm going to break up the chummery, I'm going to go and get married". So I said, "You can't do that, Nobber – it's just not on." He said, "Yes, yes I can. I am sorry about this, but I am going to marry Maria." So that was that.

Lif remembered that when Terence who was also in the tea trade, announced his engagement, a telegram was sent off to Sandy to tell him the good news. Sandy's reply was, "Well done, Jones Buyer [Terence]; suggest Heath's rep [Mark] enters the market, marking up prices for golden tip". Ever since taking on Lif as his personal secretary, Sandy was always determined that Mark and Lif should get married.

In fact Mark quickly bowed to the inevitable and he admitted: 'It had to be said that I had got, shall we say, more than just a steady girlfriend at that time, Elizabeth Mills, so I said, "Oh to hell with it, I suppose I had better get married as well if we are going to break up the chummery."'

These impending weddings prompted the idea of one final, wild party to celebrate the break-up of the quartet. The chums decided on a Bacchanalian theme at Everard Lodge. So the invitations went out, inscribed on an elaborate scroll, purportedly from Lord Bacchus, urging invitees to celebrate or commiserate on the 'breaking up' of the boys' chummery. All those invited were commanded to wear the appropriate attire. This gave rise to a rather unusual task that Lif was asked to perform for Sandy. Lif explained: 'Sandy was determined to go as some sort of a Sultan and so I was required to make him a pair of voluminous trousers, which were to have a shiny cummerbund with a dagger attached to it, in order to set them off.

'I duly produced the trousers, but being rather stupid I had made no provision for him to be able to have a pee without having to take the trousers off. And worse, Sandy had been sewn into the cummerbund, so when nature called he attempted to haul at the elastic at the bottom of the trouser leg, trying to pull it high enough to allow him to pee. It proved a tricky job apparently.'

Lif also had to apply crepe hair to his chest to make it look hairier than it was. Luckily she did not have to unstick it.

All of this was definitely not included in Lif's job description when she first started working for Sandy. He was transported to the party in a hackery that was drawn by an office junior. A hackery was a light vehicle, not unlike a rickshaw, it had two large wooden wheels, with spokes and a basic seat that could accommodate two adults. It was generally drawn by a bullock, but in this case Sandy nominated a young member of the office, Tony Savill, who was at the time the young assistant in Heath & Company on behalf of Joe Lyons. He had to perform the duty of being a 'centaur' and run when harnessed between the shafts of the 'hackery' on which Sandy was seated. Again, Lif had to sew tufts of coconut fibre on to Tony's pair of corduroy trousers. For her part Lif adopted the role of a dancing girl, and she ended up by accompanying the conveyance as it progressed through the streets. Potentially it was an embarrassing thing for young people to do, but Lif said later: 'I don't think anybody raised so much as an eyebrow as we passed them.'

All the guests responded magnificently to the challenge of the invitation and only Norman Bostock was allowed to appear in his silk dressing-gown so that he could carve the ham in style. Beth, his wife was also dressed in simple fashion. It was a great party.

According to Lif, despite her mother's rather disparaging, even dismissive, remarks about Mark's appearance, she grew to love him dearly. Sylvia however, was rather concerned when Mark reckoned his 'demob' suit was perfectly suitable for their wedding. She offered at least to buy him a new tie. As it turned out, on the big day everyone was staggered to see that Mark had been shamed into purchasing a new suit for the occasion.

Years later Mark's indignation was still apparent: 'I had in fact had to buy a new suit; they wouldn't let me get married in my demob suit!'

Sylvia had also offered her daughter £100 to spend on her wedding dress and trousseau. Trousseaux – or rather more familiarly known as the 'bottom drawer' – usually included items of linen and household necessities, but as Mark already possessed most of these, Lif decided to spend £30 on her wedding dress and the balance on her 'going away' outfit and some fancy nighties.

Mark's entire trousseau consisted of several new pairs of sleeping pants made out of Tabralco, which was a popular cotton material, and the said pants had borders of nursery rhymes. Throughout his life, Mark loved to get in to his sleeping pants on all possible occasions, and most particularly during weekends spent at their beach bungalow down the coast. This attire was lovingly described as 'Mark's Day and Nights' by our dear friend, Christine Gordon. Strange at this may seem a pair was subsequently offered and accepted by a visiting American who had accompanied Sybil Maxwell Joseph on a visit to Sandsend (Bentota). He arrived at the jetty in an immaculate while linen suit and Panama hat and looked thoroughly out of place at Bentota. Mark immediately said "My dear chap you are never going to enjoy yourself here dressed like that. You need a pair of my 'day and nights'. Once fitted out in this thoroughly unlikely 'suit', he relaxed and enjoyed the weekend.

Shortly before the wedding day, there was a visit by a touring rugby team from New Zealand, and their reputation on this tour was fearsome, apparently the team had left not a single fullback standing in the home rugby clubs thus far. In desperation a call was made to Mark to step in and play against the Tourists, even though the Colombo Football and Hockey Club's Rugby Club knew Mark was just days away from his nuptials. Naturally Mark answered the call for help, although even he pleaded for clemency and to be treated gently by the opposition in view of his impending marriage. Sylvia, of course, was horrified, but she could say nothing. Mercifully Mark survived that particular match in one piece.

That same year there was a ball at Queens Club and Mark insisted on buying Lif a new ball gown. He probably considered her not to be very fashion conscious because, soon after their wedding, he insisted she got herself some brighter clothes. In those days there were practically no ready-made clothes to be had and so fabric was bought and given over to tailors. Mark was not at all interested in his own appearance and certainly neither of his two sisters was renowned for their taste in clothes.

Sadly shortly before Mark and Lif were to be married their much loved Irish Vicar Douglas Harpur of Christ Church, Galle Face, was transferred, leaving Ceylon just three weeks before the big day. However, later on he was able to be present at three of the most important occasions in the lives of the Bostocks.

Firstly, he baptised Gillian at the parish church of Newbury in 1955. If the saying is correct that when a baby yells at his or her Christening, the devil is truly chased out of him or her, then Gillian certainly got rid of him, because she yelled from start to finish. Despite this rather unfortunate occasion, Douglas remained completely calm, and kindly consented to baptise Claire (also in Newbury) a few years later – she, it should be noted, behaved impeccably. The third family occasion was a sad one, when Douglas conducted Sylvia's funeral in 1960. Douglas had brought great comfort to Sylvia when she was in Papworth hospital in her last days of her battle with cancer, He smiled at her through the casing of the iron lung, saying "I will see you again". She smiled back at him.

During these years, Douglas was in charge of a very well-known and ancient Norman church in St. Albans which was frequently visited by curious visitors both from England and abroad. Whenever Douglas spotted a few loitering around the back of the church, he would climb up into the pulpit to deliver his sermon and very deliberately turn an hour glass upside down as he pronounced his text. There would then follow an immediate exit of sightseers.

Shortly before Mark and Lif's wedding there was the other Everard Lodge chummery nuptials to be witnessed, as Mark explained: 'First, Terence got married in Colombo. I was his best man for that. 'Then, three weeks later Lif and I were married at Christ Church, when Terence was *my* best man. Terence was a very good squash player, I think he was head prefect at Wellington and captain of rugger there, despite being a short-arsed little chap, he was their hooker and he was a damned good squash player. He always pipped me in the squash court, but when he came back from his honeymoon we had a match, I think it was the final of the club competition and it was the only time I actually managed to beat Terence because he was absolutely on his knees by then, and I was able to notch my name up on the board of Queens Club squash tournament.'

In fact the various chummeries forged lifelong friendships. In his latter years Mark reflected on further good times, long after the chummeries had disbanded: 'As we all left our late 20s and moved in to our 30s the chummeries broke up, and we all got married; but the great thing was that it didn't prevent us from continuing to have the most enormous fun just as we had enjoyed as bachelors with girlfriends. We still used to go off on shooting parties, playing rugger and hockey and going up-country and in fact led quite an exhausting life at weekends.

Shortly after Mark and Lif were married there was an up country hockey match to be followed by a black tie dinner and dance at the club. Terence and Maria were also staying with Johnny and Mary Johnson.

Mary and I were changing together when there was a knock on our door and Terence appeared asking if Mary had packed his shoes. She hadn't, but feeling rather smug I said I had remembered to pack Mark's footwear. However that smugness of mine was short-lived, because moments later there came a second knock on the door. This time it was Mark, asking if I had packed his trousers. I hadn't. The upshot of it all was that thereafter Terence, who was something of a dandy, did his own packing to make sure nothing was left behind; Mark however, was never bothered about such sins of omission and forever left the task of packing to me. It should be said that I was always a good packer, and we invariably shared a suitcase anyway.' Mark's comment on the event was "we were no longer thinking as bachelors and had passed over the packing of suitcases to our new wives" and they, in their newness to the task, had made a bloody balls-up and had given us one of everything. I remember we had to borrow like mad as between the two young wives they could just about dress one man.'

Mark also recalled a shooting trip up-country: 'We went up to the North East Coast, I don't think Ronnie Lushington was with us, so it was a pretty ham-fisted lot of shots amongst the party. We had with us Dennis Jones who had about three words of Tamil and Sinhalese, and when we got up to Mulaitivu, which of course was to become the hot-bed of the Tamil Tiger country, we found a lovely looking snipe field with a tank at the end of it.

'Dennis marched up to somebody who looked as if he might speak English and asked him if there were any *kaswatuwa*, which is the Singhalese word for snipe, and he looked a bit dumbfounded because most of them are Tamils up there, so

Dennis started flapping his arms and making squeaking noises and trying to pretend he was a snipe and this old boy told Dennis that there were some very good birds but that we would have to approach them as if were not going to shoot them, in short, we were to act as if we were all just out for a stroll. He advised to "Take your golf umbrellas, as I see you have some with you. If you put your gun down your side, so that you don't let him see your gun and you walk out as though you are just out for an evening stroll, then you can walk right up to them."

'Of course when we did this strange manoeuvre and put Dennis into the lead with his golf umbrella up, all that flew up were a few diddy doits (Mark's name for a Red-wattled Lapwing) and a paddy bird (egret) or two and one or two storks or whatever. There wasn't a snipe in sight.'

But back to the wedding, and although Douglas Harpur was unable to marry Mark and Lif, being rather a perceptive man, he did not think his successor, Rex Luckraft, would be much in tune with the young couple and so he requested that the Bishop of Colombo, the Right Reverend Rollo Campbell Graham, conduct the marriage.

As it happened Mark knew the old boy, having met him when returning from leave, the two of them were travelling back to Ceylon on the same ship. The Bishop was a very tall man and also very learned, and Mark remembered how the pair of them would pace the decks daily, discussing highbrow topics.

The Bishop agreed to stand in, but he probably had not conducted a wedding for many, many years and was not at all acquainted with the form. Christ Church had a very good choir conducted by a rather dour and serious Scot – Norman McLean – and he insisted on a rehearsal before the wedding. Some of the couple's friends thought it would be a bit of a laugh to join the choir for the day, but they were in for a rude shock, because Norman McLean did not stand for any nonsense, there was certainly no larking around and they were put through a rigorous rehearsal.

October 3rd dawned overcast and gloomy and it was not long before the heavens opened, and there was quite a strong wind, but it did not affect the happiness of the day. The groom, accompanied by his best man Terence Allen, turned up well in time; the bride, Elizabeth Mills, accompanied by her bridesmaids Judy-Jane Shattock (daughter of Gary), Tessa Greene (whose father Neville was a partner at Keell and Waldock and a cousin of Mark's) and the young Mandy Willis (daughter of André and Babs), was also punctual. The Bishop added a bit of pageantry, dressed as he was in his full attire complete with crook, crozier and mitre, he also inadvertently contributed to a moment of high comedy during the solemnisation of Lif and Mark's union, when one of the young sons of some Dutch friends, on spying the Bishop in all his High Church finery, cried out "Look Mummy, there's Father Christmas".

The reception was held at the Garden Club and, in fact, was the last social occasion before the club was taken over by the Ceylon Lawn Tennis Association. Mark remembered the day fondly: 'Ronnie and Sylvia Mills were extremely kind. Father and Mother came out and we had a marvellous gathering." In fact it was a great celebration with many friends from all walks of life. Sandy Mathewson was down to make a speech and Mark and Lif held their breath, both apprehensive of what the fun-loving chap might reveal, knowing them as well as he did. But in the event the couple's fears proved groundless, Sandy made a magnificent speech. There was another dodgy moment when it came time to cut the cake, because the top tier began to topple, thankfully it only teetered to an angle approximating that of the Leaning Tower of Pisa. Another potential disaster averted.

The method of departure for the happy couple was rather primitive, even a trifle bizarre, but Mark had been determined not to have his car festooned with clutter and tin cans, nor did he want old boots attached to it, so he had parked his car out of sight of everyone, around the corner, and the pair left the reception on a hackery, with a friend, Tony Savill, between the shafts.

The departure did not pass without incident however, with Lif almost toppling off her seat after Tony leaped in the air when some firecrackers were set off under the vehicle. A photograph of the incident shows that Mark had anticipated what was about to happen and was already leaning back to counter the sudden movement.

The first night of the honeymoon was spent in the Mount Lavinia Hotel, but the newly weds found that they were not alone. They heard a skittering, scratching noise and when the light was switched on they spotted a rat running around the picture rail.

The honeymoon proper was scheduled to start the following day and if that old romantic Mark had had his way the newly weds would have spent the rest of it somewhere up country. It was Sylvia who had been instrumental in persuading Mark that they would be far better leaving Ceylon and going abroad for their honeymoon, rather than spending it up on the Bostock family's tea Estate at Bandarawela, or wherever. She reckoned Mark was far too well known and people might well be keen to visit the young honeymooners. As a consequence Mr and Mrs Mark Bostock flew up to Kashmir to spend two weeks on the Dal Lake and moored alongside the Nagin Bagh, outside Srinagar, on a houseboat.

A chap by the name of Karanai was in charge of the houseboat, and on arrival the newly married Bostocks found, to their consternation and frustration, that their bedrooms were at either end of the boat. When it was pointed out to Karanai they were actually married, he suggested they might like to share the same room. His next suggestion was they might like a double bed. When the affirmative was given, he rushed off and presently there was a loud splashing in the lake and a small paddle boat drew alongside with the said bed perched perilously across it. The sliding doors were then pulled aside and the bed was duly posted through.

The only down side of this idyllic honeymoon was Mark's passion for climbing mountains. Lif was a bit of a reluctant starter, but was told firmly to stick to a steady pace and keep going. When the couple spent a few nights in Gulmarg at what used to be the old golf club house, Mark announced that if they climbed the hill behind the golf course they would come to a beautiful azure lake. Spurred on by Mark's enthusiasm, Lif soldiered on and eventually they arrived at the lake. However, it being October, the lake was frozen over and covered with snow. For a few terrible moments the wedding ring was in great danger of being hurled down the mountainside. Further insult was also added to this injury in that Mark insisted on regaling Lif with tales of one of his earlier girlfriends who was a keen climber and when the going became hot she would take off her top and on occasions her bra as well. Not to be outdone, and particularly on her honeymoon, Lif who had grudgingly struggled up a particularly rocky hill, on reaching the summit stripped off her bra. The evidence of this dramatic action was captured by Mark on his 8mm cine camera and later shown to a horrified cousin, Richard Pyman.

It was extremely cold at Gulmarg and the bathing arrangements were pretty primitive, comprising as they did, a tub in front of the fire. Fortunately Mark had a pair of 'long johns' with him and these he kindly lent to Lif, having first hung them up in front of the fire. Not very romantic bed garments, but they still helped against the chill. The windows in their room were in a sorry state and they were mostly covered over with brown paper, which failed to keep out the bitingly cold wind that whistled through those frames which lacked glass.

10

TEA THINGS
AND
TEETHING

During the early days of their married life, when Mark went off to the office on his scooter, Lif had few responsibilities around the home apart from the daily routine of 'doing the Cook's book', which entailed telling the cook exactly what meals were required and checking up on his shopping expenses. Even when the babies came along there was always a nanny. However, Lif, like her mother before her, was not one to be idle and she refused to join a bridge four or meet others for coffee, instead she threw herself wholeheartedly in to helping out with various charities and much-needed social work. Among her activities, she joined a committee which supported St. Margaret's Home for orphaned children, which at the time was run by Anglican nuns. Lif also joined the Child Protection Society.

Recently, when visiting an old Greek friend of more than fifty years standing, Lif shared the memories of the days when they used to visit the merchant seamen who had been hospitalised in Colombo. She and the then Dina Zarephi, later Dina Langridge, made an excellent team since the latter could speak a number of foreign languages and so could communicate with the seamen, while Lif provided the transport to take them to the various hospitals. Sometimes they would be asked to dances organised by the Missions to

Seamen, which had its headquarters next to St. Peter's Church and close to the Passenger Jetty in the Fort area of Colombo. Unsurprisingly neither Lif nor Dina was too keen on these invitations.

However, one of the more rewarding activities was inherited from the wife of the Defence Adviser at the High Commission. Every year before Christmas, all Lif's friends were invited to a coffee morning and each guest was asked to bring along a toy or gift for a child, unwrapped, so that it could be given to an orphaned child in one of the many homes that they supported. These toys were then individually wrapped and marked with a name and given to a boy or girl of suitable age to have as their very own present. The joy on the children's faces was reward enough for all the hard work.

Lif also became a supporter of the Bishop of Colombo's Christmas appeal for the two Leprosy Hospitals. Lif said: 'Each Christmas I would accompany Mrs. George R. de Silva – a wonderful old matriarch – to the hospital at Hendala to hand to the patients their gift of a sarong, small towel and piece of soap. I made it a point actually to place the gifts into their hands instead of just putting the present on the end of their bed. One year Mrs. De Silva asked me to accompany her to the Leprosy Colony on an island off the East coast from Baticaloa. Usually the money was given to the local priest but Mrs. George R. told me confidentially – "I'm sorry to say dear, but I don't always trust these clergymen." We completed the long and tiring journey uneventfully.'

The newly-weds were in no particular hurry to start a family. For a start their liquid assets did not lend themselves to feeding additional mouths. If the truth be told it was a source of deep disappointment to both of them that Keell and Waldock had not seen fit to mark the wedding with a promotion or, at the very least, a pay rise for Mark. He did receive a married allowance from the firm, but this was little short of risible. So the couple began married life living in rented accommodation in Siebel Avenue in Colombo, where they could afford to employ just one house servant, although they did pay (as did other households in the area) for an itinerant bathroom 'coolie', since the menial tasks involved in keeping things hygienic were far too lowly for someone as grand as a housemaid or houseboy.

So Mark carried on his broking, and as compensation there were always the enjoyable weekend trips up to Aislaby to look forward to. Mark was nothing if not a traditionalist and, like his father before him, took his lunch in to office each day in a 'tiffin carrier' and then had time before the work of the afternoon started to have a quick snooze in his father's old deck chair.

By this time Mark had discovered that he suffered from various allergies, which naturally bothered him, because the side effects, congestion of the nasal sinuses to name but one critical symptom, had a not insignificant bearing on his professional ability to taste tea.

He was to talk of the allergies later in his life, and concluded that they had been triggered by stress. Typically he has wry comment to one allergy in particular. The discovery was made before an important tea sale. Initially Mark had thought he was going down with a cold, so he said: 'I doused myself with cinnamon and quinine (which was my normal remedy for a cold) but it didn't seem to help.' The next was to seek medical advice. 'I went to see an ENT specialist, who just told me that I was probably suffering from a whole bunch of allergies, and he divided my arm up into segments; he then stuck needles into the skin in each segment, and, of course, tea came up in a great blister straightaway. He confirmed to me I was hyper-allergic to a number of things.

'This puzzled me because we had never had allergies in the family before, but I hadn't realised that it is this thing they call "stress" nowadays, this arises when you suddenly find yourself pushed into doing something you are not accustomed to doing, and as a consequence you worry about it. In addition to all the tea broking responsibilities I had all the finance of the proprietary planters on my hands as well and I suddenly found myself becoming totally allergic to all sorts of damned things. Unfortunately this is probably the source of the skin allergies and asthmatic problems from which my poor daughters, Gillian and Claire, and a grand-daughter suffer.'

There was stress around every corner it seemed, and not long after the wedding a tricky situation arose that Mark found himself having to deal with pretty much singlehandedly. A J Wickwar died. Now it so happened that Mark's father Norman Bostock and AJ had long ago made a gentleman's agreement that, on the death of either, the other should be given 'first refusal' to buy the other part of the property for a fair valuation.

Unfortunately AJ had made no mention of this arrangement in his will, nor was there a mention of this concord in any other document in his possession for that matter. Thus the disposal of Malwatte had to be by sealed tender. In Mark's mind it was paramount that this very valuable property should remain as a single unit, so he felt he *had* to make a successful bid. But Mark knew that most rival bidders would be aware of the pressure on the Bostocks to purchase the property; he was also further aware of the way the Ceylonese mind worked and therefore he had a shrewd idea that in certain circumstances there was no such thing as a 'sealed bid' and that once he had submitted his tender that his rivals would be shown his offer to give them a chance to outbid him. So he lodged his bid fairly early on, then *five* minutes before the tender closed, he entered a second bid, which gave his rival bidders no time to top his latest offer and he was thus successful in securing Malwatte.

Some years later, when John Keells took over the hotel called 'The Village', the directors decided that there should also be a craft shop on the premises. Lif made the mistake of saying that she would be happy to source some of the stock. To this end she used to purchase batiks – both wall hangings and lengths of batik fabric that she was confident would appeal to European visitors. She then employed girls to come to her home and take away material for sewing, then ensuring they returned with the finished article for checking. Often the locally sewn garments would not be made with matching threads and the finish was frequently not up to standard. Having put forward this idea, she then found herself largely in charge of keeping the shop fully stocked. Lif often accompanied Ken Balendra and David Blackler (directors of John Keells) to the hotel to keep tabs on activities in the shop. There had been much dispute as to possible names for the shop, until Lif finally suggested that it be called Suriya Kala (Sinhala for Sunshine Crafts), a name which was agreed upon.

Some of the most popular items in the shop were the beautiful batik silk scarves which were produced by an order of nuns who kept mulberry trees to feed their own silk worms. The scarves were woven on the spot with meticulous care.

The manager of the shop used to have a bit of trouble with some of the Italian guests, who had a tendency to hand over counterfeit Ceylon rupee notes, of which there always seemed to be a plentiful supply in those days. This was a bit of a game for them and they happily rummaged in their bags, when they were caught out, and produced the right currency.

There was a time when virtually all imports were banned. This was during one of Mrs Bandaranaike's terms as Prime Minister. However, the good that came from this was that many foodstuffs began to be made locally – biscuits, jams and chutneys, cordials and jolly good they were too. Accompanied by two male visitors to do the week's shopping, Lif was approached by the shop assistant who said, *sotto voce*: "Lady we have off-white sugar today" The boys were highly amused. A slight problem, however, was the chronic lack of toilet paper, however the airmail editions of the Daily Telegraph proved a good substitute!

Meanwhile things were progressing at Aislaby. The Superintendent on the estate at that time was a Scotsman named Alan Allan, who was a brilliant agriculturalist, but, like many planters, he was rather dismissive of the abilities of 'tea men' to taste and differentiate between the various teas. He would frequently set traps for Mark when he laid out the teas to be tasted in the factory. He was always disappointed, because he never did succeed in catching Mark out.

In those days the planters had little interest in the manufacture of the tea, so this was left to the 'Tea Maker' – the senior member of the factory staff.

Alan had previously been a planter in the Low Country where the agriculture differed in many ways from the methods practised in the hills; this was mainly due to the different weather patterns. The Uva district, in which Aislaby was situated, was very dry on the whole, whereas in the Low Country there was more rain. Much to the disdain of the local planters, Alan introduced many of the ways he had learned in the Low Country, and with great success. Mostly, the differences were in the method of pruning – i.e. not the drastic way the bush was cut back, but leaving 'lungs' so that the plant was able to recover quicker and enable earlier plucking. When the traditionalist Uva planters saw the success of Alan's methods their criticisms were soon stifled and they discreetly adopted many of them themselves.

Initially Lif found Alan's wife Ella to be a somewhat formidable personage and an intimidating presence, but her looks deceived, in fact she was anything but as self-confident as she appeared, and in any case was actually possessed of a soft centre. However Ella, for her part, was equally in awe of the senior Bostocks, and whenever they visited the Allans she was always very keen to have everything just as they would have liked it. For example, Ella knew that Mark's father Norman enjoyed his evening game of bridge, but also that he liked his supper at 7.30pm sharp. On one occasion time was marching on and Ella alerted the head boy to bring supper in ten minutes. However, on the first announcement of supper, the game of bridge had reached a vital stage and Norman was keen to complete the rubber, hence supper had to be delayed. After several attempts to serve supper the boy obviously got fed up, came in and announced "soup is on the table, Lady".

The fact that Ella was also a qualified nurse was used to great advantage on the Estate, because it meant that she was able to have a huge input, and to do a wonderful job, in, among other things, helping the expectant mothers in the labour force, both with assistance in delivering the babies and in teaching care of the babies post-natally. In fact conditions for the labour force on Aislaby were quite advanced for the era. The workers were blessed with a number of fine facilities; to begin with there was actually a maternity unit on the estate, where the mothers-to-be would be transported to the local hospital or clinic, unless they insisted on having their babies in their homes.

There was also a *'crêche'* for the babies when the mums went out to pluck. This *'crêche'* was basically a room full of slings, which were suspended from the roof, and into which the babies were placed; an older lady in the workforce was then employed to keep the slings swinging gently by prodding them with her toes in order to encourage the babies to sleep.

Another innovation for the labour's living conditions was the annual allowance for each family which permitted them to paint their door in the colour of their choice. They were also given curtains for their homes. This encouraged a great pride amongst the workers and they took care of the whole area and thus the worker who had previously been responsible to act as a sweeper for the 'lines' was redundant and the labourers made sure that the whole area was kept clean; after some years the traditional 'lines' were replaced by 'cottages'. Certainly the Aislaby workers would boast to their fellow labourers in the area of 'how we do things on Aislaby'.

The two couples naturally became very friendly, although the newlyweds did find that socially, staying with the Allans was a trifle inhibiting, because the older couple were rather punctilious about the social niceties, and Mark and Lif were ever mindful that they had to be on their best behaviour when they were guests. For all that they used to enjoy themselves immensely and Alan taught Lif an unusual trick for meal-times. He revealed to Lif how he always managed to keep his pile of salt to the side of his plate. In order to prevent it sliding in to the gravy he would put a drop of gravy or sauce on the side and *then* pour the salt on. Lif immediately adopted this trick and continues to use it.

Mark had learned much under Alan and so was devastated when Alan announced that he intended to retire, and that he and Ella wanted to go to South Africa to be near their daughter, Elizabeth.

The word 'indispensable' sprang to mind as Mark contemplated the daunting task of finding a replacement for Alan. He spent long hours racking his brain and trying to think of where he could find a suitably experienced person. Eventually, not knowing where to look or even how to go about recruiting in the first place, he gave up. But, fortunately for Mark, Fate did not surrender so easily, in time-honoured fashion, he decided to give himself a break from the worry and stress of it all and took himself up to Nuwara Eliya for a round or two of golf, and to spend some time seeking consolation and inspiration at the 19th hole. It was while he was there that he bumped into an old mate, Ronnie Lushington, who was also looking very gloomy.

On inquiry, Ronnie revealed that he had just lost his job with Ceylon Tea Plantations. For his part Mark said he had just lost his Superintendent on Aislaby. There might have been a slight pause at that point, before he asked Ronnie if he might agree to work on Aislaby, provided Mark's father Norman was in agreement and could foresee no difficulties in his son employing a friend. Norman duly agreed to the arrangement and Mark had found himself a soul-mate. The pair of them had met years before on the rugger field. Their first meeting – or rather more aptly – their first encounter was hardly the foundation for what was to become a lifelong friendship. Mark had recently arrived in Ceylon and was representing the CH & FC, whereas Ronnie was playing for the Kandy Rugby Club. In those days Ronnie was known as the 'Kandy flyer' as he was pretty swift on the wing. However, during the match he fell victim to one of Mark's bone-crunching tackles. This physical assault on her husband greatly displeased Ronnie's glamorous wife,

Bobby, who was among the spectators on the touch line. Bobby later revealed that she always hated every player who felled her beloved husband. However she did forgive Mark in time and indeed became very fond of him and one of his greatest admirers. Naturally a few years on Mark and Ronnie worked wonderfully together. Ronnie was always open to new ideas, of which Mark had plenty, and thus he proved the perfect foil for Mark's fertile imagination. Aislaby was on the move.

Initially, there was just the one bungalow on Aislaby, Kirchhayn, which was the residence of the current planter. It had previously been the home of the District Judge and was situated on the first area of land bought by Norman. It was a spacious house and surrounded by a large and beautiful garden. Later a small bungalow was built in the garden to house the head clerk and, later still, two rows of sheds for the poultry were constructed. A bungalow near the factory was in due course constructed in order to house the Assistant Superintendent. There was also a sports hall.

1954 was to be a spiritual landmark in the lives of both Mark and Lif. Bryan Green who was Canon of St Martin's in the Bullring in Birmingham, and a well-known evangelist, visited Colombo to conduct a mission. Lif went along to the first session, which was held in the Ladies' College hall, and, after hearing all Bryan had to say, she walked forward and gave her life to Jesus. She came home thrilled, and Mark accompanied her to the second session held at the Methodist church in Lipton Circus. Lif had by then explained what happened to her the day before and Mark also went forward that evening. This marked the start of their Christian journey. They both continued to attend all sessions of the mission. Lif was so joyful that she used to go round singing in her tuneless voice the old mission hymn "He lives, He lives, Christ Jesus lives today. You ask me how I know He lives? He lives within my heart".

Bryan became a great friend and on a subsequent visit to Colombo he even braved a weekend at the family's bolt-hole in Bentota, where he was subjected to the traditional "well shower" by the children. True to his nature he took it in good part.

When Bryan died, Lif and her sister-in-law, Ruth, drove up to Birmingham to be present at his memorial service. Bryan was quite controversial in some of his views which may have prevented him for attaining the status of Bishop, but what a tribute to the man, when of the six Bishops attending his memorial service, five had acted as his chaplain.

The wife of another of the vicars at Christ Church, Galle Face, was particularly keen on acting. Although she was unable to take part herself, having been stabbed in the back while working in India and was crippled, Mollie Milford organised some theatricals at the church. One Christmas a lorry was hired on the back of which the nativity story was portrayed. The 'float' went to different districts of Colombo each evening and the gospel story was read in the language prevalent in that particular area and the actors had to learn their cues in all three languages. Lif performed as the angel Gabriel. In fact, all three Bostock girls – Gillian, Claire and Lif have at one time or another performed as Gabriel. On another occasion, there was a very moving re-enactment of the crucifixion. On this occasion the whole church building was utilised with the crowds coming up all three aisles with the denouement up near the alter. Lif was privileged to be given the part of Mary.

It was not until they were into their second year of marriage that Lif fell pregnant and Mark immediately laid down the law as to where his first child should be born. Fearing that any child born in Ceylon, as he himself had been, would find gaining British citizenship difficult because they would be second generation born abroad, and therefore removed from the entitlement to hold a British passport, Mark decreed that Lif should return to England to have the child.

It was around this time towards the end of 1954 that Mark was finally invited to become a partner of Keell and Waldock. Although the couple had limited liquid assets, thanks to the foresight of his father Norman, Mark had ample collateral to raise sufficient capital to buy into the company. Mark was well aware that it was this which made him an attractive prospect for the continued prosperity of the firm. Instead of leaping at the offer and accepting it immediately, Mark revealed his business acumen, simultaneously stunning the partners, by requesting to see the accounts of the firm, prior to making his decision to accept the offer, since he felt they were just keen to have his financial contribution, which would not have been insubstantial. In the end their reluctance to release the accounts forced him to turn for help to the Registrar of Companies. Once he had studied the figures and seen what he wanted to see he finally accepted their offer.

It was not long after gaining the partnership that Mark was able to reveal his commercial prescience when he suggested to the other directors that Keell and Waldock should buy its own stores' premises rather than pay rent to another company. This sparked a great deal of intense discussion among the partners, before it was finally agreed that the firm should put in a bid for Dodwell's stores on Glennie Street. The bid was successful and, years later and after much renovation and additional building it stood for many years as a wonderful site for John Keells and Walkers Tours and Travels.

On the domestic front the plan, when he discovered that he was to become a father, was that Mark would accompany his pregnant wife back to England to be present at the birth. However, rather cruelly at the last minute, his immediate boss in the tea department, Maurice Murdoch, insisted that *he* had to go on leave. Maurice was a cousin of the well-known radio comedian, Richard 'Dickie' Murdoch, who kept everybody cheerful in the dark days of World War II with his weekly programme of 'Much Binding In The Marsh'. Maurice's decision meant that Mark, as his deputy, inevitably had to remain in Ceylon. This caused the young couple a great deal of sadness and also resentment as they both felt it was such an important time in the early years of their married life. As a result, Lif had to travel back to UK alone while Mark waited anxiously for news of the birth. This incident served to underline the selfishness of Maurice, who would occasionally appear late in the office on the excuse that he had been detained by clients. However, the tell-tale slick of red paint behind his ear would give away the fact that he had been working on his boat down the coast at Bentota.

So the very pregnant Lif had to make the long sea voyage back to the United Kingdom on her own. She was miserable when the day of departure finally arrived, partly because they were simultaneously giving up their rented home in Siebel Avenue, so there were very few of their own things left in the house. However they did manage to salvage a bottle of Babycham and some cloyingly sweet sherry, which were poured in turn into a plastic picnic mug that Mark had unearthed, and with which they toasted Lif on her forthcoming journey back to Blighty.

On the first day out to sea on the SS Willem Ruys, Lif found herself feeling rather down, so she took herself up to the sports deck where she started practising deck quoits. Lif was already quite a competent player due to many games on the verandah of Pellew House in Trincomalee. She was quite surprised when a young man approached her and asked her if she would partner him in the ship's quoits competition. Lif's pregnancy was not at all obvious from her figure and nobody realized the situation until she appeared that evening in a very voluminous smock. Her poor partner must have been extremely embarrassed; however, the couple went on to win the event. During the last two rounds, some of the onlookers, on realizing Lif's condition, took to picking up her quoits from the deck for her.

Lif was met by her parents and went off to stay with them at Dockyard House since, by that time, Ronnie was Captain in Charge of Portland dockyard. Ronnie was very proud to be the only Post Captain to have his grandchild's pram in the hall. The Portwey Maternity Hospital was identified as the place where the birth would take place (despite having been the Workhouse in an earlier incarnation) and an eminent obstetrician was chosen to attend to Lif privately. However, the baby was late in making her appearance, and things became a trifle tense because the obstetrician was due to go on holiday, so he introduced his locum to Lif.

Unfortunately Lif reacted very adversely to the proposed change in specialists and was extremely upset. So Ronnie then consulted the Navy doctor in the Dockyard, who said that it would be in order to insist that the consultant delayed his holiday until Lif's baby had been born. Eventually, ten days after the due date, Gillian made her appearance on 4th August, 1955 and while Lif was still in the delivery room the doctor promptly asked her if he could have permission to go on his holiday. She graciously allowed that he could.

Lif's little private room looked like Covent Garden with all the flowers, and the Sister was sure a bigger and better bouquet would soon arrive from the proud father. Mark, of course, had never heard of Interflora and the only response to Lif's ecstatic telegram announcing the good news of a 'beautiful daughter...' was replied to by 'beautiful query'.

By the time he eventually arrived in Portland on leave his daughter Gillian was six weeks old. Much to Lif's consternation, the first thing that Mark did was to go straight out in to the garden and lifted the baby out of her pram. Impressively, but perhaps understandably given his sporting prowess, he did not drop her, nor did he even look remotely like doing so.

In true Bostock tradition, not only the new born baby but also Lif herself had to be shown all around the greater family and Gillian became very uncertain with being handled however lovingly by so many strange people. Mark and Lif had employed a temporary nanny, Betty while they were in England, and her presence enabled them to do some socialising as well.

Lif had just one concern about the early months of her baby's life and that was how she was going to cope with the weaning process; breast feeding on a four-hourly basis was all too easy. Lif's fears were allayed when she attended the local baby clinic in Portland and she looked around at the other young mums and thought to herself 'if they can do it, so can I.' Needless to say, there were no problems. Farex and Farley's Rusks were the staple diet for babies or an egg mixed in with the bottle.

There can be very few babies of three months old who have spent a night in the Savoy Hotel in London but this happened to Gillian, courtesy of Norman Bostock. Norman was so delighted to have his son and his two daughters all in the UK at the same time that he treated the whole family to a night at the Savoy and to a performance of 'Salad Days' at the Vaudeville Theatre just across The Strand from the hotel. This was really the first popular musical to hit London after the end of World War II and did a lot to raise spirits in England.

It was quickly apparent during these few weeks of going around the family, that Gillian was only happy with Lif and Mark and the lovely nanny Betty. So there were, understandably, a few misgivings about how she would react when they returned to Ceylon where she would be surrounded by an admiring sea of dark faces. The fears proved groundless. When Gillian finally arrived in Ceylon, aged six months, she beamed and gurgled at the new nanny, Mary, a Ceylonese, and then at all the fuss made by the rest of the household servants in the new family home at 425/11 Havelock Road. Mary had been chosen by Mark's sister Ruth, because she was a close friend of her own nanny, who was at the time looking after their first son, Luke. And the climate did not seem to have any effect on the bouncing baby girl. She revelled in the heat and the humidity, contrary to the expectations of the members of the family back in England.

The Ceylonese love all babies, but they were especially fond of fair-haired children, and although when she arrived Gillian actually had no hair, when eventually it did grow (according to Lif she had her first hair cut aged two years) she did turn out to be fair-haired, and was naturally much-loved by everyone.

Gillian was an easy baby and Lif took quite naturally to her new role as a mum, even worrying her own mother in the way that she tackled the baby's first bath at home when she followed the nursing home's instruction to soap the baby on her lap and, having done one side to seize an arm and leg and flip the baby over in order to soap the other side before finally putting her in to the water.

The cheerful cherub that was Gillian seemed to be a happy little soul, with smiles for everyone, and when she was finally able to talk she even christened herself 'Jolly on' and she soon became known to many friends as 'Jolly One'.

Soon after the Bostocks returned from leave with little Gillian, Lif's parents came to stay. At that stage Gillian had developed a most upsetting habit of refusing to be put to bed at night by Lif. When the final moment came for 'lights out', she would cry out 'Mary, Mary' and until Mary, the nanny came, she would not settle down. This was much to Mary's delight, but was a source of great sadness and distress to Lif. Fortunately, Sylvia came up with some excellent advice in which she said "Forbid Mary to answer Gillian's cry". The first night this rule was applied, Gillian shouted at the top of her voice for a good twenty minutes. The same routine was adopted the second night and the crying went on for only ten minutes and this gradually eased off until it stopped altogether when Gillian obviously decided she was wasting her breath. Peace reigned.

Gillian was always a very independent child and never let an adventure go by without accepting the challenge. At the age of around eighteen months she would leap off the side of the swimming pool at the Galle Face Hotel, trusting that the adult standing in the pool would rescue her. She went down in to the water and came up spluttering but with a broad grin on her face. Likewise when the family had a beach property with a river on the land side, she would plunge in and come up smiling. During this stunt she would swallow massive amounts of river water and when it was approaching time for her to come out, Lif would line her up and see how fat her tummy was and give the verdict. Mark and Lif insisted that their nanny Mary must also learn to swim. Like all Ceylonese women, Mary was very modest and insisted on being fully clad, even down to her petticoat.

A few months later as a young toddler she was playing about when she fell out of her cot. When questioned by friends during a walk along the breakwater as to how she acquired her black eye, her quick response was 'I was just fooling about'.

One of the pastimes Gillian and her nanny enjoyed greatly was calling in the various pedlars who would come down the lane offering their different wares. Lif recalled: 'One of the most popular of these was the man with a large aluminium box on the back of his bicycle. He used to shout something that sounded like "nylo pattinpad", which was actually supposed to mean "envelope, writing pad". He also had all sorts of buttons, ribbons, cottons, stationery and everything else you could imagine. Nanny used to ask him to open them all up, but then invariably would buy nothing. But it was all a happy way of passing the morning. There was also a beggar who would come around making very strange noises in his throat and indicating that he was mute then holding out his hand for a donation. Later he was found near the kitchen having a totally normal conversation with the cook.

"The 'Fudge Man' was another favourite with his delicious 'milk toffee' and he would invariably make a sale. He was also popular with Ronnie Lushington and he must have had a telepathic sense as he invariably coincided his visits when Ronnie was staying. Other vendors sold 'live' crabs, which were transported in baskets hung at each end of a long pole. These fellows were rather clever at manipulating the crabs with their fingers to make them look as though they were still alive. Others would put the creatures down on the doorstep and then they had to be 'chased' and 'captured'."

11

PEERS,
PLAYERS AND
PARADISE

Thanks to the generosity of his father Norman, in the year following Gillian's birth, the Bostocks, Mark and Lif, and Mark's sister Ruth and her husband Mike Thornton, acquired a property on the South West coast. It was modest enough, a simple beach house for weekend and holiday use, but what it lacked in size and space was more than compensated for by the idyllic setting. 'Sandsend', as the house was called, (in memory of Sandsend near Whitby in Yorkshire where Mark had spent so many happy holidays with endless cousins) was located some 25 miles south of Colombo, at Bentota, a coastal village. The house was situated on a strip of land, with the sea on one side and a river on the other. It was as close to a bathing paradise as one could get, because even in inclement weather, when the South West Monsoon was in full swing and the sea was too rough for swimming, there was the river offering safer waters to all bathers.

Mark recalled: 'Our property at Bentota was situated between the Bentota Ganga and the sea. It was a sand spit which had been built up when the road and rail bridges were constructed at Bentota, at the turn of the century. The construction had had the effect of swinging the river north, because prior to that the river used to go out right beside the old, Portuguese fort, which is now the Bentota Beach

Hotel. By making a separate island and swinging the river around it meant the currents built up this long spit. So anyway we eventually ended up buying this little property, the last but one from the end of this spit.'

Not that the purchase was an especially straightforward process, as Mark explained: 'I had a particularly unpleasant time trying to buy the property because the owner was a very eminent dentist from Kandy, who never went there, and he had let it be known that he wanted whatever it was, I think something like 20,000 Rupees, for it, and so I offered him what he was asking. Now it just so happened that a director of an agency house was also looking to buy the property, however he had offered considerably less than I had, and so he had been turned down.

'So the purchase went ahead, but before it was completed I was summoned in to see Fred Waldock, the number one of Keell and Waldock. He told me that this shipping director had been on to him, apparently absolutely furious that "that pipsqueak Bostock had offered the owner of this land the asking price" and that as a consequence this shipping director had been squeezed out. He therefore suggested, or rather demanded, that Fred Waldock should tell Bostock that he should withdraw his offer and let this chap proceed at the lower price.

'Naturally I said I would not back out of the deal. And Fred, being Fred, backed me up, so we ended up with this strange little house at Bentota.'

Strange or not, Mark was evidently more than happy there. 'We did most of our entertaining at Bentota in a marvellously relaxed atmosphere,' he said. 'We were very fortunate in that the other owners of houses, or shacks, down the spit were all great chums of ours, so there was continual movement between one bungalow and another.'

However, Sandsend was fairly basic when the two families first took it over. The lighting was by kerosene lamps, while the water for drinking and washing was drawn from a well in the garden. The well was one of the more memorable aspects of the house for Mark, who said: 'The well was the most lovely central point between the main house and the annexe and we didn't need to bother about showers, even though there were showers in the house, you just had to tip a bucket down at the end of a long string into the well and had your shower there and then, and by Jove it was most refreshing.' The depth of the well had been judged with great care so as not to let the saline water percolate through.

Everybody enjoyed their invigorating 'well bath' after a swim in the sea, to remove the saltiness with the sweet fresh water. As time went on this became something of a tradition, one that was especially enjoyed, as they grew older, by Gillian and Claire in particular, who both relished pouring buckets of ice cold water over everybody's heads, regardless of their social standing or professional status.

It was the 1950s so naturally there were no such luxuries as refrigerators, instead in those early days there was a zinc-lined cabinet, which took a hundredweight of ice from Colombo Cold Stores (Elephant House) which had to be brought down in the boot of the car along with all the food and drink for the weekend. Careful planning on Lif's part ensured there was never a shortage of cold beers and drinks not to mention butter that did not melt.

A large wooden chest provided storage for the pillows and the cotton mattresses to be used on the canvas camp beds. Furniture was minimal and fairly Spartan, consisting of cane chairs and tables and a solitary, rather basic, dining table. Mark applied his practical brain to things and reached the conclusion that changes had to be made, not all at once of course, but over a period of time. He said: 'The coconuts out on the sea side had only just been planted and were barely two years old, they therefore gave no protection at all from the weather, and so the south west wind would roar in and the rains would hammer against that side of the house, with its horrid metal window frames, which of course rusted up in no time.' Thus, as the years went by, a proper bar was built, while the side of the house which faced the sea was opened up to give access to whatever breeze might be there, to be locked up with large aluminium shutters when the family decamped.

The only access to Sandsend was by boat across the river, which heightened the sense of isolation, but Mark had that problem covered. He said: 'We were spending one of our leaves with Lif's parents in Weymouth while Ronnie was Captain in Charge at Portland and I bought three boats from Todd's yard. They were making glass fibre boats and there weren't many boats being made from that material in those days. They were producing a rather splendid "nestling set", which comprised a 15-footer, into which nestled a 12-footer and into that a nine-footer. I bought this set and shipped it out to Colombo.'

This nest of boats was also filled by the Bostocks with curtaining material for their new home in Colombo, thus maximising freight space.

The little matter of transporting the boats down to Sandsend from Colombo was solved by Mark's great friends. 'The chummery decided that instead of putting the boats on a lorry and shipping them down to Bentota, that we would sail them down,' and this obviously appealed to the Viking in Mark, a venture which was reinforced by the knowledge that if things did not work out under sail, he could always call on the back-up of internal combustion. 'I had a couple of little Seagull outboard engines,' said Mark, 'one was a four-horsepower and the other a six-horsepower engine. We strapped these on the backboard of the 15-footer and sailed it across the Beira lake and thence out into the harbour, through the locks, before finally taking it down the coast to Bentota, towing the smaller ones behind us.'

The voyage took the chums about four hours and Mark admitted: 'I think one or two of us were feeling rather seasick on the way down. It might have been caused by the sea, or possibly the piss-up we'd had the night before – it was a fairly hairy journey, though, I do remember that. But anyway, we got into the Bentota river and there the boat resided for the next 25 years or so.'

It was here in the river, that Gillian and later her sister Claire, used to spend many a happy hour rowing up and down. Competence as a rower was essential because there were strong ebb and flow tides and the mouth of the river was quite close so they could have easily been swept out to sea. They were usually accompanied by one of the family dogs, especially Digger who was a comical English Pointer and a particular devotee of the river, where he would readily dive for stones tossed in by Gillian for as long as she wanted to throw them. Digger always knew when a trip to Sandsend was on, because he recognised the beer crate when it was being loaded into the car, and knowing what was in store, he would become impatient for the journey down south to get under way and would invariably howl with joy as the party finally set off down the coast. He would roam at will along the spit all weekend and Christine Gordon, who was a neighbour would regularly be woken up feeling two jets of warm air on her face and on opening her eyes would find herself looking into two yellowish eyes staring at her through the mosquito net. The name Digger was extremely apt and he would spend hours digging in the sand on the beach in the full sun with his tail endlessly wagging, forever hopeful of finding a stone. At the end of each weekend Lif would have to anoint his balls with after sun cream or Calamine lotion as his family jewels were extremely tender from prolonged exposure to the sun and sitting in the boot of the car on the return journey, rather painful.

Gillian remembered vividly the scavenging hunts that the family had at Bentota whenever there was a gang of youngsters staying there. On one occasion a wheel was on the list and one enterprising competitor had spotted an unattended bicycle on the other side of the river so took a boat across and hi-jacked the bicycle.

There was another hi-jacking of sorts as well, one which involved their neighbour across the river. The owner of the land on the opposite bank of the river went by the name of Karunaratne, known to the family as 'Curried Rats'. He allowed the family and their friends to use his garden for parking, but, that one good deed apart, he was in general, a pretty unsavoury character. On one famous occasion he 'dognapped' Digger. Mark went across the river in search of the dog and heard Digger howling in his characteristic way, but when challenged, Curried Rats initially claimed it was a goat. Mark managed to persuade Mr Karunaratne to see reason and Digger was eventually returned. Another incident occurred during a curfew, when the boat and outboard engine were stolen under cover of darkness. In due course boat and motor were found and returned to base.

It might have been an idyllic place, especially for children, but Norman Bostock announced that he would not accompany the families on trips to Sandsend if it meant he was to be surrounded by numerous grandchildren. Mark was instructed by his father to build a separate, small annexe a short distance from the main house so that he and Beth could have some peace and privacy; needless to say this construction drew the children like moths to a candle flame, so much so that it quickly came to be known as the 'children's wing'; and on his visit after the completion of the annexe, Norman found himself sleeping in the main house, while the children took over, and enjoyed hugely, the annexe.

Sandsend was a wonderful place for Mark, because he could escape the hurly-burly of the big city and shake off the rigours of the working week. Once ensconced in the beach house he was able to relax and unwind immediately.

He also took great pleasure there in honing his skills as a boatman. As it turned out he proved an excellent sailor, and frequent trips would be made out to sea, through the rather hazardous mouth of the river. On one occasion a friend, Pam Fernando, was on board when the boat had to be steered through some pretty treacherous waters. Finally, when they docked and Pam stood up, her trousers looked decidedly wet, and she instantly quipped, "It was fright, men." On another occasion Mark and a friend went to rescue some youngsters who had got into trouble when they found themselves taken out to sea unexpectedly by the powerful currents. Unfortunately, one of the boys – a non-swimmer – was drowned and his body was washed up shortly afterwards; it was thought that he had probably had a heart attack since he had always been very scared of the water.

For all the fun they had at Bentota Mark and Lif still found time to explore and enjoy other parts of Ceylon. In 1960 they went on a five-day shooting trip to Irainativu, an island in the Gulf of Manaar, off the North West coast of Ceylon. Lif had clear recollections of that time. 'We set off from Jaffna in a *dhoni* (a traditional sail boat, with or without an engine, that is built of coconut palm wood and has lateen sails), courtesy of the local Customs and Excise Officer – our destination was the remote island of

Irainativu where we were due to stay at the house of the local Roman Catholic Priest.

'Our party comprised, Mike and Ruth Thornton, Ronnie and Bobby Lushington with Mrs. Beauchamp (Bobby's Mother), Vincent Cox, Mark and me. We were also accompanied by the faithful Pathan servant of Ronnie – the handsome Allah Bux. If Bobby and I wanted to annoy Ronnie and Mark we used to keep on saying how gorgeous he was.'

The voyage was scheduled to take a good four or five hours down the coast to Manaar, so the prudent Mrs Beauchamp decided it would be circumspect to take along a commode. It so happened that her son-in-law Ronnie Lushington was able to come to her rescue, as Mark explained: 'Ronnie had inherited a wonderful old thunderbox from his father.' The thunderbox was, conveniently, a portable one, which had a lid that closed down tightly; it also boasted a lovely seat, beneath which sat the bucket. Mrs Beech, as she was known familiarly, sat herself on the thunderbox for the duration of the sea voyage, treating it as her throne, and indeed according to Mark, looking not unlike Queen Victoria.

Mark added: 'Because there was only this one loo and in the early morning there was of course a queue to go the loo, Mrs Beech became, by default, the arbiter of who could use the facility, and when.' Apparently the seafarers had to form a queue in order to use the loo, and Mark said: 'If anyone wanted a second go, she would say: "No no you get to the back of the queue". She really ruled the roost there.'

It is little wonder that Mark and Ronnie mischievously dubbed her 'Queen of the Biggies'. In fact the only people who attempted a second visit were Mark and Ronnie as Lif revealed: 'She was appointed to monitor the queue to make sure Ronnie and Mark didn't sneak in for a second turn before the rest of us had had a chance.'

There was one odd incident on the outward voyage as Lif explained: 'Mrs. Beauchamp's husband had died exactly a year previously and she was wearing his old wrist watch. And during this trip to Irainativu the watch stopped, and at the very hour and minute that he died.'

On arrival at Irainativu they decided to set up camp outside the church – the priest not being in residence at the time – because it was apparent that the accommodation that had been arranged for them was totally inadequate for everyone to sleep, as well as to live, in. Lif again: 'We had brought a large tarpaulin with us, plus camp beds, of course, and a very adequate dormitory was soon set up. Allah Bux, as well as being chief shikar (stalker) on these shooting trips, was also the camp cook, one who excelled at conjuring up delicious dishes from the day's 'bag'.

Mark revealed what a day's 'bag' comprised: 'There was some marvellous duck shooting and also some very splendid partridge shooting. We had red legged partridge on the North West coast these are long-legged chaps, who prefer to run rather than take to the wing and they live in clumps of bushes. We persuaded the girls to beat all the bushes with sticks that we handed to them. The theory was that this would flush out the birds and we would be waiting on the far side to bring them down with our guns.'

Not everyone was as sharp a shot as Mark and Ronnie though. Mark said: 'We had some rather inept shots with us. My brother-in-law Mike Thornton and Ruth were with us on that occasion and he really had not much clue about shooting but when the partridge were put up from a thicket over Thornton he would blaze off and had no idea about shooting etiquette and he used to run off after a bird and say, "That's mine!" even though Ronnie and I knew perfectly well that he had been nowhere near it; but anyway he'd roar off, breaking the line, and when he came up to this poor flapping bird he'd say "Oh my poor dear chap, I'm frightfully sorry, I didn't really mean to hurt you, but couldn't you have just dropped down and died? I have to put you out of your misery, but how do I do it?" We could hear all this going on, then he would put another cartridge in his shotgun and, from point blank range, he didn't only blow its head off, he would blow it to pieces, thus rendering it completely useless for the pot. Then old Thornton would claim it was his bird and that would make his day.'

After the partridge drive, came the duck shoot, and here Mark and Ronnie revealed a deal of fieldcraft, before demonstrating their proficiency with their weapons. 'Each day Ronnie and I would go up to these brackish little tanks on the edge of the island, where there would be absolutely swarms of duck feeding on the seaweed; we would creep up to the edge (bloody uncomfortable it was too over thorns, jagged rocks and pebbles) and then we would suddenly leap to our feet and clap our hands, and the whole of the tank would erupt with a great noise of beating wings as the birds took off; and although we would actually be aiming at a particular bird, between us we would probably bring down ten or fifteen birds each with just that first, and only, left and a right, because of course after that initial flight they would all be away; but I remember we would return to camp each time with some 20 to 30 birds dangling from our belts.'

Then, of course, it was the turn of Allah Bux to take centre stage, as Mark explained: 'While we then went off for a swim, the chaps we had as servants and boat boys would make up a wonderful sort of game stew with the duck and the partridge we had shot, every night that we were there. We really forgot about lunch, because we would take the dhoni out to another island and swim through lunchtime, so would just have one huge meal in the evening.'

'Irainativu had a population of approximately 100 and, of course, we were a great curiosity for the local inhabitants who were always there to greet us on the shore after we returned from a day's fishing.

'The island abounded in partridge and these were our prime targets. On one occasion a poor wretched bird got up from under our feet, there was a barrage of fire and it plummeted to earth where it was greeted with a glad cry from Mike – 'My bird!'

He was instantly challenged by the neighbouring gun – 'You're *not* claiming that bird, are you?

'Why, yes, aren't you?' was Mike's retort.

'We met the delightful French Roman Catholic priest at the end of our stay, and he told us that he had been amazed to find his own grave in France, this was because he was thought to have died there during World War II.'

According to Mark, this French priest, who looked after five churches, three on the mainland, the one in Irainativu and one in India on the opposite side of the Palk Straits which was only about 40 miles away, was something of a rogue. 'This lovely padre was the biggest smuggler on the North West coast,' claimed Mark, 'and he always had a great bunch of the most wonderful Indian cheroots, which were totally unobtainable in Ceylon; and he had a dug-out boat, which had a huge outboard engine that meant he could outpace any police or other vessel on the coast.' They duly returned to Manaar, and thence to Colombo having had a truly memorable and wonderful time. Lif was rather proud of the tan she had acquired but was greeted with great disapproval by nanny Theresa who said 'Lady's very dark' Most Ceylonese people love fair skins.

Mark remembered another hunting trip, when he and Ronnie ran into someone who had clearly irritated him. 'There was this idiot of a young planter, a new boy, staying at Hambantota rest-house,' said Mark, still indignant many years later. 'Ronnie told him that if he got to Ridiyagama tank, (a 'tank' is a small lake), by about 7.30am, when the sun was up, he would be bound to find a croc lying on an island or promontory in the tank, sunning himself with his mouth open and he couldn't really miss it. Ronnie got out a map and showed the young fellow how to get there, pointing out how close the tank was to the main road. The chap's mouth was all agape. He was extremely excited at the prospect of bagging a croc.

'Ronnie and I set off very early the next morning, taking not only our shotguns, but also our rifles. We shot several snipe around Ridiyagama, before driving to the tank. Once there we motored around it until we were opposite an island that we knew, which was quite close to where the main road came in. Sure enough, just as we had predicted the previous evening, there was a twelve-foot croc, sunning himself first thing in the morning on the bank of the tank.

'The tank crocodile is called a "mugger", he's not vicious, he really goes after the frogs and rarely tackles a deer coming down to the tank, in fact they are relatively harmless. But there was this one chap, sitting up with his mouth open, so we shot him and rowed him out to this little island where we then skinned him. You really only skin the tummy, it's the only thing that is useful on a mugger and is used for making handbags. Then we turned him back over onto his tummy again, propped his mouth open with a stick so he looked as if he was baring his front teeth and upper mandibles, and we left him looking like a live croc that was basking in the sun.

'We left the island pretty smartish and returned to the car, which we had left some way away. We then found ourselves a nice shady patch and sat down and had a cup of coffee. At 7.30 on the dot we heard another vehicle coming along the road. He parked and sure enough this idiot got out of the car. We could see the delight on his face the instant he spotted the croc, just as we had described it to him, all lined up about 80 yards out on the little island.

'So he began to stalk it; down he got into some pretty nasty scrubby jungle and crawled on his tummy, closer and closer to the water's edge. Once he got himself into position he must have fired I should think about a dozen shots at the mugger, and we could see this poor old creature sort of heaving over every now and then as each bullet thwacked into it.

'This cretin must have shot the stick out of the creature's mouth as well, because its jaw clamped shut suddenly. By this time the mugger was lying very still. Then there was a roar of delight from this young fellow and he charged into the water, reloading his rifle and approached the croc with his rifle poised to finish it off if necessary, but it was obviously stone dead. The young fellow then produced a huge hunting knife; he turned the croc over only to find that it had already been skinned and he was suddenly rather crestfallen. At that point we did feel that perhaps we had been rather shitty to play a trick on him like that, but he was such a bumptious young fellow, he needed to be put in his place.'

Sadly long before his death outstation jaunts such as these were no longer possible, because as Mark said: 'Of course all that area subsequently became a stronghold of the Tamil Tigers, so no-one could go near it. We were very privileged to go there.' But he did admit: 'Ronnie and I had a few expeditions up to the North West coast, there was another place called Pooneri, where again there were a lot of partridge, duck and snipe, although that is now a huge army camp, the northernmost on the West coast, thought to have been used in the campaign against the Tamil Tiger terrorists.'

Squeezed somewhere into all this activity was Lif's brush with the Silver Screen. In 1957 the film 'The Bridge on the River Kwai', which was directed by David Lean and starred Alec Guinness, Jack Hawkins and William Holden, was being shot on location in Ceylon. The action was focused on a village called Kitulgala – Kitul is a form of treacle extracted from the kitul palm and 'gala' means rock. The sharp-witted timber merchant who supplied the wood for the building of the bridge, knowing that the bridge was to be blown up in due course built a dam further down the river and was therefore able to collect all his timber as it floated downstream to his cannily placed obstruction.

Lif was among a lucky group of people who had been invited to be an 'extra' in the film; in it she had to play the (non-speaking) part of a Naval nursing sister in the hospital scene which was shot at Mount Lavinia. To create the illusion of a hospital ward beds were arranged along the veranda of the Mount Lavinia Hotel with other locals drafted in as extras posing as the patients.

Lif said: 'As nurses we were instructed as to what we were required to do; such as not looking at the cameras, and carrying on doing our bit of the action until the director told us 'cut'. I had been instructed on how to administer an injection for my bit part, and I have to say that my poor "patient" looked increasingly nervous as he awaited the word 'Cut!' to be called out. It seemed to be delayed endlessly, because all the while I was getting closer to being in a position when I would have to administer the injection. Fortunately for all concerned the instruction 'Cut!' was finally given, to the considerable relief of my petrified "patient".

The most exciting part of the day for Lif was when she had to appear – for a very brief second – on the 'set' with Jack Hawkins. Any watcher of the film would have had to have been extremely alert to catch this fleeting moment. A dreamy-eyed Lif recalled fondly: 'Jack Hawkins was such a lovely and unassuming man, and this was demonstrated perfectly when the husband of the Ceylonese matron asked if he would pose with his wife for a photograph. Jack was all too willing, but went off to get his military cap and baton so that he was fully dressed for the photo. He and his wife were occasional visitors at the Colombo Cricket Club, and everyone who encountered them during this visit found them to be particularly charming.'

Generally, though, it was Sandsend which occupied much of the Bostock family's leisure time, whether it was for a weekend or longer. However, the frequent family trips there were not without excitement. The road down the coast had to cross the railway line, and on one occasion, at night, when the crossing gates were closed, an impatient Mark decided he could not be bothered with waiting and announced that he knew a short-cut through the coconut trees. As the coconut trees seemed to be planted closer and closer together, he eventually ended up with the car straddling the railway line and the train about to leave the small station. A slight panic ensued as the train headlight picked up the chaotic sight of the family trying to heave the car off the tracks. However, in true Ceylon fashion, the train pulled up short of the obstacle and the engine driver got out of his cab and helped to lift the car off the track, all the while with his train blocking the level crossing, much to the enragement of the other law abiding drivers who were patiently waiting to continue their journeys. Not surprisingly that particular route was not chosen again.

As the years went by Mark and Lif were able to have a hand in acquiring the neighbouring property for some close friends of theirs, as Mark explained: 'Our wonderful friends George and Christine Gordon were very frequent visitors. One day George said to me, "Look old boy, is there any chance you could acquire that plot of land next door to you, – rather than have us coming and staying in your house all the time?" So I said that I did know the gentleman who owned it, but he was never going to build on it because he had pledged it to his three sons. But George said that he would love to buy it, and so I took it upon myself to go and talk to the owner, who was the Minister of Justice in that particular UNP government. He had a lovely residence down near Mount Lavinia and asked me to go and negotiate. I had to come up with a scheme that involved some tax-dodging that would benefit him and his sons, and so I bought the land and George built the "Hunter Hilton" as it was called alongside. Many, many were the parties we had and the path between the houses was a well trodden one.

'We had a tradition that we spent New Year at Bentota and most of the other bungalows were also full down there with friends. On News Year Eve we had a grand firework display, which actually was watched by all the people on the village side of the river. George was a great pyromaniac and he just loved setting off the most wonderful but, in some cases pretty dodgy fireworks, supplied by the Fireworks Palace, including most explosive rockets and things that went crash and bang, all with extremely short and in some cases dubious fuses. It actually took us quite a long time to set up the fireworks. It was always done on the Gordon compound down near their jetty because their coconut trees hadn't grown up as much as ours, so we had a fairly clear sky in which to send off all these rockets. There was one marvellous incendiary which was a sort of mortar. It was the size and shape of a coconut and you had to go and slip it into a mortar tube which had to be dug well into the sand. It went off with a real *whoomph!* and as it headed skywards all sorts of things shot out of it, and it went on sending out new incendiaries as it came down.' On one occasion when Norman Bostock was amongst the on-lookers, seated in the front row, a rocket fell over as it fired out of the bottle and exploded rather too close for comfort, finally emitting a great deal of smoke. When the smoke finally cleared and the other nervous onlookers returned to check on the damage, he wryly remarked 'It was never like this at Passchendaele'. The letting off of a fire-balloon on New Year's Day also became a tradition and caused much amusement, including an incident when one of the 'fire lighters' – a rather hairy young man – had the hairs on his chest and his eyebrows singed.

One of the other traditions at New Year was the attacking of one of the other bungalows on the 'spit' with rockets using a two-pronged assault from river and beach. The start signal was from the beach party by launching a particularly powerful rocket. This rocket had to be held upright in a bottle, half buried in the sand. On one occasion it failed to leave the bottle, hoisting the whole thing out of the sand, only to fall to the ground several feet away, much to the embarrassment of the beach party. Fireworks manufactured in Colombo and sold at the Fireworks Palace certainly would never have passed the health and safety regulations. Mark's father Norman added to the lack of safety by igniting some of the rockets with his cigarettes while rocking around in the boat as part of the river attack party.

A less dangerous sport was turtle watching. At regular intervals turtles would come up the beach and lay their eggs (sometimes as many as 100 or more) in the sand. It was a fantastic sight and once mummy turtle was dropping her eggs, nothing would disturb her. The local lads would come down the beach and try to locate the nest by following the turtles' tracks, then probing the area with sticks. The family used to gather the eggs whenever they could and re-bury them on their property. The date was duly recorded on a calendar and the weekend when they should hatch was carefully calculated. Baby turtles are prey to many hazards such as crows and large crabs and last but by no means least, the female turtles, who, having expended so much effort in laying their eggs, would be waiting out at sea to gobble up some of them. So later on the family adopted the policy of digging a small pit in the sand and filling it with sea water, letting the little ones get in some swimming practice, before attempting their long trek to the sea. It was interesting to see how they would all bang against the sea side of these pits, this instinct of the baby turtles was remarkable, but it was what was always guiding them.

Family members were not the only visitors to Sandsend. As the visitors' book bears testimony, it proved to be a popular place for an impressively large cross-section of people, and was an easy way of entertaining friends and visitors to Ceylon. Among the many people who enjoyed the charms of Sandsend were touring parties of well-known, and not so well-known, British sports clubs. Rugby clubs in particular availed themselves of the stunning facilities, including London Welsh, boasting British Lions and Wales' internationals JPR Williams, John Taylor, John Dawes and Mervyn Davies, among others. There were also boisterous visits from Oxford and Cambridge Universities' rugby fraternities.

The London Welsh tour of Sri Lanka was preceded by that of Paris Universities. A member of the London Welsh Rugy Club, Dai Llewelyn, who was staying with the Bostocks in Colombo prior to the arrival of his fellow club members, attended the last rugby match played by Paris Universities at the Ceylon Rugby & Football Club (CR&FC) ground. During the course of the match, Dai commented to the family members that he thought the London Welsh could score at least 100 points against the Sri Lankan national team. Unfortunately this comment was overheard by a sports journalist and Dai's prediction was published in a local paper. When the London Welsh played their first match, the ball was passed to Dai to claim their 100th point. Sunburn, particularly on the shoulders (making scrums even more painful) and the tops of feet (causing problems with rugby boots) plus gastric effects of hot curries were the only means by which Sri Lanka managed to keep future scores restricted to less cricket like proportions.

Dai had attended a wedding in the Caribbean prior to his arrival in Sri Lanka and having an olive skin had acquired an extremely healthy tan so it was decided that he would be dressed up in a sarong and shirt to greet his team mates at the airport, carrying a large leek that Lif and Gillian had made with crepe paper. Mark also dressed up but in an old (and rather tight) striped cricket blazer and Panama hat in an attempt to look like an archetypal colonial, to meet the team. Some of the team members were heard saying how hospitable it was for the Sri Lankans to send out a welcoming party, only to realise belatedly that the "local" was in fact their fellow team mate.

MCC parties, on their way back from a gruelling tour also made Sandsend a regular stopping off point, much to the delight of the family's old Tamil cook, Ramsamy, who would usually accompany the family on their trips south. Despite the Spartan state of the cooking facilities he was always able to conjure up delicious curries on the kerosene-fired cooker. As a serious cricket devotee Ramsamy was thrilled when any cricket teams arrived at Sandsend for some much-needed, post- or mid-tour R&R. His particular favourite player was Kent and England's Derek Underwood.

In the winter of 1973-74 Tony Lewis, while captaining MCC on a tour of Pakistan and India, paid a brief visit to Ceylon, and more specifically Sandsend, and he later wrote: 'The only way the Ceylon cricket team could beat the MCC was if the visiting side had spent a weekend with the Bostocks!' In the visitors' book Lewis described it as 'Paradise', while vice captain Mike Denness decided it was 'Too good to be true, will be back tomorrow to make sure!'

In fact Lewis had visited Sandsend for the first time three years earlier, as he explained: 'I first met Mark and Lif Bostock when I captained an MCC minor tour that included matches in what was then Ceylon in 1970. In my side were some players who would graduate to Test cricket: Geoffrey Boycott, Keith Fletcher, Bob Taylor, Geoff Arnold, Pat Pocock and Don Wilson. The Bostocks were wonderful hosts, though I made an early judgement that the "no-sleeping-on-tour" Old Marlburian, Mark, was far more 'dangerous' company than his wife.'

His memories are sharp and his recall of Mark captures the essence of the man. 'You could not be an England team in Colombo without walking into the hospitable grip of Mark Bostock, a true Brit, passionate about rugby and cricket, no mean golfer, especially when competing under The Lucifer Society flag.

Although, in truth, over the following years, it was easier to beat Mark at golf than it was Lif, who was Lady Captain of Royal Colombo Golf Club more than once, including the Centenary year of 1979. Lif said her rather dubious invitation to be Lady Captain was that she was the oldest member of the Ladies' Section. In her opening speech she quoted Katisha's song in the Mikado, "There's a fascination frantic in a ruin that's romantic. Do you think I am sufficiently decayed.' About 20 years later this was even more relevant when Lif was invited to be Lady Captain of Royal Ashdown Golf Club.

So, when as captain of the MCC touring side (England by any other name), to the sub-Continent, Lewis was more prepared for the Bostocks' brand of hospitality. He wrote that the cricketers were exhausted after a five-match test series against India as well as a full three-day match fixture list against all the State sides, before they wound up the programme with the first unofficial test against Sri Lanka, a three-day game that the Tourists had won with more than a day to spare. By the time they arrived at Sandsend they were shattered, and in need of some serious R&R. And they certainly got that.

Lewis referred to an entry in his diary for the time. 'Tuesday 20th February: Great day for the exhausted boys: the best. A day at Bentota on the beach with a running picnic. Lif treated us to a flawless display of water-skiing, making it look so easy that some of the team wanted to give it a go. Barry Wood showed us how tenacious he was by heaving his body half-way out of the water to a crouching position behind the motor and boat. He hung on, but was still submerged below the thighs and had to collapse. He did this four times. Lif had become the patient instructor, but the Lancashire opening batsman confirmed that he was more skilful on land than in water.'

On returning to Colombo that evening it was decided that the Bostocks, Lewis and Mike Denness would go out for dinner, before dropping into the local night club. Unfortunately the two England cricketers were inadequately clothed for such a jaunt and so they had to be 'kitted out', one in a pair of Mark's trousers, the other, which happened to be Mike, in a pair of Lif's trousers; the jackets that they borrowed were not exactly bespoke either.

Lewis remembered the occasion well: 'We were wearing shorts and had to embrace the slight formality of wearing long trousers. I fitted into a pair of Mark's with the help of a firm belt; but the only trousers to fit Mike were a pair of Lif's. He was entirely pleased with this until he discovered that the zip was at the back!

"I can't help you, mate, you are on your own." are words very rarely spoken by a cricket captain to one of his team, but that is what I said to him that night.' The off-the-peg outfits were still sufficient for a good night out.

An MCC touring party to India, Sri Lanka and Australia (for the Centenary Test in Melbourne), which was captained by Tony Greig and managed by Ken Barrington was similarly entertained in March 1977. A few days earlier they had drawn an unofficial test against Sri Lanka and Sandsend represented a perfect stop-off before they headed Down Under. The cricketing party also brought a glitter of celebrity to Bentota in the person of the actor Bernard Cribbins and his wife Gill, the latter describing their visit to Sandsend as 'lovely'.

The mystery as to why Cribbins and his wife came to be among the MCC party was explained more recently by the man who also had hit songs with "Hole In The Ground" and "Right Said Fred". Cribbins is a great cricket fan and also, as he said: 'Ken Barrington was an old friend of mine and someone with whom I played golf.' When he learned of the tour Cribbins decided it would be a good idea to take a holiday coinciding with the MCC party's time in Sri Lanka. Barrington then played the part of good friend with a single gesture. Cribbins added: 'Ken said I could sit in the MCC dressing room with the players during play in the match, and I spent three happy and interesting days.'

As for Sandsend, he had fond memories of the various players disporting themselves. "It was a lovely day,' he said, 'and my abiding memory of the day in Bentota is of the MCC captain Tony Greig, who was determined to go surfing. The surf was quite big. We had been paddling in it, but Tony was body surfing, wearing a pair of flippers. At one point all you could see of him was a one bent leg sticking out of the water with a black flipper on the end. On returning from his surfing, Tony was intrigued by a game being played by the family which seemed to include a sun hat from which came a sound akin to dice being rolled. Dice taken from under the hat and then passed on to the next player with a claim that a 'full house or four of a kind, etc. Later the ritual of liar dice was explained to him. Another memory Lif has of Tony was an amusing remark he made which ran thus – 'If I had a daughter, I would never allow her to go out with a chap like me'.

The Leicestershire and MCC wicketkeeper Roger Tolchard had a go at scuba diving. He was swimming up the creek, which was on the other side of the land, and someone, either Lif or Mark, said, 'I hope he's all right, we get sharks in there.' The water in the creek was very muddy, you couldn't see very much. Luckily Tolchard did not run into a shark, although he did scratch himself on the pilings of the jetty.'

The most distinguished visitor to Sandsend was Lord Louis Mountbatten. The resident High Commissioner in Colombo had asked Mark to entertain his Lordship to lunch. Naturally there were specific and special instructions for the aristocratic lodger, his aides stating quite clearly that his Lordship would like a breast of chicken and a glass of chilled white wine for lunch. In his own inimitable, and uninhibited, way Mark replied that Lord Louis would be given beer and curry, just like everyone else at Sandsend, and he would just have to like it.

This visit coincided with Lord Louis leaving his post as C-in-C Far East in 1964. Mountbatten was accompanied by his elder daughter, Patricia Brabourne, who unbeknown to Mark at the time, was pregnant with twins – one of whom was later to be killed with Earl Mountbatten who was assassinated when his boat was blown up by the Provisional IRA at Mullaghmore, off the coast of Sligo in the Republic of Ireland in 1979.

At Sandsend the noble Earl was determined to go spear-fishing around the rocks that lay about a mile off the coast, and he insisted that his daughter accompany him through a dangerous passage in the rocks towards the open sea, saying in his stentorian voice "follow that man". Mark later took him to task, when Lord Mountbatten had graciously invited Mark and Lif to a reception in London.

The illustrious guests' departure was somewhat unusual because Mountbatten suddenly realized he was running late for a dinner with Ceylon's Prime Minister Mrs. Bandaranaike and he ordered Mark to take him across the river. By this time the family's boat, by now fitted with a very powerful outboard motor, took some handling, and when Mark realized he was coming in to the jetty on the far side much too fast he leaped over the side, in so doing managing to impale his bathing trunks on the gear lever and doing a nose dive in to the river. Mountbatten commented rather dryly "I won't ask you to do that again Bostock". After the VIP guests had left, the party began with his staff, most of whom had been left behind, letting their hair down and really enjoying themselves.

Two days after his visit to Sandsend Mark received a letter headed, Chief of Defence Staff, from Government House in Aden, which reads: 'Dear Bostock, I am writing to thank you and your wife very much on behalf of my daughter, my party and myself for your kindness and hospitality to us on Sunday at Bentota.

'My tours are usually hectic and crammed full of official occasions, so that lazy Sunday at your lovely beach house was all the more delightful.

'Thank you particularly for taking Patricia and me out to the rocks to schnorkel [sic] and see the fish. We couldn't have enjoyed ourselves more and are deeply grateful.' The letter is signed: 'Yours sincerely, Mountbatten of Burma'

Quite apart from well-known guests visiting Bentota, a host of friends and family members enjoyed the relaxing and informal atmosphere of Sandsend and many happy weekends were spent there until it was "acquired" by the Tourist Board.

12

BOARDING
PARTY

Not long after its acquisition the Bostocks' and Thorntons' idyllic days at Sandsend were rudely interrupted. There had been lots of rumblings and mutterings of discontent with the political climate of the country, and possibly as a consequence there was also a great deal of industrial unrest almost from the moment the country achieved Independence in 1948, when the first Parliamentary Elections, which apparently lasted some four or five weeks, saw Don Stephen (DS) Senanayake, the leader of the United National Party, invited to form the first Cabinet. February 4th was subsequently designated 'Independence Day'.

Lord Soulbury GCMG, GCVO, OBE, MC, PC, was appointed Ceylon's Governor-General, holding the post from 1949 to 1954; he had been sent out from the United Kingdom to help to draft the new constitution for the island.

Unfortunately, D.S. Senanayake (DS) came to an untimely end; he died after suffering a stroke when out riding and falling off his horse. That was in 1952. The Governor-General appointed DS's son, Dudley Shelton Senanayake, to be his successor and the island's second Prime Minister. At the time Dudley was Minister of Agriculture and Lands. Elections soon followed and the UNP was returned to Parliament. Dudley had no lust for power and resigned in 1954.

Two years later Solomon West Ridgeway Dias (SWRD) Bandaranaike, who had previously left the UNP Cabinet, formed a new Party – the Mahajana Eksath Parumuna (known as the MEP or Sri Lanka Freedom Party) and had been elected as Ceylon's fourth Prime Minister (which was the start of a remarkable dynasty in the country's governance) in a landslide victory in 1956.

SWRD was a reformer and quickly brought in various measures to help the poorer citizens of the Island, such as a free rice ration, a type of National Health and other benefits. Unfortunately the country could ill afford such luxuries and quickly lost many of the benefits of the British rule. Fundamentally SWRD was a good man and someone who did his best for the country in his own way. He was a dedicated worker, however, he crossed swords with some of the Buddhist hierarchy who held a great deal of power and wielded enormous influence in the country. The subsequent assassination of SWRD coupled with the increasing frequency of the strikes and the Sinhala Only Act, brought to the fore the existence of an undercurrent of unrest, with commerce frequently being severely disrupted, thus exacerbating the Island's troubles. Sadly, the introduction of the Sinhala Only Act, whereby the state official language was Sinhala and all state business was conducted in this language, thus precluding a large number of Tamils from holding certain positions which would necessitate speaking, reading and writing Sinhala resulted in the first uprising of the Tamils. This linguistic division was largely responsible for the Civil War which waged for so many years.

So just 11 years after gaining independence a strike, called by the workers in Colombo Harbour in 1958, brought trade and industry in Ceylon to a standstill, and as a consequence threw commerce, both domestic and international, into disarray.

Nanayakkarapathirage Martin Perera DSc, better, and more simply, known as Dr N M Perera, one of the founders of the Sri Lankan Trotskyist Lanka Sama Samaja Party (LSSP), was behind the industrial action. Dr N.M. Perera was subsequently to become the first Trotskyist to become Minister of Finance in Mrs. Bandaranaike's Government.

The effect of the strike left the tea trade in particular extremely hard hit, something which had a direct and significant impact on the island's economy, since the exporting of tea was vital to Ceylon's fiscal well-being.

As Mark recalled: 'The communists were making a mess-up of trade and commerce, and so rendered the harbour totally strike-bound, this meant one couldn't export any produce, and there were no imports either of course. However, the tea trade was determined to go on, and so, under considerable duress, we all knuckled down and kept the auctions going, for a while at least, but eventually of course a problem arose when all the stores in Colombo were full and we therefore couldn't get the tea out.'

As a consequence the Government under SWRD, called on Sandy Mathewson, he being a senior man in the tea trade, to gather together a team, which was to head up to Trincomalee with the aim of transforming the Naval Base into a trading port. Trincomalee had never been used, at least not formally, for commercial purposes, so there was no infrastructure in place, and therefore a great deal of work had to be undertaken by this team.

Unsurprisingly given his growing expertise in the industry, Mark was called upon by Sandy to head up the team. 'Sandy rang me about 10pm one night.' It just so happened that the whole of our area was burning, because everything had been incinerated and looted, anyway he said, "Mark, get in your car and go up to Trincomalee tonight and set it up as an export port".

'I did complain a bit, saying we had a baby with us, and what sort of staff would I find. He said, "We have conscripted staff from all the houses in Colombo, business houses and brokers and you will find them all being assembled up there and I want you to take charge of it."'

Mark said he would only agree to the move provided he could take his family with him, since he was afraid it might become dangerous in Colombo, given all the unrest in the Capital. Sandy agreed to Mark's condition.

'So at about midnight Lif and I got into the car with Gillian, I don't know what age she was then, she must have been about three years old. I drove us all up, Lif, Gillian and nanny Vera, to the Sea Anglers' Club, where we stayed, along with everyone else on the team, for the duration and we more or less took the place over. The Sea Anglers Club was traditionally a popular, if rather basic, holiday club for many tea planters' families.'

It just so happened that Lif's brother, Ken, was also in Trincomalee, in command of HM Submarine Tudor at the time, so a modest family reunion was able to be staged.

The problems were apparent to Mark from the outset. 'The first thing I had to do was to put together the organisation and machinery to open up Trincomalee, which had never been a commercial port in its long existence. We decided to set up our office in Mud Cove, which was at the end of the railway line and close to China Bay. And we called ourselves the Trincomalee Tea Administration (TTA).

'On the morning I arrived there were about 200 railway wagons, each filled with tea, and nobody to unload them. So the first thing I had to do was organise some manual labour and fortunately Sandy, being a rugger minded chap had conscripted a lot of rugger players from all the agency houses, so I had a good strong crew to work with and we managed to disintegrate this huge line of wagons and gradually get them shunted back down to the wharf where we could put them into the warehouses and sort them all out for various destinations.'

The shunting operation was hampered by the fact there was only one shunting engine up in Trincomalee and only one very decrepit and senile engine driver shunter.

Still Mark and his band put the old boy to work and for a couple of days everything went smoothly, then tragedy struck. Mark explained: 'Unfortunately about two days later the engine driver was leaning out of the cab to look back to hitch himself onto the next line of wagons he was going to move down to China Bay wharf and he fell out of the train and obviously hit his head and the train ran over him and that was the end of our shunting expert.'

It left the humans having to put the puff into the shunting of the rolling stock and do the work of a steam-driven loco. Not the easiest of tasks. 'We had to do the whole of the rest of the shunting by hand,' said Mark. 'I am sure this was when I started to get the most awful tennis elbow and various shoulder problems. There was a slight incline on the gradient there and we had to line up about half a dozen wagons on the split line to go down to China Bay, then run a wagon into the back of this lot of six, get them off the points and on the move; then, with the gradient, we were able to get up enough speed for this lot to be taken over by the next group of rugger forwards, who were about 300 or 400 yards down the line and they then would give the wagons another nudge to get them down to the unloading area. So the beginning of the morning was spent doing about four or five hours of shunting by hand all of the wagons that had come down the previous day, before getting the empties onto the parallel line, so that the next train down that night could hitch itself onto the enormous string of empties and cart them back up-country.' That operation would appear to be the antithesis of the old British Rail advertising slogan of the 1970s, which was 'Let the train take the strain'.

The area of Trincomalee known as China Bay had previously been an RAF station and another of the early jobs confronting Mark, once he had organised the road transport, was where to leave all this tea. He decided that the hangars should be converted into 'go-downs' or stores, but that was not as straightforward as it seemed.

Mark assessed the task that faced him and his team. 'All the roofs had disintegrated, while the floors were sodden with water.

'Luckily we had found some old Naval tarpaulins and these made the roofing just about waterproof, but I certainly couldn't have left any of the tea chests on the ground in the warehouses because they would have lapped up the moisture.

'Thankfully I found a very friendly sawmill close by on the Trinco road, and the owner sold me all his waste cuttings and standard lengths of wood, which he had in vast quantities, and these we transported to the warehouses. We were then able to stack the tea chests on all this timber and thus keep everything dry.'

There was a personal bonus that arose from this deal, as Mark explained: 'The sawmill owner was an exceedingly pleasant chap and he was so grateful to me for taking all his rubbish off his yard *and* paying it for it, that he said, "Look I have all these wonderful logs of satinwood, but no-one wants to use it because it is so hard that it completely blunts the saws. I don't know what to do with it and it has been here for generations."

'So I told him that I was just about to build my own house in Colombo and if he could arrange to send it down then I could get Don Carolis' yard, where they had a proper sawmill, to size it up for me and I could use it as a parquet floor. This was all duly cut and sized up for me by Don Carolis at six cents a foot, which of course in those days was a little bit of money, but still just a fraction of what it otherwise would have cost, and we ended up with this wonderful satinwood parquet floor in Sweden Bank, our new home.'

The conversion of Trincomalee was still fraught with snags. After sorting out shunting, storage and road transport Mark was confronted with yet another obstacle. The port could accommodate only one ship berthing its length along the jetty, which was the only way the tea chests could be loaded onto the ships. 'This one "alongside berth" was the oiling jetty berth,' Mark explained. 'It was most inconvenient because although there was a jetty there, one had to move all one's tea out to the end of it.

'Anyway we fashioned that as the only alongside berth, while all the rest of the ships had to anchor out in the bay.' That posed yet another problem for Mark and his team. 'Of course we hadn't got any lighters to ferry the tea out to the anchored ships, and we couldn't get them up from Colombo either. It so happened that there was quite a fleet of the old sailing boats coming down from India, mainly with tiles and building materials, as well as a lot of grain, so I commandeered a lot of these craft and told the skippers that we would pay their owners more than the going rate, as a consequence they were very happy to lend themselves and their vessels to me.'

That should have been that, but no, the commandeering of these vessels threw up a technical obstacle. 'Unfortunately these were round-bottomed boats, and therefore the tea chests being rectangular, scrunched together, making loading inefficient and also causing some damage, so we had to refashion the bottom of the boats, filling them up with planks so as to get a stable, flat base on which to put our tea chests. The Ceylon Navy was wonderfully helpful in lending us tugs and other small powered craft so we were able to tow these Indian sailing boats out to the ships in the harbour.'

The practicalities out of the way, Mark then stumbled into what was potentially a more serious, indeed more dangerous problem – local politics in the shape of a rather thuggish person. 'All the Indian boats were from Madras State and Tamil Nadu,' said Mark, 'and were therefore owned by Tamils; the sort of "mudalali" – Tamil – in charge of the commercial side of Trinco harbour, and therefore responsible for looking after all these vessels, had a very tight hold on all the marine comings and goings.

'He began to commandeer the boats working for us when sugar and rice supplies came in; he was looking to transfer the cargoes to the lighters in our charge and ship the sugar and rice off to the China Bay jetty. Essentially he was pinching all my lighters.

'In fact he turned out to be a rather nasty thug. I found out his movements and noted that, at a certain time of the day, he always went along the sea-front at Trinco harbour to organise his commandeering of all my craft, so I waited for my moment, then I shot out of a side entrance and blocked his path, and I told him that if he didn't mend his ways I would put him in the hands of the police and lock him up, because I was virtually the *gauleiter* of Trinco harbour.'

He had his thugs with him and so he told me what he thought of me, but I was rather larger than he was, and I was also very angry, so I gave him a very hefty thump, a second such thump would have sent him into the harbour.

'After that I had complete compliance, although he kept on trying to niggle away at things behind my back and he still tried to pinch my lighters from time to time.'

Typical of the traditions and philosophy of the island's culture, the bureaucrats from Colombo inevitably felt the need to interfere and interrupt operations, to the intense irritation of the hard-working team that was toiling from dawn to dusk to get the job done as quickly and as efficiently as possible and without trying to attract too much red tape and bureaucracy. Early on in the Trincomalee project, in a bid to boost the flagging morale of his workforce, Mark had put up a notice in dog Latin in the little TTA office, which read 'nil illegitimi carborundum' which loosely translated means 'don't let the bastards grind you down'.

Mark took up the tale: 'They were very confused days at that time and at one point in the operation the government decided to pop up to see how we were getting on. Their representative was R G (Dicky) Senanayake, someone I'd known for a long time. He was the Minister for Trade. He turned up one morning on the Heron flight that came up daily to us with all the shipping papers, and said he wanted to look around to see how the new port was looking. So he came into my office, which was in Trincomalee town. He was very amiable, and despite a permanent limp, a legacy of polio, he wanted to walk around and see what we were doing. When we returned to my office he asked, "What is that strange insignia over the top of your door there?" I said, "Well Dicky, I don't know whether you were a classical scholar at Cambridge or Oxford or wherever you were, but it's in dog Latin, which, when translated, says, "Don't let the bastards grind you down". He gave me a puzzled smile then asked, "All right old chap, and who are the bastards?" So I replied, "I'm not going to tell you who the bastards are, you know perfectly well." Fortunately, we left it at that.'

Gradually the trading picked up in Trincomalee, but not without the odd upset. On one memorable occasion Mark had a heated confrontation with the captain of a German ship, who refused to accept a cargo because, he claimed, one or two chests of tea were not up to weight. Mark took up the tale: 'The ship was bound for Hamburg, Rotterdam and the German captain was complaining about the state of some of the tea chests, and I said they had all been inspected before they were hoisted aboard, and that they were all intact; in fact anything that was ever damaged, we would repair in our makeshift carpentry shed. But he was trying to give me a dirty bill of lading, which would have meant that the cargo of tea would not have been accepted anywhere.

'I told him that he had to sail that night because I had to have the berth ready for a ship bound for South Africa the following day. But he insisted he was going to give me this dirty bill of lading, and he sent me off the ship. I was exceedingly angry, because I had a whole load of tea waiting to get onto the ship that night.

'As soon as I had disembarked he raised the gangplank, so there was no way I could get back on board by conventional means. But once on the jetty I could hear the very unpleasant, and large, first mate or chief officer or whatever his title was, stamping around in the hold, bashing our tea chests, in order to reinforce his captain's reasons for giving us an unacceptable bill of lading. Naturally I became even more incensed, this was all really getting to me now.

'I looked around trying to think of a way to get back on board, and quickly before too much damage was done. Then I spotted the forward mooring line which went from the capstan on the jetty to the bow of the German ship. I didn't hesitate, I swung myself onto it and, hanging upside down, rather like a sloth, I used it to climb my way back up onto the ship again. And sure enough, once I was aboard, I found the first mate stamping around, smashing up our cargo. I shouted to him that I had seen him doing this. He asked me how I had got back on board, but I ignored his question, and instead told him to leave the tea chests alone, and that I was going to see the captain. I informed him that I had already told the chief harbourmaster to come around and check the cargo, and that I had requested that the pair of them be put under arrest if they didn't comply with my orders. And I insisted that I saw the frightful captain. By now they were beginning to get a bit scared. I told them they were now under the jurisdiction of me and the chief harbourmaster, who also happened to be the Government Agent at the time, and I explained that their ship would be impounded and that they would be sent to gaol on a charge of damaging our cargo.

'Thankfully I finally got some sense drilled into these fellows and I said "If you get that gangplank down I will get our carpenters to repair those chests that you have damaged and you will bloody well pay for them and you *will* sail on tonight because I have to have this berth ready for tomorrow". The captain, after he had given me a beer or two, asked "How the hell *did* you get back onto the ship?" I told him that I was a nautical fellow myself and that I had climbed up his forward mooring line. So we finally got that ship out.

'But they were difficult days, and although one was dealing mainly with charming people, who understood what we were trying to do, we still ran into the occasional awkward situation, which would turn unpleasant when one met the odd nasty fellow like this German master, and then things had to be done differently. Somehow we managed to get through it all and within the first ten days we had loaded and sent away about twelve or fifteen ships, which, when you consider that was from scratch, was a quite remarkable achievement.

'We had such a motley crew, a wonderful rag, tag and bobtail lot manning the TTA; but the labour all tried to help and the documentation went on apace, and Lif was my secretary because every day I had to get this ship's documentation done and sent down to Colombo. We had a little flight every morning at about 6am and so Lif had to get a load of documentation and other bumph from the TTA down to Colombo so that the recipients at the various destinations knew that such and such a consignment was on its way.

'There was one occasion when we thought were going to have real problems, because Sir Oliver Gunatilake, who was at the time the Governor General and had been working with Admiral Sir Geoffrey Layton during the war commandeering ships and food ships and who therefore knew the ropes whenever there was an emergency, found out that there was a Bibby cargo boat coming out from the UK *en route* to Rangoon, with relatively little to discharge in Colombo. So Sir Oliver intervened and diverted the ship, as part of his overall responsibilities for Ceylon, to Trinco, where he ordered that it be loaded with tea for export.

'Fortunately for everyone concerned, Carson Cumberbatch, the owning managers and agency in Colombo, agreed to this rather draconian action. So when this Bibby boat came in I had to go and load her with the most enormous amount of tea which was to go back to the United Kingdom, but I was only given a day or so's warning and I had an APL ship, a huge vessel, tied up at the oiling jetty loading tea for the United States Eastern seaboard, and we were trying to ship an enormous backload of tea, because we hadn't had an American ship in for about two weeks, so my warehouses were absolutely chockablock with all this tea, which I had to get it out.

'This of course meant that I couldn't get the Bibby boat alongside, so I was desperate. I eventually got onto a great friend of mine, Anton McKayser, whose brother Irvine and I had played rugby together for Ceylon. The McKaysers were two strapping great chaps. Anyway it just so happened that Anton was the Government Agent in Trincomalee at that time and he was also Queen's harbourmaster, "Poobah" and generally seemed to be in charge of everything. So I was able to say to Anton, "Look here old cock, I have a bit of a ticklish problem, because this Bibby boat has come in and she's got buses for Rangoon on all her cargo hatches, so I can't do anything without a crane and somewhere to park these bloody things – can you help?"

'Now at that time I was still in the RNVR and I was meant to be in Trinco for what was called JET exercises, Joint Exercises Trincomalee, I had to go and do about a fortnight or three weeks every year. Anton invited me to pop over to see him and discuss the matter. When we met he told me that the fleet was out and it was going to be over at the Andaman Islands for a few days, so he thought he might be able to help me. It transpired that the Admiral's floating jetty was moored alongside Admiralty House, and Anton said: "If we tow that across to you, can you get those buses offloaded onto the Admiral's jetty and do all your necessary work, offloading everything and repacking in 36 hours?" I assured him we could. He said he would organise things at his end, but he explained that we then had to get all the floating jetty's cables repainted, because it had to look as if nothing had happened by the time the fleet returned.

'So we got this ruse going, in came this Bibby boat and Anton gave me a crane to go and offload these buses onto the Admiral's jetty, so I could get into the hatches and we reloaded the hatches so we got everything destined for Rangoon out so that I could get my tea into the boat down into the bottom of the holds, and this fairly scant consignment for Rangoon was popped onto the top of the forward hold. I think she had about four holds in total. We carried out this whole operation throughout the day and night, then we reloaded the buses onto the sealed hatches and the Bibby boat sailed 36 hours later; the buses were duly unloaded in Rangoon and the boat then shot back to London, as fast as Bibby boats can shoot (about 12.5 knots) and so we got this consignment of tea back in time for distribution in London.

'Meanwhile dear old Anton had had this Admiral's jetty towed back to the Admiralty House jetty all ship-shape and newly painted, and nobody suspected that we had done this dastardly thing. But all that was only possible due to the wonderful cooperation between the GA Trincomalee, who was the complete Poobah, as I said earlier. But it was proof, if proof were needed, that if the German captain had turned nasty we could have imprisoned him, because with the help of Anton, we had complete control of Trincomalee harbour at that time.'

The team that Sandy had assembled was, of necessity, only an *ad hoc* one, and yet they achieved everything they had set out to do at Trincomalee. Half a century later Mark looked back on that time and reflected: 'It was I suppose one of the most remarkable achievements of the private sector to keep the trade running, despite the efforts of the government, despite trade unions and despite having to enlist the help of the shipping lines that came into Colombo and were then diverted to Trincomalee. I had drafted into my team in Trinco people from all the agency houses, the shipping lines, brokers, buyers, they were drafted up there at short notice, virtually overnight, yet everyone turned up, and suddenly we found ourselves all working together, although invariably we were competitors in our everyday business; yet up at Trinco we knuckled down and worked side by side.'

So finally the time came for Mark and everyone in his team to pack up and return to their day jobs in the capital. Mark said: 'We had a splendid party just before we left at the Sea Anglers Club where I was able to thank everybody for their most enormous contribution.' So the Bostocks finally returned home to Colombo, where life was restored to near normality.

13

A
GROWING
FAMILY

It was shortly after their return to Colombo from Trincomalee that Lif fell pregnant for the second time, so plans were once more laid for an extended trip to the UK scheduled for early 1959.

This time Lif was accompanied not just by her husband, but also by Gillian. The trip to the United Kingdom was to ensure, as had been the case with Gillian, that their second child could be born in England and thus have the automatic right to a British passport.

The whole family set up home with Lif's parents, who were by now living in a delightful Elizabethan cottage in High Halden, not far from Tenterden in Kent.

It was during this home leave, when the family was awaiting the arrival of Claire, that Gillian developed an idea of hiding things, usually under a cushion or underneath a chair. As soon as everybody realised her little game, they only had to ask Gillian for something they had lost and she would go straight to the hiding place and produce the item with a flourish.

There were at the time some very nosy neighbours living opposite Ronnie and Sylvia Mills; these neighbours always liked to know the news before it happened. Mark, however, was absolutely determined that they should *not* be the first to hear the news of the new arrival before anybody else, indeed he did not even want them to know that Lif had gone into labour and into hospital. Accordingly, very quietly in the early hours of 26th, Mark and Lif slipped out of Verrall Cottage, the Mills' home, unseen and unheard.

Thus it was that at 4.00pm on February 27th 1959, Elizabeth Claire Bostock was born, at the Kench Hill Maternity Home just outside Tenterden, a sister for Gillian. There was also a minor triumph for Mark, because he even managed to get the birth recorded in the following morning's newspaper and was delighted with himself when he learned that the news was a surprise to those neighbours.

As the family was only going to be in England for three more months after Claire's birth, there was no point in investing in a lot of baby equipment. Sylvia had been offered an old pram by a friend. Being a coach-built pram, it would not fit into a car so Sylvia and Lif were dropped off by Ronnie at the friend's home and wheeled the pram back to Verrall Cottage. It was extremely rickety and they felt like a pair of rag and bone merchants. However, once fitted with a new chassis and the inside lined with 'Fablon', it was transformed into a pram fit for a queen. In those days all small babies were put outside in their prams for a large part of the morning for fresh air.

Sadly Claire had inherited her father's allergies and suffered badly from eczema and had to have her hands encased in cotton gloves to minimize the effect of her constant scratching of her skin. Unfortunately, before going back to Ceylon, the medics insisted that she had the diphtheria jab. This resulted in a nasty eruption behind her ear and her arm was then encased in a home-made 'splint' – ie a loo roll – to prevent her scratching. Fortunately, to a great degree, the eczema was controlled by ayurvedhic treatment out in Ceylon.

Claire was a happy baby, just as her sister had been, and she adapted well to life in the tropics from the moment she arrived in Ceylon at the age of three months. She also appeared to enjoy being looked after by the diminutive nanny, Vera. The family had hoped to move in to their newly completed home in Bullers Lane on their return from leave but, yet again, they had to seek rented accommodation for six months. The builders of Sweden Bank had taken advantage of the Bostocks' six months' absence from the island and were using their time and the Bostocks' house to construct a circular staircase for another client. However, as soon as the kitchen was completed the family moved in and were there to monitor progress properly and the project was eventually completed in time for Christmas that year.

Claire's early days in Ceylon were not without incident. There was one occasion when Lif was driving in to town with Claire in the front seat beside her. There were no seat belts, let alone baby or child seats, in those days. Suddenly Lif had to brake hard. Claire shot forward from her perch on the seat and her head collided with the choke button, which protruded very prominently from the dashboard. The result was a nasty gash below her eye, which began to bleed profusely.

Unfortunately, the sudden braking did not prevent Lif's car running into the car in front. This just happened to be a police car. Much to Lif's dismay the police constable who had been driving the car got out immediately, but the moment he saw the problem with the child he leapt into Lif's car and ordered her to drive to the nearest hospital. While Claire was lying on a stretcher awaiting medical attention, several nurses came up but all they could say was

"My, look at all the blood". As soon as the doctor on duty saw the wound on the lower eye-lid, he realized that it was the job of a surgeon to sew it up. Thus it was that the family met the well-known Dr Anthonisz, who was the surgeon at Colombo General Hospital, who attended to the Prime Minister S W R D Bandaranaike's gunshot wounds but was unfortunately unable to save him.

At an early age Claire showed signs of being dress conscious and refused to wear any dress or sunsuit that did not have matching pants. Lif used to make all the children's clothes (even the matching pants) since there was no shop such as Marks & Spencer on the island in those days. Claire was to remain very fashion conscious throughout her childhood, and was blessed as an adult with the sort of figure on which all clothes look good.

The two girls were distinctly different. Gillian had a broad streak of independence running through her from her days as a toddler. One example came when she was invited by a nursery school friend to spend a weekend with him and his parents in Trincomalee. She accepted with alacrity, without ever having met Patrick Barker's family beforehand.

The only time when she was home-sick was when she first went to the Hill School in Nuwara Eliya at the age of eight. She was excited about going to boarding school and getting decked out in her uniform, but when it came to waving goodbye, she looked thoroughly forlorn, and Lif remembered seeing this very little girl standing pathetically in the doorway of the school and looking as if her whole world had fallen down around her ears. A kind older girl – Jane Scott – came to her rescue but Mark had to drive round and round the lake in Nuwara Eliya before Lif mastered her tears and could face going on to the Hill Club for the night. At the beginning of each new term Gillian had most of the parents of the other children weeping as the school train pulled out of the Fort Railway Station in Colombo en route for Nuwara Eliya, regardless of the fact their own, dry-eyed, children were waving farewell quite happily.

Claire and Gillian were good friends in a way, but they did use to annoy each other. There would be frequent scuffles since each would want to have the last word, and there would invariably be a punch, a pinch or a slap, or all three at some point during any altercation. So much so that Mark said "why don't you try and kill each other?" On one occasion they were tussling for a screwdriver while trying to fix in the last screw while erecting Claire's cot. Claire being the less strong, relinquished her grip on the screwdriver, which as a consequence caught Gillian in the eye. Fortunately no damage was done long-term, although at the time Gillian was terrified that she might go blind.

There was no shortage of anecdotes and adventures with the two lively young girls. Often during the summer holidays, the family would make wonderful trips to the game reserves as well as heading up to Trincomalee where they would stay at the Sea Anglers Club. On one memorable occasion, a group of friends and the Bostock family decided to do a trip down the Mahaweli River. They embarked at Kantalai, several miles away from Trincomalee, and took their three boats upriver disturbing basking crocodiles which roused from their peaceful sunbathing, launched themselves into the river. The intrepid group then spent the night on the way in makeshift tents in an area where plenty of wild elephants roamed. Fortunately, one member of the party had lit a huge bonfire and kept it alight all through the night as in the morning plenty of elephant footmarks were found uncomfortably close to the camp-site. One of Gillian's school friends Sue Dinnis, who happened to be holidaying with the family, made some brilliant batik T-shirts with "Up the Mahaweli" printed on their fronts and a large hand with a V sign on the back. The group chugged victoriously into China Bay and greeted those who had come out to meet them with their "Up the Mahaweli" sign which unfortunately was taken as being something of a brush-off by the welcome party.

The Bostock family also loved their trips to the game reserves, Wilpattu being their favourite in the Dry Zone. There was wonderful, if slightly Spartan accommodation in the park bungalows. Guests had to take all their provisions but there was always a resident cook. On one such memorable trip, the men of the party had been shooting outside the strict game reserve and came in with a whole lot of snipe. Once at the bungalow, these were strung up on a coir rope between two trees for the night. The following morning the snipe were full of red ants and had to be thrown (rope and all) into the nearby 'tank'. Soon after a croc smelt them and went in to enjoy an unexpected breakfast. However, the rope got entangled in his teeth. At that moment another croc swam up and attacked the rope and snipe and a marvellous tug of war amused the family watching from the safety of the bungalow verandah.

Mark was always full of ideas for expeditions during the holidays and was always the 'leader of the pack'. This was particularly evident when some of the lads on holiday at the Sea Anglers Club used to follow him when fishing for crayfish. Needless to say, Mark always caught the largest one!

In 1967 the family headed off on a home leave, and for a change opted to travel by sea. The Cathay stopped at Aden and passengers were advised not to disembark as there was still fierce fighting with British troops involved. Small arms fire could be observed from the ship which was anchored off shore, but needless to say, Mark ignored the Captain's advice and went onshore as an "observer". Mercifully he returned unscathed. When the ship arrived at Port Suez, Gillian, who could have been no more than eleven at the time, announced that she wanted to disembark and go with some of the other passengers by land as she wanted to see the pyramids and Cairo. Mark and Lif had to remain on the ship as Claire was too young to go on this adventure. Gillian's request was granted, and consequently she became the only member of the family to have visited Cairo. The journey through the Suez Canal and the Bitter Lakes was very tedious as there was a backlog of oil tankers and the Cathay was not a priority. As a result, when the ship finally came through to Port Said it was so behind schedule that it was not allowed to stop, so in the middle of the night the group that had visited Cairo had to leap from a launch which came alongside the ship and precariously mount a ladder while the ship was still moving.

As had been the case with Gillian, there were tears from Claire when she started school. She did not immediately take to the idea of education, certainly not in an establishment that was not home, and she used to cry when she was left at Nursery School.

However, she did very well under the eagle eye of Dulce Perera, who ran a little primary school in the CH&FC pavilion. Dulce summed Claire up and realised that she needed to be kept under control and thus Claire became proficient in reading, writing, and elementary arithmetic by the time it was her turn to follow her older sister Gillian to the Hill School at the age of eight.

Here, unfortunately for Claire, she came up against the first Ceylonese teacher the Hill School had employed. This particular woman took an instant dislike to Claire with the result that even the slightest misdemeanour would see Claire dismissed from the class for a period of time as a punishment. Consequently after just one term at the Hill School, Claire had completely lost confidence in herself and used to say, "It's all too difficult, Mummy". So Lif instituted a little book which recorded how many places up from bottom each girl had come and for each place they had improved they would receive an extra one rupee in their pocket money. This little scheme did not break the bank, but it certainly helped to focus the girls' minds on their studies.

Eventually, at the age of 12½ Claire went to Benenden School in Kent, again following in her sister's academic footsteps.

The year Gillian went to Benenden Lif stayed in England in order to be at home for Gillian's first half-term holiday. This meant that Claire had to return to Colombo on her own as an 'unaccompanied minor'. This was an occasion when Claire showed great character as she was taking with her a birthday present for Mark which was a very fashionable pink shirt from Carnaby Street. This street in the West End of London was the epicentre of fashion in the 'Swinging Sixties'. At the Customs, the officer asked her if she was carrying any presents. When she replied "Yes", he asked her what it was to which he got the summary retort: "I'm not going to tell you, it's a secret".

Gillian's independent character caused problems for Lif when she was travelling home with the two young girls by air, they all three found themselves in the transit area heading for a connecting flight. Gillian raced ahead. By the time Lif had arrived at the departure gate there was no sign of Gillian. She was eventually discovered, and just in time, by observant fellow passengers when she was on the point of boarding the bus for the plane to New York.

Gillian had experienced no problems when settling in to life at Benenden, and she enjoyed her school days there. That was not quite the case with Claire, the impression being that she did not settle in quite as happily. It was not until she entered the Sixth Form there and undertook a course on "How to make the best of yourself" that she seemed to gain a far greater degree of self-confidence and self-belief.

Gillian's academic career was to follow a marginally more conventional path than her sister's. On returning to England after travelling around India and Nepal with her cousins Jenny and Andrew Holloway, she went to an interview at the School of Oriental & African Studies in London. The thought of spending the next three years in London after the vibrancy and heat of India did not inspire her despite the interesting course. Mark had recently returned from a business trip to South Africa and told her what an exceptional city Cape Town was, so she decided to investigate the possibilities of attending UCT. She applied for a place and was accepted. She went off on her own from Sri Lanka, emerging with a degree in archaeology and anthropology after her three years there. She was extremely fortunate in that wonderful friends Theo and Marie Madeleine Curchod, who had been stationed in Ceylon as Swiss Charge d'Affaires in the '60s were by then posted to Pretoria/Cape Town as Swiss Ambassador, so she was not totally without friends. They gave her a fascinating introduction to life in South Africa especially during the time of Apartheid. Her Archaeology and Anthropology course also allowed her to visit many unusual areas. She also, in a somewhat cavalier fashion hitchhiked through what was then Rhodesia in the middle of the "Bush" war with an American friend, meeting many courageous, interesting and extremely hospitable people along the way.

After returning to England, she completed a post graduate secretarial course and was then involved with the Indonesian Tourist Promotion Board in London, followed by a stint with Grants Scotch Whisky. Gillian then took the equivalent of a gap year, sailing from Fiji to Brisbane with two doctor friends in a 35' yacht, followed by a year spent in Australia working. She reluctantly then made the brave decision to head for England.

She recalled: 'Coming back to a cold dark England in February was rather depressing but, having sworn never to work in the City or for a bank, I was extremely fortunate to get a job at Flemings the merchant bank.

'Our great family friends Tony and Joanie Lewis also fortuitously asked me to "house sit" for them in their lovely home in Putney while they were to be away for several months as Tony was commentating for the BBC during the MCC tour of India that winter.

'The Sri Lanka connection was again apparent not long after settling down in London when I was invited down to Kent for a weekend by the wonderfully gregarious Tommy Candler. She was a freelance photographer, who had been staying with my parents in Colombo while doing some fashion shots on location in Sri Lanka. Tommy's houseparty on this particular weekend was invited to join Martin and Judith Miller (Miller's Antique Guides) at their house, The Grange, in Benenden for Sunday lunch.'

'Tommy had met the Millers while they were travelling in Sri Lanka, and, having established that they all lived in Kent, a great friendship blossomed and invitations were exchanged. The Millers were well known as very generous and hospitable hosts and their house was full of a great cross-section of people – all interesting in their own right.'

At this lunch Gillian found herself sitting with a group of people among whom was a photographer called Graham Kirk. He was someone Tommy had heard of in her professional capacity. According to Gillian the lunch was extremely animated and great fun. 'It was very strange to be quaffing vast quantities of wine in Benenden, quite legally, rather than sneaking off into the bushes as we had done while at the school. Conversation was lively and I seem to remember waxing lyrical about Australia and my experiences while living there.'

Back in London, a couple of weeks later, Gillian received a phone call from Graham, during the course of which he invited her out to dinner. He was clearly very keen to meet with her again since he had displayed a great deal of initiative in tracking her down. First he had telephoned international directory inquiries to try to get Lif and Mark's telephone number in Sri Lanka, but inexplicably they did not seem to feature in the directory. Gillian takes up the tale: 'Having drawn a blank there, he had then telephoned Lords, since our conversation at lunch had obviously included the fact that I was house-sitting for the Lewises. He told the person at Lords that he was an old friend of Tony Lewis, but that, after various moves, he had misplaced his contact telephone number.

'Remarkably, and obviously this was prior to data protection legislation, he came away from the call armed with Tony's home telephone number. With all that investigative work just to track me down, it would have been churlish not to go out to dinner with him. I later discovered that he disliked everything about Australia declaring it was, among other damning qualities, without culture (an opinion formed despite his never having been there), so I assume it was just my general enthusiasm which appealed to him.'

They now have two daughters, Catherine and Alexandra and celebrated their silver wedding anniversary in 2011. Their wedding in Crowbourgh having been memorable and full of incidents, mainly due to the presence of The Right Hon. George Younger, married to Diana who is Gillian's godmother. George was at that time a minister in Margaret Thatcher's cabinet and thus required security personnel. The house, garden and church were thoroughly searched and sniffer dogs were employed to further check the area as it was during the height of the Provisional Irish Republican Army (IRA)'s activities and only a couple of years after the bombing of the Grand Hotel in Brighton where George had had a close shave, along with Margaret Thatcher and her cabinet although others were not so fortunate. Much to the delight of one of the guests George's "minder" at the time was a particularly tall, handsome chap and had his job slightly compromised by a female guest who had no idea of his profession and was flirting outrageously with him.

Once she left Benenden Claire's life followed a completely different route from that of her sister. Acting on the sensible advice of the then Headmistress, Miss Betty Clark, she followed a Hotel and Catering Management course at Guildford Polytechnic, which she thoroughly enjoyed, and then went on to forge a successful career in this line.

Working initially at a Trust House Forte hotel at London's Heathrow Airport, Claire started in the kitchen, where she was perceived by the rest of the kitchen staff as a bit of a stuck-up girl, a 'nob', probably because of her cut glass Benenden-influenced accent, but she soon dispelled this image when she spilled some piping hot gravy over herself as she was endeavouring to bring a dish out of the oven. This happened at the very moment that the unpopular man in charge came in to the kitchen. Claire uttered a loud and not at all ladylike 'bugger'. Thinking she was referring to the manager her colleagues' attitude towards her changed and her stock among them rose and finally she was 'in' with the rest of the kitchen staff. It was at this hotel that she also discovered the joys of the "stock pot" which she had to clean out. This appeared to be the base of all soups served at the hotel and was constantly being added to while gently simmering away. To her amazement when she got to the bottom of this pot on one of the rare occasions it was totally emptied, she found several tea towels adding to the flavour.

Gillian decided to take Claire on a trip to South India, this after Claire had finished at Benenden. Much to Lif's delight, her daughters invited Lif and one of her great friends, Christine Gordon to make up a travelling quartet. Christine was a bit more pernickety than most regarding cleanliness, and throughout the trip she would always insist that the toilet facilities be fully checked out before taking a room. By all accounts the foursome had a wonderful time on this 'back packing' adventure, travelling by third class on the railway and staying in the most unlikely of places. Gillian, as the leader, had insisted they were not going to spend more that 10 rupees per night. On one occasion, they were convinced they were staying in a brothel as the concierge looked thoroughly surprised when these four English ladies checked in. One of their best nights was spent in the station rest room in Pondicherry, courtesy of the very charming Station Master.

Claire soon learned that Food and Beverage was very much a male dominated side of the hotel industry and so she changed to PR work, at which she excelled and she went on to hold responsible jobs at the Meridien chain of hotels, in London, Colombo and ultimately at the Changi Meridien in Singapore. It was there that she met and fell for an airline pilot Tony Oxlade, who was at the time on sabbatical from Qantas and was working for Singapore Airlines. The crews were accommodated at the Meridien.

Having met in Singapore, the couple decided they wanted to be married in Sri Lanka. So Mark and Lif approached the vicar of their old church – Christ Church, Galle Face. However, the vicar put up all sorts of difficulties, because

Tony was a divorcé. Mark eventually called on his old friend the Bishop of Colombo to officiate. Kenneth Fernando was more than happy to do so. Nearer to the date of the wedding Lif suggested to Mark that he checked with the Bishop to ascertain that all was still in order for the big day. But Mark pooh-poohed the idea saying: 'Oh no, Kenneth will remember'.

Unfortunately, as it turned out the Bishop appeared for the service a week ahead of the wedding and was more than puzzled to find nobody around. All was not lost, however, and the Bishop's Chaplain conducted a lovely service a week later based on a New Zealand prayer book. This had several wonderful elements the first of which was that Claire was accompanied up the aisle by Mark on one side and Lif on the other. Both families were further involved and invited to stand on either side of the happy couple and support them in the vows. Gillian's two little daughters – Catherine and Alexandra – were rather shy little bridesmaids. Tony's Dad and his stepmother and son, Jeremy, had bravely come up from Australia and were welcomed in to the Bostock home.

On the Friday before the Service the Registrar of Marriages had arrived at Sweden Bank to conduct the registration. Quite a few of Claire and Tony's friends had flown in from Singapore for the occasion and all gathered in the house. The Registrar was an odd little man, but he assured the family that he had conducted many marriages. His opening words were addressed to Claire to be repeated after him and ran thus "I Claaaire...do not know...why I...should not be married to this man". Everybody was having a hard job containing their giggles which was made all the more difficult when the "why I" scenario was repeated by Tony.

The reception was held in the garden of Sweden Bank which was beautifully decorated in true Sri Lankan style with decorations in tender coconut leaves. On entry to the house the young couple lit the brass oil lamp and others also lit the wicks dipped in coconut oil – a tradition in the country for all special occasions.

Claire had originally wanted to be married on the beach but was dissuaded by her parents and a compromise was reached when the visitors from Singapore and the family all went down the coast to Bentota and celebrated the same evening at the Ceysands Hotel. When the newly married couple were about to leave the party they discovered that a State of Emergency had for some reason been declared in the Southern Province and consequently they were unable to cross the Bentota bridge in order to reach their hotel as planned. Each of the provinces was under a different set of laws – one being British and the other Roman Dutch. Consequently, they had to walk down the beach instead of by road. They were slightly alarmed when they kept seeing flickering lights and expected at any moment to be pounced upon. It turned out that the lights were intended to guide them to their hotel and they walked down a beautiful flower-strewn path to the hotel. Part of Claire's honeymoon was spent at Aislaby, again accompanied by the rest of the family.

On returning to Singapore Claire and Tony soon moved to Australia, much to Claire's delight as she had fallen in love with Sydney on a previous short visit, seeking employment there but had been unable to obtain a work visa. Tony always used to say she only married him in order to live in Australia. They soon found a lovely home in which to bring up their two daughters, Olivia and Indiana.

14

D'YE KEN
JOHN
KEELLS?

It was not long after the Bostock family had returned to Ceylon, at the end of that summer of 1959 that the country was thrown into further turmoil by the assassination of S W R D Bandaranaike. The 60-year-old, who had introduced the contentious Act of Parliament which made Sinhala the official language of the country, was in his third year of office. It was widely held at the time that the assassination, which took place on September 26th, was carried out by a Buddhist monk Taldue Somarama Thera. Initially it appeared that the monk had acted alone. But reports about the assassination were laced with rumour and riven with wild speculation. According to some sources two different calibre bullets were found in the Prime Minister's body by the surgeon who operated on him. Others thought that it was the result of an affair by the Prime Minister; still more believed that the assassination was the result of a conspiracy, which was ultimately held to be the true version of events.

The plain facts were these. Somarama had visited the Prime Minister at his private residence the day before; when he returned to the residence in Rosmead Place 24 hours later, possibly because of his visit the previous day, coupled with the fact that he was a member of the Buddhist clergy, he was not searched for weapons. Somarama was given ready access to Mr Bandaranaike, who was just beginning his routine meetings with the public.

On being informed of Somarama's arrival the Prime Minister went out on to his verandah to greet the monk in the traditional Buddhist manner. It was while the Prime Minister was prostrate, and therefore unable to defend himself, that the monk pulled a revolver from where he had concealed it under his robes and fired it at Mr Bandaranaike. The shot (or shots, depending on which version is true) was not immediately fatal, but despite six hours of surgery and intensive post-op care, Ceylon's fourth Prime Minister died the next day.

After a police investigation it was discovered that Somarama had plotted with two others to assassinate the Prime Minister, and after an eight-month trial the Buddhist monk was found guilty of murder and sentenced to death. His two associates, Mapitigama Buddharakitta Thera and Hemachandra Piyasena Jayawardena, were found guilty of conspiracy to murder and were likewise sentenced to death. However, on appeal, their sentences were commuted to 'rigorous imprisonment for life'.

It was not until four years later, in August 1963, that a commission was set up to investigate the assassination, with particular reference to the conspiracy theory and to ascertain whether any organised body, ie: rival political parties, had been involved in setting up the assassination. In the end the commission was unable to establish a political connection to the three plotters and the assassination.

The following July, SWRD Bandaranaike's widow Mrs. Sirimavo Ratwatte Dias Bandaranaike won the election and became the first female Prime Minister in the world. She was also to become the first Prime Minister when the

Republic of Sri Lanka was born in 1972. And even after her political career was over the country was to see another Bandaranaike in office when her second daughter, Chandrika Kumaratunga became Prime Minister in 1994.

The political front, in the guise of civil unrest encroached from time to time on the Bostock family and their business interests. Tony Whitham, the first Assistant Planter on Aislaby, the family's tea estate, recalled some worrying moments for Mark, Ronnie Lushington the Superintendent and their employees. 'During the People's Liberation Front of Sri Lanka (JVP) uprising we had one of our Senior Field Officers taken in as a suspected insurgent. He was locked up for years, but when he was released I gave him his job back. Those were worrying times with daily curfews. Many estate managers were killed including my successor Hetiarachchi who was shot in front of the factory.'

That was in 1988, when the JVP, a brand of extremely aggressive 'angry young men', decreed that any factory superintendent on the island, who flew the Sri Lankan flag from the factory on Independence Day would be shot. Unfortunately for Aislaby the JVP had a very active 'cell' in the Bandarawela area, so when Nimal Hetiarachchi, Aislaby's superintendent at the time, refused to comply with their diktat, they sent a hit squad to the estate, broke into his bungalow in the early hours of the morning of February 4th, 1988 and marched him down to the factory. On the way there they shot him from behind, which was their particular way of showing it was their handiwork.

Fortunately overall security was not a real problem at Aislaby, which by this time had been nationalised by the Sri Lanka Government. The watcher at the factory was a Pathan named Allah Bux. Ronnie and Mark used to take him on their trips to Yala and the jungle. Bux was apparently a crack shot, so other than the JVP murder squad, there were never any other serious security problems in the factory.

As previously mentioned, it was Mark's suggestion that John Keells should acquire their own stores. Thus the property previously owned by Dodwell's was bought. The property also included a house at the gate of the property – the house subsequently known as Keell Hall, almost certainly a wordplay, based on a particularly cruel and barbaric form of punishment known as keel hauling, which was prevalent in the Royal Navy during the 17th and 18th Centuries; a line would be tied to each arm of the convicted sailor and he would then be put overboard at the bow of the ship when it was under sail and he would then be hauled along the length of the barnacle-encrusted keel, under water, to emerge – provided he had not drowned – with body badly lacerated, at the stern.

Keell Hall became the residence of Alan Henricus, the Head Storekeeper. Alan had been a key member of Mark's team during the setting up of the Trincomalee Tea Association. Later on David Blackler, who was the only bachelor on the board at that time, took up residence and conducted extensive renovations and improvements. These stores were in an idyllic location on the edge of the Beira Lake. The modern and very prestigious building housed the offices and stores of John Keells and Keell Hall was subsequently used for guests and office functions after David Blackler vacated it. The site is currently in the process of a major building development.

The firm's long history had culminated with the amalgamation of Keell & Waldock and E. John Thompson White Ltd; initially it adopted the very cumbersome name of John Keell Thompson White Ltd. However, Mark changed this when he became Chairman of the company in succession to André Willis, in 1969. An eye-catching advertisement appeared in a London Times' supplement of a picture of the legendary huntsman John Peel on horseback and followed by his pack of hounds and the caption "D'ye ken John Keells".

Mark had always taken tea seriously, and although, in his professional life, he was responsible for broking other commodities as well, it was the fragrant leaf that held his heart and his attention, and occupied much of his leisure time, as he explained. 'A lot of my weekends were spent visiting Ceylonese-owned tea estates, because they needed help in the field, the factory and also in finance.

'By the very act of visiting these estates we at John Keells established ourselves as the number one company, looking after the Ceylonese-owned properties, and as a result more and more Ceylonese proprietors came and asked us to sell their teas for them.

'It was very hard work, but most rewarding, because when you are selling tea for instance or rubber, you have to get to know the manager of each estate. You have to understand and appreciate his situation, and you have got to know what facilities there are in the factory because there is simply no good to be gained by going in and criticising (the word criticise is possibly not the right word, but I can't think of a better one) a chap for making a bad tea if he simply hadn't got the equipment for making a good tea. It was only by going and assessing the situation that you could help the chap make a better tea with the facilities he had at his disposal.

'There are so many ways of doing this. For instance if a chap hasn't got enough power – in those days most factories were driven by a generator or engines and if a fellow hadn't got enough power to go and do all his manufacture correctly at the proper time, he couldn't make a good tea and it was no good going and screaming at him saying you've got to go and do this and do that, if when you visit the estate you find that he is hopelessly under powered. You have to write out a programme specifically for him so he is using various parts of his factory machinery at different times which enables him to possibly and hopefully do a proper programme to make a decent tea. There was one factory I was asked to visit in the Uva district, and it should have been making some lovely tea in the season when we get dry winds and very high ambient differences, that is the difference between the wet and dry bulb thermometers. All of which means that if you have an ambient difference of 25 degrees Celsius, it is virtually scorching, and we sometimes experienced that situation in Uva. In these conditions you can make a really lovely tea.

'Anyway this factory I had been asked to go and see was managed by a very good friend of mine Tusker Ted; he was a wildlife expert and his wife was equally keen about nature and what is now known as 'the environment'. They were lovely people. I discovered that dear old Tusker had an enormous tulip tree growing right outside his factory, and it completely blanketed his central bulking chamber, as a result he couldn't get a decent wind volume through in order to help with the withering of his leaf. I told him there was only one thing for it. With reluctance I said, "The only thing that can be done, I'm afraid, is to have that tulip tree taken down, because you will never make a decent tea with that impeding your airflow." He was naturally against such drastic action, and informed me that the tree would come down "over my dead body".

'Matters came to a head and I had to report to the agents that there was this impediment barring the air intake, but that probably, if they hacked it down, we should be able to make some decent tea. So of course, down it came; but I then had an awful struggle, because for a couple of weeks

Tusker would not let me make a tea which proved me right and him wrong, until I had to get one of the executives from the agency house up and we then spent all night working on it. It was worth the effort as well because we made a really rather lovely tea.'

Mark was nothing if not dedicated and he said: 'As a result of visits such as these I got to know all the planting districts really well", so much so that he could point out each one as the family travelled around the country. "At that time I was visiting about 100 estates per year, paying special attention to the Ceylonese owned plantations, and it was not just a matter of advising them on manufacture, I realised that they also wanted me to go out and tell them what to do in the field for their agricultural improvement as well. So it was a very busy time. It was a very exciting and worthwhile time for me as a tea broker."

But as important as tea was to Mark, he always had the firm's interests at heart, thus it was that he saw an opportunity to diversify, and expand, when he took advantage of a bit of a depression in the early seventies to buy a controlling interest in Walkers Tours & Travels, and then bought Mackinnon Mackenzie – the P & O agents – in 1974. It was at a time when Mrs Bandaranaike's government was in the process of nationalising tea and rubber estates and were toying with the idea of also nationalising the brokers and agency houses. Mark had met Mrs Bandaranaike socially (possibly at Westminster House, the official residence of the British High Commissioner – see photograph with Alistair Wilson) and she had told him that she was taking on the position of Minister of Tourism and that she intended to actively promote the tourist trade. A couple of newly appointed directors – Derek Samarasinghe and Tissa Molligoda – objected strongly to the acquisition of these new companies as they felt especially Mackinnnons was not a good buy. However, they were eventually overruled. Unlike Ken Balendra, they had not yet caught Mark's sixth sense for business. Mark's way of conducting board meetings was to let each director have his or her say and then announce, "Thanks to you all for your contributions, but this is the way we are going to do things." If that seemed somewhat autocratic, it was at least effective, and anyway, in the event, these two particular purchases served to underline Mark's commercial prescience, because it sparked a whole chain of diversification into the tourist trade, which would also prove to be lucrative.

Mackinnon Mackenzie had a prestigious office in the Fort area, but later there were problems, because under J R Jayawardena's Executive Presidency, the building was taken over by Government. Later there was an unexplained fire in the adjoining bank building which leaped across to Mackinnons when amateur fire fighters opened all the windows in the bank building and the fire extinguishers were faulty and a whole chain of disasters ensued. The building in its current state of considerable damage did not suit the Government and they later handed it back to John Keells, with the proviso that the company would not sue the Government for compensation. This was because whatever insurance there might have been was held by another Government organization – the Ceylon Insurance Corporation.

Part and parcel of being in the Travel Trade entailed being a member of ICCA (International Conferences & Conventions Association – a prestigious organisation involving all aspects of the multinational travel trade). Conventions were held annually and the first one which Mark attended was in Vienna in 1980. It was there that, after what Mark considered to be the important part of the agenda had been completed, he decided he would search for a nearby agreeable wine bar. He thought he had slipped out unnoticed but the following day some of his colleagues decided to follow his trail. This was the foundation of what was named The Thirst Club. Several of his colleagues subsequently decided that this was decidedly the best forum in which to talk serious business and enjoy a drink at the same time.

Lif was fortunate in being invited as an 'accompanying person' to Vienna and there enjoyed two very memorable experiences the first of which was a private invitation for the group to attend the college of the Vienna Boys' Choir and to learn all about the training given as well as listening to the boys, all decked out in their sailor suits, singing in the most wonderful way.

The second occasion was dancing in the Schonberg Palace. Mark and Lif always considered themselves to be rather 'hot stuff' at the quick waltz and what better place to enjoy it. Their visit to the Opera House did not quite match up to expectations when the heroine in Madam Butterfly was a soprano of uncertain years who did not quite seem to fit the role, albeit a wonderful singer

Other capital cities that the Bostocks enjoyed together were Istanbul, and Athens. Lif was not accompanying Mark to Salt Lake City where Mark ended up in hospital after a night out when he was catapulted out through the revolving door onto a pavement covered in sheet ice. His colleagues thought they had killed him. When he awoke in a strange place he had no idea what had happened, with all sorts of tubes inserted in to him and a rather suspect bottle of red liquid on the floor beside his bed. This turned out to be his own blood! The nurse explained that as Mormons they did not give blood, so any non-Mormon patients were bled in order to provide for blood transfusions. Some months later he received a rebate on his hospital bill of $80.

In 1982 the convention moved to Torremolinos and was described by Bent Hvidt as probably the most disastrous ICCA Convention ever. "The venue was a very modern but inhospitable concrete bunker. The peak of mishaps occurred on the Gala Night in the mountains, hosted by the local Mayor of Malaga. When the delegates arrived they found the solitary restaurant was closed and no Mayor to be seen. In marked contrast the convention held in Sri Lanka was an outstanding success. The Thirst Club was instituted in Vienna and Mark's usual way of saying "Cheers" was adopted. This consisted of raising one's glass to shoulder height and saying "First of the Day" no matter what time of day it might be and no matter how many previous drinks had already been quaffed. Anybody can be identified if they should quote this.

Mrs. Bandaranaike's conversation with Mark, inferring that she could not promise her Government would not nationalise the broking houses was not a hollow threat. John Keells, as a prominent broking house, did indeed come on to the Government radar. Furthermore, Mark had heard that a team of Government officials was due to come round to John Keells with a view to seeing if the premises were ripe for requisitioning, and so he went into action to try to ensure that there would be no danger of the firm falling into Government hands. John Keells was situated down a very narrow lane called Glennie Street, and Mark requested the Head Storekeeper to summon as many lorries, bullock carts and sundry other vehicles, to occupy both sides of the street, thus effectively totally blocking vehicular access to all the offices located there.

Mark's strategy ensured that the Government representatives had to leave their cars at the wrong side of the railway line, and continue their journey to Keells on foot. They eventually arrived, very flustered and 'out of sorts', and then they were further angered to discover that neither the lifts, nor the air-conditioning, was working. They arrived dishevelled, sweating and out of breath in Mark's office, at which point he innocently asked them if they had had a good journey. Of course they complained about the traffic congestion, to which Mark replied, "Oh, you should have come yesterday and seen what it can really be like on a bad day." He also said the buildings suffered frequent power cuts. The ruse worked and the government's team produced a negative report on the suitability of the building for requisitioning, thus the day was saved for John Keells and their wonderful property remained with the firm for many years.

As Chairman of John Keells, Mark's time was very precious and he was horrified when he was called upon to do jury service as he knew he could not spare the time away from the office for what was expected to be a very long and involved case concerning a well-known member of Colombo society who had been accused of murdering his wife. Mark could not think how he could wriggle out of this jury duty, so he appealed to his friend and sometimes protagonist Colvin R de Silva who was the former Cabinet Minister of Plantation Industries and Constitutional Affairs, Trotskyist leader and most importantly as far as Mark was concerned, an eminent and very well respected lawyer. Colvin R's suggestion was that when Mark was paraded with the other members of the jury in front of the legal representatives in the case, he should develop an awful twitch and act as if he was not of mentally sound mind. This he did with great conviction and he was considered unsuitable for jury duty. Mark had previous experience of putting on such a performance when as children he and other members of his family would appear at the window of their railway carriage in order to repel others who might want to join their compartment.

No history of John Keells under Mark's Chairmanship would be complete without including the last of his wonderful personal Secretaries, Grace.

Grace was someone who really understood Mark well, and on occasions, when, for example, he might have written a letter in a certain amount of ire, she would decline to bring it in to him for his signature at the end of the day, saying, "I thought you might like to reconsider the wording in the cold light of day."

Grace retired at the same time as Mark and later worked in London. She came to visit Mark and Lif at Spring Cottage and, much to her surprise, was told she was going black-berrying that afternoon. Her remark after this unusual experience for somebody wearing a sari, was, "I knew retirement would be hard for the Boss, but I never thought I would be going out to the hedgerows to fill his winter store cupboard."

An amusing story is told by Nimmie, a young colleague of Grace's who had just joined the company as a holding board secretary. Grace instructed Nimmie as to how she should behave while receiving dictation from Mark and Nimmie was understandably nervous taking a letter from the Chairman for the first time. Grace told her not to look up at Mark as he would lose the flow of his dictation. However, when she heard Mark opening one of his desk drawers, she did look up and to her horror saw that he was slowly extracting a pistol. He then appeared to take aim straight at her and she thought her last day had come only to find he was aiming at a crow on the outside verandah rail right behind her.

There is no doubt that Mark Bostock was a man ahead of his time, he was someone who was always very keen to promote and encourage the younger men and women in the company, and by creating a large number of subsidiary companies under the general umbrella of John Keells he was able to make many people directors of the smaller boards. He was one of the first businessmen in Sri Lanka to have women directors in his company, and he also brought in the rule for retirement whereby everybody had to retire at the age of 60, thus giving further encouragement to the younger people, most of whom still remember him with great affection.

Mark was always generous with his advice and loved nothing better than to discuss tea and ways of improving the production and manufacture. As Chairman of John Keells his door was always open to anybody of high or low estate to come in and share their problems with him. He was resolute in achieving his aims and 100 per cent honest in all his business dealings and remained a-political throughout his 17 years as Chairman.

At the time Mark took over the Chairmanship, Keell & Waldock it had been a single entity, solely concerned with freight and commodity broking. By the time he retired in 1986, there were more than 40 companies under the umbrella of John Keells.

But even after his retirement Mark continued to spend about six months of every year in Sri Lanka and kept up his enormous interest in all aspects of tea and was always ready to give of his expertise. He also developed a system for solar-heated hot air for use on factory roofs, mainly for the manufacture and processing of tea, rubber and coconut products. Sadly, he did not live long enough to see this reach fruition on a large scale.

15

HOME
FROM HOME

Visits to the United Kingdom were an important aspect of the Bostock family's life and featured more and more prominently as the girls grew older. Mark and Lif had spent their first two home leaves staying with either the Bostock family at their home Greenham Court in Newbury – where Mark was able to indulge in the passion he shared with his father, that of fly-fishing, and he was able to spend many a peaceful and contented hour on the River Kennett – or at the Mills' homes of Dockyard House and later Verrall Cottage in High Halden, Kent. But Mark and Lif realised that they wanted a little more independence on their visits to the United Kingdom, and the freedom to choose when it was convenient for them to return to their home from home, so eventually they decided that, with the two growing girls in tow, it was now time to find a more permanent place of their own.

Initially they rented the ground floor flat of a large and very cold house called "The Farthings" on the outskirts of Horsham in West Sussex, the town where Mark's father had been born. This must have been one of the coldest possible temporary homes with the only heating coming from the Aga cooker in the kitchen. Lif's brother Ken had lent them a Valor kerosene heater and on one particularly cold night this was left burning while all the doors around the hall were closed. At some unearthly hour of the night the nanny, sporting an extremely sooty moustache, knocked on Mark and Lif's bedroom door and said she thought there must be something wrong with the stove. By the time they had sorted out the problem they had all acquired matching moustaches. The following morning the hall looked like the opening scene of Great Expectations, with soot-coated cobwebs hanging like wispy black streamers from the ceiling and adorning every corner. Naturally, all the coats, jackets and other outdoor clothes hanging in the hall reeked of kerosene.

For much of their married life up to that point Mark had been very dubious of Lif's ability as a cook, so when, on the first evening at Farthings, he peered into the Aga oven, it was with genuine surprise that he said of the dish within: 'It looks as if we are going to be able to eat it.'

The Aga proved not quite so successful when the Bostocks hosted a house-warming party; several sticks of bread, which were warming up in the oven, were forgotten, and by the time they were discovered they had been transformed into charcoal. Neville Greene (Mark's cousin) picked one up and knocked it on the head of the kind friend who used to help them in the house; the poor woman was scraping charred breadcrumbs out of her ears for some days to come.

It was during this home leave that Mark did some serious rugger refereeing. He had by then served his 'apprenticeship' in Colombo. After retiring from playing he had decided to try refereeing in order to maintain involvement with the sport he loved and which had been central to his life. After completing the requisite courses, he was duly certified as a fully qualified referee by the Ceylon Rugby Football Union.

But his apprenticeship had made Lif extremely nervous at times, especially early on, since she had no idea what to expect from him. He did not disappoint. On one occasion, when put in charge of a tense needle match between two neighbouring Up-Country clubs, he felt a sudden, painful sting on his backside as he was bending down to peer in to the scrum. He immediately stood up and spotted a tea coolie with a catapult in his hand hiding in the tea bushes. Mark immediately gave chase, and the game had to wait until he had caught up with the offender and given him a piece of his mind. Workers from the estates took a keen interest in the rugger games, and probably had a bet or two on the side.

Thus when he came over to the UK he offered his services to the county RFU and before long Mark found himself placed in charge of some fairly challenging matches, in particular university games, he was also asked to take charge of local games in the Horsham area.

At that particular time Mark was undergoing some homeopathic treatment for the allergy which had been causing his catarrhal problem and he had been told by the doctor that he had to keep off alcohol. It goes without saying that he became the butt of post match ribbing and ribaldry by players from both sides, who, when offering to buy the ref a drink, heard him ask for lemonade rather than a beer. He came through that 'dry' spell unscathed, and was greatly amused by the humour it engendered.

The rather unusual nanny, whom Mark and Lif employed at that time, had an Indian boyfriend. She was later confirmed as being pregnant and she insisted on marrying her Indian friend; Gillian, aged about six or seven was equally insistent that she wanted to be a bridesmaid.

It was when they were on their fourth home leave that Mark and Lif decided it was time for them to buy their own home. Mark's sister, Eve, invited them to stay with her and her husband Tor at their family home in Maplehurst, West

Sussex. Gillian and Claire were able to attend the village school, which arrangement meant Mark and Lif were left free to scour the countryside in search of their ideal home.

Gillian and Claire attended the local primary school, which was more of an education than they anticipated. One class was learning about everything that went into a cup of tea, including the china cup, sugar, milk and tea and Mark was volunteered to give them a talk about tea. He duly arrived in his gardening corduroys to deliver his talk and Gillian was apprehended later in the loos by one of the girls who had attended the talk who said "Cor your dad's wearing the Dave Clarke Five trousers"! Another said "Ain't yr dad 'ansome", which certainly hadn't entered Gillian's reckoning before and Mark certainly hadn't been noted for keeping up with the latest fashion. Lif also overheard Gillian telling Claire the facts of life, which she had gleaned from her class mates and after some lurid details, Claire said "Oh don't be silly Gillian, nothing like that could possibly happen".

They had already decided on a particular part of East Sussex because they felt that it would be reasonably convenient once the girls were established at Benenden School. Also many ex-pats on home leave lived in the area, to such a degree that it was known affectionately as "Srilankashire". This area was in and around Crowborough.

It was only after they had purchased their new home, that Mark and Lif learned that the young Ronnie Mills used to come down to Crowborough from London every Easter with his parents to enjoy the healthy air and it was on the Crowborough Beacon Golf course that Ronnie started to learn to play golf. Further, Sylvia Mills' elder brother Lionel Gurney was for many years the Honorary Secretary of the Golf Club. At the time they were living in Croft Road in Crowborough. Uncle Lionel had been gassed in World War I and as a result survived on one lung.

After some time and countless viewings, in the end, on a miserably cold and wet day, their diligent house-hunting was rewarded when they stumbled across Spring Cottage in Crowborough.

The trees were dripping wet, the garden had clearly been neglected for years, while the house itself looked thoroughly dejected and neglected. However, Mark, at least, saw the potential in it as a family home-from-home straightaway and almost immediately the two of them, Mark and Lif, made the decision that this was what they wanted. They duly submitted an offer, which was accepted by the owners, since the house had been on the market for many months with very little or no interest having been shown.

Typically, almost the moment that Mark and Lif's offer was made, than another better offer suddenly came in, with the additional incentive to the vendors that the rival purchasers would be willing to buy the adjacent paddock, which belonged to the property and was also being offered for sale, but as a separate lot. Fortunately, the vendors' estate agent came in on the Bostocks' side. He told the owners that Mark and Lif had all along acted in good faith, and that if the owners changed their minds, they had better look for another estate agent. Mark was duly allowed to make a renewed offer, which matched the rival one and the Bostocks therefore also acquired the paddock, which, with his business acumen, Mark very quickly managed to sell on, and at a profit.

By now there was only a month remaining of this home leave, before the couple had to return to Sri Lanka, yet a lot of hard work and organisation lay ahead of the couple. To begin with they had no furniture, apart from a few pieces donated by Norman and Beth. Mark was able to rectify this by attending the Gorringe's furniture sale in Uckfield. He was very fortunate as on one particular day the train bringing down the dealers from London had been delayed and Mark was able to pick up many bargains. Being a broker by trade, he knew exactly the strategy of the bidding process. On one day he virtually furnished a six-bedroom house for £1,000. Large removal vans would appear at the house and disgorge alarming amounts of furniture etc. and on one occasion Mark had bid for a "job lot" as a hotel was selling up, luckily the "lot" included bedding and various kitchen equipment as well as unwanted hat stands and other paraphernalia, which were duly returned to the auction house for resale.

Mark then turned his energy to sorting out the garden, which was large, being somewhere in the region of three acres, including an area of woodland. To assist him in this work he employed a singular man who had been doing some work for Eve. His name was Ernie and in truth he was a bit of an eccentric. The joke in the family was that he had probably had to bail out of a plane during the war and had forgotten to open up his parachute and had landed on his head.

Be that as it may he turned out to be a good hard worker. He set up camp in the garden shed for the duration, so Gillian and Claire were always terrified when they had to take cups of tea to him. The grass was standing about three feet tall and the 'lawn' was littered with small trees and hedges that needed to be cut down and dug up.

Lif, in the meantime had to set about making curtains and sorting out the inside of their new home. Mark suggested to the girls that they went and called on some of the neighbours with a wheelbarrow of lilies from the pond to see if they could find homes for them. They made friends with a dear old lady – Miss Herring – who lived in the next house and they used to do little jobs for her. Miss Herring was quite a legend in Crowborough and used to go everywhere on her horse.

Some friends called the Knopps, also from Ceylon, lived up the lane with girls of roughly the same ages as Gillian and Claire who linked up with them and spent part of the day with them. By the time it came to 7.00pm Lif thought she had better go in search of the girls. But by this time the girls had moved on from their original destination and had gone to the home of another couple Ted and Audrey Leigh. As Lif entered their drive, Ted came out and said "Oh, yes, the girls are here. Come in and have a drink. What do you drink? We only serve gin and whisky here". There then began the most wonderful friendship which has lasted well into the 21st Century.

Sadly Ted died, but Audrey, or 'L'il Aud' as she was lovingly nicknamed, survived him and eventually emigrated to Australia. She had always said that when the Bostocks sold Spring Cottage, she would sell her home in the lane and move to Australia where her son lived, and she kept her word. The Leighs inevitably introduced the Bostocks to many of their lovely friends and so suddenly they found they had acquired a social circle as well as a new home. Gillian and Claire became firm friends of the Leigh twins – John and Louise. They had wonderful times building camps in the woodlands.

It took just under a month of hard work and judicious purchasing to make Spring Cottage fit for habitation, the place was then let for the next two years. This was much to the chagrin of the previous owners who were annoyed that they themselves had not thought of the idea of letting, as they had really wanted to return to the house once their next assignment was finished, having completed the interior décor to their own satisfaction, some definitely not to the Bostocks' taste, most notably the enormous bathroom which boasted wallpaper featuring green, rather than pink, flamingos.

Spring Cottage was the scene of many a happy gathering and family celebrations, including the Bostock's ruby wedding anniversary, Gillian's wedding, Catherine and Alexandra's birth and Mark's 70th birthday party, although on this last occasion Mark did suffer a mini-stroke. That birthday party was just about the last family celebration to be held in Spring Cottage, since by that time anyway Mark was finding the stairs increasingly difficult to cope with.

Lif finally persuaded Mark that Spring Cottage, their first lovely home in England with its six bedrooms and extensive garden and woodland, was by now far too big for them. So, after 32 years, the Bostocks decided they had to move on, after Mark reluctantly conceded that she was right and following much discussion and thought, the best option in their view seemed to be a bungalow.

Mark had three criteria which had to be applied to every property, did it have a view? Was there a handy local shop nearby? Was there a smaller garden?

It took a while and a lot of viewings but they eventually came across Tree Tops in Tubwell Lane, in the Jarvis Brook area of Crowborough, which certainly met the first two criteria, unfortunately though it still had quite a large garden. However, the view straight across the fields to Rotherfield church was spectacular, and ultimately that was what persuaded them to buy it. It was the first house with a view that Lif had ever lived in throughout her varied life, and she would ever after stand looking out of the window each morning and say to herself, "I can't believe I am here".

Like most house moves, this transaction did not go as smoothly as it might have. The Bostocks had already agreed to move out of Spring Cottage by a certain date, but the vendors of Tree Tops kept delaying their departure. Mark and Lif therefore found themselves homeless for about ten days; it took the intervention of some kind friends who offered them their one-room cottage as a temporary home.

Once established in Tree Tops, Mark and Lif set about a few alterations and additions, including the building on of a lovely conservatory. Mark then embarked on another of his crazy ideas, that of constructing a table which could sink down into the floor and rise up at the press of a button in the same way as old-fashioned theatre organs in cinemas. At last the engineering side of it was completed and the table itself designed, Mark went back on his annual trip to Sri Lanka, leaving Lif to deal with the carpenter. Mark's original idea was that the table legs would fold up under the table top, thus only requiring a shallow hole to be dug in the ground to accommodate them. The carpenter disagreed with this concept and so a hole of about four feet was dug, in order to ensure that the table and attached legs would be stable. Mark was not amused when he saw it. However, the whole idea worked well and was always a good conversation piece, although in the process of its completion it looked as if Tree Tops had become a Baptist church with an enormous oblong hole prepared for complete emersion. Lif was always terrified before the table was installed that someone would step back into the hole.

Contrary to the negative thoughts friends had had about Mark adapting to a much smaller home, he was supremely happy at Tree Tops and even went back to listening to his much loved classical music. Mark would also sit at the end of the garden in the evening and we all thought he was just enjoying a quiet gin and tonic, but he would actually be working on new ideas. Like his father before him, Mark enjoyed shucking peas and slicing runner beans from the garden. He claimed it slowed down the drinking of his gin and tonic. Lif was not always too pleased as the vegetables would be presented to her for freezing just at the time she reckoned her cooking for the day was over.

Mark was to live there until the end of his days, while Lif stayed on for a further four years, until she felt it was time to move nearer to the town centre, to be within walking distance of the shops and church and her many friends.

16

MISADVENTURES
IN THE
MALDIVES

With each home leave they made the Bostocks became aware of ever more changes to life in Ceylon. As the 20th Century surged towards its close on a wave of technological and social advancements things grew more and more unstable on the island.

One of the first things to change during these turbulent years was something very close to the Bostock family's heart. In 1979 their coastal idyll of Sandsend was taken from them. The property was requisitioned by the Government, which then handed over the lease to a German company, one similar to the Club Méditerranée. Although the Bostocks were given a 10-year lease on the property some years later under a different Government, it was not a long-lived deal and they eventually lost their beloved hideaway at Bentota for good.

The weekend prior to this painful act a nest of rats had been discovered in the chest among the pillows and cotton mattresses; Danny, the watcher-cum-cook at the property was most distressed when he saw the baby rats being deliberately drowned in the river reckoning this was a bad omen, and so it turned out to be.

Of all the family, Mark was undoubtedly the one most affected by the loss of Sandsend. For many years it had been a refuge for him, a place of peace where he could relax and shrug off the cares and responsibilities of the business world, and instead just enjoy life and have some fun, take in the sea air and revel in the company of friends and family.

Never one to be down for long Mark had soon thrown himself into a project that was to take his mind off Sandsend. John Keells had recently entered the travel business and were about to build their first hotel from scratch. With this in mind the company had purchased an old Walawa (a Sinhalese ancestral home) on the outskirts of Kandy. At first sight it looked an unlikely place for a large hotel, since it was perched on a small hillock above the Mahaweli River and there was consequently little surrounding ground that was suitable for building.

However, under Mark's guidance 'The Citadel' soon began to take shape. Mark had a remarkable talent for 'time and motion' study and, in this case, a coachload of tourists would be directed to their rooms and their luggage would follow. He even thought how a toilet should be placed in the area of Reception, which is now common practice. Even the finer points, such as the height at which a mirror should be placed above a hand basin and the convenient location of light switches, were carefully considered by him. Often these details had not been taken into account by the architects or so-called interior designers.

With all this in mind Mark and Lif made the journey, not down to Bentota, but rather up to Kandy, almost every weekend to check on all the details of design and construction. The hotel proved popular as it was away from the hustle and bustle of Kandy itself and yet remained easily accessible from this popular tourist attraction. Consequently, in due course a further building was constructed, this one with air-conditioned rooms and rather more up-market accommodation. Drivers' quarters were added and a limited number of parking lots also featured.

But civil unrest was never far from the surface and ethnically everything really came to a head in 1981 throwing into question the country's future socially and economically, when Velupillai Prabhakaran the leader of the LTTE movement (Liberation Tigers of Tamil Eelam, known more familiarly as the Tamil Tigers) led an ambush of two Sinhalese soldiers in a jeep on the Kankesanturai Road. There then followed further attacks on police stations. The violence escalated throughout 1982, before reaching boiling point in 1983, when the bodies of 13 soldiers, all of whom who were Sinhalese, were brought to Colombo for burial. Colombo erupted in flames and crowds of unruly Sinhalese burned, looted and smashed any Tamil home or business that lay in their path.

The Executive President J R Jayawardena appeared initially to be reluctant to reassure the populace that the Government was in control, but finally decided to cancel the military funeral of the 13 Sinhalese soldiers, returning the bodies to the families, before eventually declaring a dusk-to-dawn curfew.

Rather worryingly Lif and Claire found themselves caught up in the action on the streets of Colombo on one frightening day. Lif recalled this harrowing incident 'Mark was away in South America at the time on travel business, but fortunately Claire was staying with me, because she was working for the Meridien Hotel in Colombo at the time. Some Tamil members of John Keells took refuge in Mark's and Lif's home and so terrified were they that they remained in the little passageway between the kitchen and dining room of Sweden Bank, steadfastly refusing to move elsewhere, since that was the only place they could not be seen from outside.'

The problem facing Claire and Lif was that the refugees were all strict vegetarians and the household had run out of vegetables. However, a quick, though risky, trip to the local market sorted that out to a certain extent. While this Tamil family was staying with the Bostocks their own home in Kirillapone was ransacked and badly damaged and all their stocks of rice and other staple foodstuffs were looted.

Once the curfew had been lifted, Claire and Lif and the little Tamil son of the houseboy set out to collect some bread from the Prima factory – the only source of bread in Colombo, and so each person was rationed to one loaf per day. Claire and Lif were joined by their 'sewing lady'. They had almost reached the head of the queue when a whole stream of cars, vans and lorries came racing down both lanes of the dual carriageway, shouting, 'The Tigers are in the Pettah. Go! Go! Go!' The hysterical shouted warnings caused utter panic and confusion

Lif said: 'It seemed to us that there was not much point in gathering a small amount of bread if our lives were in danger, so I reversed the car and joined the stream of traffic, which was unfortunately headed away from Sweden Bank, but the volume of traffic was such that there was no way we could drive against it. Fortunately I knew the back roads, although several were blocked with people shouting and waving, warning us not to go down them. We managed to drop off the 'sewing lady' near to her home and with the little Tamil boy quivering below the back seat of the car, we eventually joined the High Level road which leads out of Colombo. We were not out of the woods though, because here again, there were lines of vehicles all going in one direction – the one we did not want – out of town. By eventually crossing over towards the sea and by a very circuitous route, we eventually turned in to Bullers Lane. However our relief at getting back on home turf was rather tempered by seeing fires at the top of the lane. However, we reached home safely.'

Practically every household employed Tamil servants and drivers, so the unfortunate newly-arrived British Airways representative and his wife were completely deserted by their entire Tamil staff. To add to their troubles, neither of them could drive and they were totally unfamiliar with the roads, so their chances of collecting what meagre rations were available were practically non-existent. Eventually the son of one of the members of the British High Commission came to their rescue and drove them around, but it was not an ideal welcome to Sri Lanka.

For Lif the wanton destruction of the city she had come to love was particularly shocking. 'It was a terrible sight to see so many fires around town and buildings and little shacks such as the one which housed the man who collected paper and bottles for recycling, being smashed to bits. Admittedly, many Sinhalese families were very good to their Tamil neighbours and took families in to their homes but there was still the underlying antipathy as expressed to Lif by a Sinhalese friend "Well, the Tamils had it coming to them, didn't they?" Lif remembered writing to a friend who was on leave in the UK at the time that life in Sri Lanka could, and would, never be the same again.

Underlying the unrest was the Sinhala Only Act, which had been introduced under the Premiership of SWRD Bandaranaike back in the 1950s. It was an act which made Sinhala the sole official language of Sri Lanka, relegating English to a secondary role. Sadly it was eventually to lead to the destruction of the post-independence 'ethnic status quo'.

Another impact of this act was a general exodus from the island of many of the Burgher families. This was a great loss as most of them were professional people, such as doctors, lawyers and accountants whose services were much needed.

Of course there were other factors which further heightened ethnic tensions, not least the government's internal colonisation policies. Thus there grew a determination to create an independent Tamil state.

The all-day curfew that was imposed briefly did, on one occasion, have its lighter side. Claire and Lif were getting bored being stuck in the house so they gathered a couple of male friends and decided to go and play golf, thinking nobody would spot them on the course. They managed to rustle up a couple of young caddies and set out on the course. They were at the furthest point of the course from the club house, where a helicopter seemed to be hovering too near for comfort and they all dived into the nearest bunker until the danger was over. Needless to say, they quickly made for home. Sadly some of the young Sinhalese caddies were rather ridiculed by their peers if they had not attacked a Tamil property, and so the problems escalated; it became a matter of honour to inflict damage and hurt on anything to do with the Tamils.

Claire and Lif in the meantime played hostesses to near neighbours and enjoyed many 'Curfew parties'.

Being a very loyal employee of the Meridien Hotel, Claire whenever it was possible went in to work. Many members of the hotel staff were not able to make it in to the City, so at one point Claire found herself working the switchboard, and one of the calls she received during her stint with the headphones was from the General Manager of the hotel, Stephan Pfeiffer, who was away in Singapore at the time. He was very surprised to find one of his executive staff doing such a humble job and Claire explained the situation, that there was nobody else who could do that particularly important job.

Eventually the 'state of emergency' was lifted and life returned, more or less, to normal, albeit with certain differences, but it was not the end of the troubles and altogether the civil war was to persist for more than a quarter of a century.

Shortly before all this excitement there was a royal red letter day for the Bostocks. It happened in October 1981, The Queen and Prince Philip had arrived on the island by invitation of the Sri Lankan Government. Although this was not, by any means, an official Royal visit, nevertheless the then High Commissioner, John Nicholas, very generously threw a party at Westminster House for senior British figures in the Colombo business world. Thus it was that Mark and Lif found themselves amidst the throng of the island's VIPs, ready to rub shoulders with the Royals. The date with the Royals was not without its stresses for Lif, particularly when she noticed, with dismay, that some of the senior ladies present were wearing gloves. She had not been asked to wear gloves and therefore assumed she and Mark were not due to be presented to the royal couple. Resigned to being merely a bystander, she therefore wormed her way to the front row of spectators, reasoning that that would be as close as she would get to Her Majesty. However, as the Queen moved past her, the High Commissioner whispered to Lif, "You will be presented to Her Majesty later."

In a state of high excitement, she rushed over to the other side of the garden to find Mark and tell him the exciting news. However, typical of the man, although he had known all along, he had not thought to inform his Royalist wife that their turn would come. The Bostocks had a wonderful meeting with the royal couple, which included some five minutes chat. Lif had to keep pinching herself in order to make sure that she was actually talking with the Queen just as if she was one of the Royal couple's good friends.

John Nicholas was knighted on this occasion at Government House, while his butler, Siniah, received the MVO. An amusing story was related by John Nicholas as to how Siniah had come to be the butler. He was originally employed by Mike and Ruth Thornton and in due course they passed him on to Sir Michael Walker the previous High Commissioner, who was delighted, especially since Siniah's predecessor had had to be dismissed because, while the Walkers were away on leave, he was found to be running a very up-market, air-conditioned brothel in the High Commissioner's residence.

Lif's previous, and only other, royal encounter had been at the end of December 1941 when her father, Captain Ronnie Mills, had been summoned back from duty in the Mediterranean to Buckingham Palace to receive his war medals at an investiture. Only two visitors tickets were awarded to members of the various families so, naturally, Ronnie's went to his wife, Sylvia, and Lif's brother, Ken. At the very last moment, one of those to be invested had a spare ticket and so Lif was able to join the family in the 'white and gold corridor'. Her memory is of being in the back row but right in front of the dais on which King George VI was standing. It was an altogether great experience for a ten-year-old schoolgirl.

It was also around this time, in the early 1980s that efforts began to be made to open up the Maldives, a double chain of some 26 atolls in the Indian Ocean, to tourism. In the early days the only way to access the islands was via Sri Lanka; and the only tourist agency was Walkers Tours – an off-shoot of John Keells. Consequently, Mark found himself heavily involved in the project aimed at bringing tourists to the archipelago.

One of the most influential among the Maldivian families, who were also connected with tourism, asked Mark if he would help them with developing the island of Gan, which had previously been home to an RAF station. The inhabitants of Gan had been highly trained by the RAF and with the closing of the station the authorities were concerned that due to lack of employment there could be problems leading to general unrest and it was felt that Gan and its people needed encouragement and most of all employment.

Consequently Mark went to tremendous lengths to help out. He got in touch initially with a company which could lengthen the existing, but inadequate, runway, with a view to it being transformed into a staging post for Concorde on its way down to Australia. He also made contact with the owners of a hotel chain which was prepared to invest in developing tourist accommodation on the island; and through a friend working for British Airways in Colombo Mark shared his ideas of making the island accessible to commercial air traffic. As all this research started coming to a head, more and more Ministers in the Male Government started to demand 'back-handers'. It was at this point that Mark's original contact told him that Maldivians would never believe that anybody would work for nothing and said that the only way that Mark would be able to prove his credibility and convince them of his credentials would be if he invested personally in a project of his own.

In those early days, all islands were leasehold only and the lessee had to be a Maldivian. Mark rather liked the idea of an investment there and accordingly was granted Kunfunadhu for his project. To get around the leasehold clause Mark's 'partner' (the legal lessee) was a man from Gan; Jaleel was short in stature and unbeknown to anyone, held a grudge against the United Kingdom for his supposed ill-treatment by the British. Mark only learned much later, and to his cost, that Jaleel had a chip on his shoulder.

Kunfunadhu was a much larger island than most but was at a considerable distance from Male and only accessible by dhoni which meant a long boat trip.

The first experience Mark and Lif had of the Maldives was travelling there by a Ceylon Air Force plane which had been organised by a friend, David Blackler. A number of American families were also on the trip. The plane was heading for Hulhulé Island (now Ibrahim Nasir International Airport), and midway across the ocean Lif looked out of the window of the plane and noticed to her horror that one of the propellers was gradually slowing down. One of the children onboard had got over-excited when visiting the cockpit and had bounced up and down and in the process had inadvertently hit a vital switch, the one which turned off the engine, with his head. Fortunately, the pilot was able to re-start the engine and on the homeward flight the seat-belt sign remained firmly on. In those early days of tourism, the Maldivians had little idea of money matters and everything from a can of Coca Cola to a two-hour boat trip cost one dollar. Things changed rapidly.

The Bostock family made several visits to Kunfunadhu and the one in December 1981 was quite memorable, as Lif recalled: 'Two friends of Gillian joined us, together with others and we slept in make-shift huts constructed of woven palm fronds (*cadjans*) and on camp beds. There was a girls' and boys' dormitory. The outside loo was a small square of *cadjans* to give a degree of privacy for the hole in the ground, and there was a white flag for users to hoist to indicate that it was occupied.

'One night one of the workers crept in to the girls' dorm and sidled up to the sleeping Gillian and whispered "Darling,

darling, give me a kiss". Poor Gillian was scared out of her wits and rushed out. The worker found himself at the end of the jetty the following morning with his bags packed and awaiting 'deportation' in disgrace. Thereafter a member of the party, Geoff Cox, slept across the doorway to the girls' dormitory to deter all unwanted intruders.'

Later on when the chalets had been constructed, Chris and Vicky Holloway and friends joined the Bostocks, having arrived in a very flash motor cruiser, courtesy of 'Hong Kong Gillie' who was looking after her boss's vessel. Gradually Kunfunadhu took on more of the look of a resort island, but still the problem of easy and quick access from Male remained.

Things were taking an unhappy turn on the business front and reached such a pitch that on one of his trips on his own, Mark convinced himself that Jaleel was plotting to have him thrown overboard as he made the night crossing back to Male by dhoni. As a consequence, Mark tied himself to the vessel's mast so that he could sleep on his feet without fear of being thrown over the side before he could defend himself.

Gradually the situation with Jaleel became untenable; Jaleel kept asking Mark for more and more money to pay mythical ship's chandlers. While Mark was negotiating for someone else to take over the lease, he was put under house arrest in Male, on trumped-up charges, all written in the local language, and therefore completely incomprehensible to a foreigner; but Mark was still required to put his signature to the documents, no matter that he understood not a single word save his name.

Finally, he told the authorities that he had run out of his heart pills and that they would be held responsible should anything befall Mark as a consequence of him not having his medication, unless they released him. This ruse worked, but all the same Mark confessed that he was still extremely nervous as he awaited the arrival of his plane to take him back to the safety of Colombo, and until it landed he made a point of hiding himself as best he could.

Now, Kunfunadhu is one of the most sought-after resorts and owned by the Six Senses Group and re-named Soneva Fushi and, no doubt, charging several hundred dollars per night. This was yet another instance of Mark's prescience.

The pain of the loss of Sandsend and the disaster of the Maldives misadventure gradually receded, and a few years after losing his bolthole in Bentota, Fate took a hand by steering Mark towards another little plot of paradise.

He happened to be accompanying some German investors who were on the look-out for a suitable beach property up the west coast, when he spotted another idyllic island, this one at the mouth of the Dedruhoya just outside Chilaw.

Mark kept this very much to himself, but it certainly seemed to be the answer to his need for a hideaway. The island was about 16 acres in extent and had been planted with coconut trees, but, as was the case at Bentota, it could only be reached via the river. The property belonged to a Muslim family living in Chilaw and the Bostocks soon began negotiations with Mr Moulana and his extended family for the purchase of Seedalopitiya (cool place of sweet water). Before the deal could be agreed many cups of over-sweet tea and 'sweet meats' had to be consumed by Mark and Lif.

It was some months before construction of a proper house began and, in the meantime, Mark and Lif happily spent weekends in a crude, small shack built from palm fronds. There they kept the most basic supplies, including two camp beds, a small cooking stove and a few items of crockery and cutlery. There were no other amenities, and even fresh water had to be scooped from shallow holes dug in the beach.

Initially access to the property was through the village of Korakopane, with a local fisherman then ferrying them across the river on his boat. Later on the family was able to use their own boat, leaving their car at the local ice factory under the care of Robinson, the manager. However, occasionally it was *just* possible, at certain times of the year, to approach the island via the beach and when this was possible Mark would insist on testing the Toyota four-wheel drive vehicle to the limit by driving through Korakopane village and then along the spit of sand which had formed across the mouth of the river. Lif said: 'It always proved to be a hairy adventure and our hearts were always in our mouths until we had arrived safely on the island.'

Once, during the early days at Chilaw, Mark was asked by a friend to look up his son, who happened to be on holiday in Sri Lanka with a fellow pupil from Eton College. The boys had been staying with a fisherman in his hut on the beach, and they must have been mildly surprised to find the chairman of John Keells was also spending his weekends in similar circumstances. The intention had been to show the boys the island and also to have a picnic lunch there. Accordingly Lif had not taken any eating instruments with them, nor mugs nor glasses for that matter. For some reason, Mark decided to change the arrangements and have the picnic on the way up to Habarana. All was well until it came to gin and tonic time for Mark, at which point he discovered that there were no glasses. The outing looked to be on the brink of disaster, with the alcohol there but no vessel from which to drink it. However, one of the boys was a member of the Magic Circle and he sidled up to Lif and said that he had some little goblets for one of his tricks, would they do? Thus the day was saved.

Korukapone was an interesting village where 90 per cent of the community was Roman Catholic and spoke a language of their own – a mixture of Sinhala and Tamil. The Bostocks soon made friends with the local schoolmaster, who pointed out that this language was a uniting factor, but it inevitably created problems for the children when they went to schools outside the village.

The population was all fishermen and when fishing became impossible on the west coast of the island, they migrated over to the Trincomalee area. The village priest was definitely the leader of the community, and once, when the Bostocks were having a problem with their coconuts being stolen, the priest preached a sermon on the subject and left no one in any doubt as to the identity of the culprit.

In due course work commenced in building a permanent residence on the island and this consisted of a basic central column of bricks and concrete, completely encircled by a wide wooden verandah on the upper level.

This verandah was supported on coconut pillars, through which a metal pin had been driven in order to ensure that the columns were partially in suspension away from the sand into which they were dug; this piece of engineering was followed on the advice of an architect friend (a Dane, believe it or not) who was currently working in Sri Lanka under the famous Geoffrey Bawa.

The ground floor of the new dwelling housed the kitchen and a store room, while upstairs there was a bedroom, a simple bathroom and toilet. The corrugated asbestos roof was completely surrounded by a gutter, with pipes leading down to large concrete water tanks to enable the Bostocks to collect the rainwater and provide the household with another source of fresh water. There was also a well which provided a small quantitiy of brackish water for the loos.

Quite apart from the construction of the house, Mark was also keen to improve the immediate surroundings of the property, while simultaneously developing the coconut areas, and so to this end he visited the local Coconut Research Board, which was based in the Chilaw area. There he bought what were called 'tall dwarf' plants, especially grown from good stock, and which were renowned as being prolific fruit bearers; being a dwarf variety meant it was far less hazardous when harvesting the crop. In fact when compared with harvesting from the normal, often very tall coconut palms, this variety was almost revolutionary. There was no necessity for a 'plucker' to tie his feet together with a piece of coir rope – made from coconut fibres – before putting his arms as far around the trunk of the tree as he could and begin to shin his way to the very top. Of course when a plucker arrived at his destination there was added peril for people standing below the tree, when the heavy fruit, nature's own missiles, would be tossed casually to the ground, woe betide anyone who stood in its path; this dwarf variety obviated the need for that, if one wanted a coconut all one had to do was merely reach up to pluck the fruit off the tree. When the nuts were harvested they were tied together and a sort of raft was formed and this would then be towed behind the boat across the river, then taken to market. Mark also gave some of these trees to the ice factory, whose land bordered the river as a "thank you" for allowing the family to park on their land each weekend. When the family returned in 2011 Robinson the manager was still there and said he remembered the family well and was reminded of them each time they harvested the coconuts.

The weather occasionally threw up the odd problem, for example, sometimes when the island flooded porcupines would regularly be washed up on the shore, and they proved to be a real menace because they would burrow down alongside the young palms and then eat the roots of the plants. Another animal that was sometimes in evidence was an estuarine crocodile but its existence in close proximity to the island did not deter the family from swimming in the river, somewhat to the horror of Graham when he found that his young daughters had been playing in the water.

Once Claire and Mark had to approach the house by boat because the floodwater was so high, but although the kitchen was temporarily underwater, the rest of the house was above the flood.

When the river flooded and the village was at risk, the villagers would come and dig out the sandbar, which allowed the flood waters to flow out to the sea.

As had been at Sandsend, so it was at Chilaw, with friends joining Mark and Lif for some fun times and simple living. Mark was at his happiest armed with a gin and ginger beer sitting on the balcony in a cooling breeze, looking out for 'the bird', a glorious White bellied sea eagle which used to frequent the opposite bank of the river.

17

AISLABY

Apart from all the home-making and the broking, the Bostocks were also working hard improving conditions and output at Aislaby, their tea estate. Production increased sharply under Mark's careful, innovative care and the time came when an SD (Assistant Planter) needed to be added to the staff. Naturally he and his family had to be housed, so a dwelling was built for him close to the factory which was situated at the lower end of the Estate.

Tony Whitham was the first Assistant Planter on Aislaby and he was subsequently to succeed Ronnie Lushington as superintendent. Tony was a 'local', as he explained: 'I had known Aislaby from the time I was about two years old, which was when my father Eric left Colombo to take up the position of Manager of Tidenham Barrow Farm, a 26-acre property owned by Foster and Agnes Marshall. The farm was about three miles beyond Aislaby, when travelling from Bandarawela. As we frequently drove into the town, we always drove past Aislaby, which with Malwatte were the only breaks in the *patna* lands of the area. Little did I imagine that one day I would work at Aislaby and at Malwatte.'

He had served a fairly thorough apprenticeship in the tea industry and had reached the position of assistant on the Haputale Estate by the time he joined Mark. It was Bobby Lushington who suggested to Tony's wife Nola that her husband should apply for the position at Aislaby.

Tony's first meeting with Mark, the day of his job interview, was etched indelibly into his memory. 'We were asked to meet Mark at Kirchhayn, and I duly turned up very smartly dressed in jacket and tie to be greeted by Mark in his blue shorts and tennis shoes.' And as things turned out there was no interview, as Tony explained: 'We just talked and had a few drinks and dinner and that was it.'

In early 1964 the Whithams moved into Greenham Bungalow on the estate and straightaway Tony fitted in perfectly. He recalled his immediate superior: 'Ronnie was a good boss, very laid back, and he gave me a free hand with all the field work.'

Aislaby was in competition with Uva Highlands, Neluwa and St James for both yields and prices, and the four properties were generally acknowledged as the best in the island. At the time of Tony's appointment all four estates were yielding around 1600 to 1700 lbs per acre. Mark thought it would be rather nice if Aislaby became the first to break the 2000 lb/acre barrier, which was the industry's equivalent of athletics' four minute mile at that time. They set about it with a will. Tony quickly realised that they needed many more hands for plucking if they were to bring in that size harvest, so he recruited about 500 village girls, which cranked up the work force to about 2 workers per acre, an unheard of figure in those days.

Tony said: 'It was touch and go, hoping for rain but not too much, and anxiously looking at the numbers each day. It was seven days work a week every week. By Christmas I was able to send Mark a cable saying: "2000 achieved" – Mark and Ronnie were both on leave at the time.'

Mark was very keen on diversification and so over the years the estate was to develop its own thriving farm, with chickens, pigs and rabbits, as well as a cow or two to provide sufficient milk for the bungalow and staff. The chicken farm (the laying birds were housed down near the factory as layers and broilers are not supposed to be near each other) had a de-feathering machine and after the birds were gutted and cleaned they were stored in a freezer room, ready for despatch to various customers. Pigs were also a feature of the farm, one creature among these, a very large boar, was named 'Mark'. Fortunately, they drew the line at naming the largest sow 'Lil'. Starting the farm was to prove providential, since it became an essential part of Aislaby Estate and Farm after nationalisation. Gillian remembers at the end of each term being sent curious parcels to bring back to Sri Lanka in her baggage allowance, including rubber 'fingers' for the de-feathering machine and a canister of bergamot essence when Mark was experimenting with flavoured teas.

Tony admitted: 'I didn't enjoy hearing the chickens squawking when they were being stunned prior to slaughter. We kept up regular supplies to Nuwara Eliya and Colombo in our insulated van. My father had run PPP (Poultry Proprietary) for many years.

'Our senior Field Officer Dharmalingam was in charge of the pigs, and one day I told him to select some good animals for breeding. I told him the pigs needed good straight backs and plenty of teats. I happened to go back to the piggery that day and heard a pig yelling blue murder with Dharmalingam astride of it, his hand in its mouth. "Dharmalingam, what are you doing" His reply was perfectly logical, given that the letter 't' has two pronunciations in the Sinhalese language; one is the straightforward t-sound, the other is the equivalent of a 'th' sound: "Why Sir, you told me to count the teeths."

Later on Dharmalingam left as he was having some difficulty with the workforce, and with Mark's help, he received a generous gratuity. He invested that in a guest house near Bandarawela, and it soon became popular with the Muslim population. Dharmalingam started to prosper, and very soon he was building a hotel in India at Mahaballipuram. I visited him and was pleased to see how well he was doing.'

Tony's initial impression of his boss Ronnie Lushington was reinforced the longer he worked at Aislaby. 'Ronnie was a real character,' he recalled, 'and one of the best story tellers I have come across. The trouble was that when I walked into his office he would regale me with all his stories, puffing away non-stop on his cigarettes – and I had little time then to get my work done, to say nothing about the effects on my lungs.'

There were other characters at Aislaby besides Ronnie. Tony recalled the Teamaker Dawson: 'He was an excellent craftsman, but had a fiendish temper. His assistants were always in fear of a tongue-lashing. When he tasted teas he would solemnly remove his dentures so that his palate could taste the glory of his tea.'

'Each week the phones would run hot after the tea auctions, and if we beat Uva Highlands we would be very pleased. During the flavoury season in July and August things would become very intense as the prices could rise by anything from tenfold to twentyfold, sometimes even more.'

It was not just tea which grabbed Tony's interest, he also developed a fascination with roses. 'While at Greenham I got a little nursery going in my garden. I did my own bud grafting, and very soon my collection of roses had grown. Bobby wanted her own rose garden up at Kirchhayn, so the pond at the bottom of the garden became a rose bed. The climate was perfect for the plants.

'We even grew mushrooms using the spent poultry litter as a medium. These were primarily grown for the use of the estate and Mark was thrilled to receive his share of fresh mushrooms.'

He also remarked on Kirchhayn's contribution to the estate provender. 'Kirchhayn had a wonderful vegetable garden and one year when there was a food shortage we even had a successful rice crop.'

But inevitably it was tea which occupied the mind for the majority of the time, and Aislaby found itself at the forefront of innovation in the industry. Tony said: 'Mark was ever willing to have a go at any half reasonable idea. We played around with rotorvanes, essences, paper tea sacks and also produced a cooling machine to keep the fermenting tea cool. Heat is the enemy of quality. We could do many things which the Tea Research Institute could not do, because the scientists were hamstrung by bureaucracy.

'The more money we spent on innovations the more money we made by way of higher yields and prices. Those were exciting days and hardly any "Tea Man "of significance visiting the island failed to come to Aislaby.'

Further improvements to the factory were the installation of a fermenting machine and a new way of blending the tea after firing. This method was subsequently used in many other tea factories around the island.

On the agricultural side, Mark was often thinking about the soil and how it could be improved as most of the fertilising programme concentrated on the tea bushes. He then conceived the idea of the widespread use of worms. This led the team at Aislaby, via Dr. Dicky of Wakehurst Place, to Wales, where an Irish vermiculture expert was introducing worms to slag heaps in order to convert them to pasture land. However, he said he was no expert in tropical worms and directed Mark to Professor Patrick Lavelle in Paris. Nothing daunted Mark headed off to Paris.

There he discovered that in order to cultivate worms one needed three generations – the adults, teenagers and babies. He also learned that different species of worms work differently; one kind works horizontally, ingesting the leaf mould while another works vertically, bringing the ingested leaf mould down in the lower levels of the soil. Undeterred Mark had a worm concrete 'tank' constructed and the worms were cultivated, working their way through the compost. Mark often used to delight in telling visitors to the estate that when they were deep-fried, worms made a tasty snack.

Claire carries on Mark's fascination with worms and their efficient way of improving the soil and cultivates her own "wormery" in Sydney. She finds it an excellent way of recycling her kitchen vegetable waste and the worms occasionally receive a "special treat" of her dog Mung's poo, but not too much as it was rather rich for the worms. The end result is a liquid feed which she uses on her flowers and vegetables.

Aislaby Estate flourished under the joint expertise of Mark and successive, far-sighted and imaginative estate superintendents, until it became indisputably one of the very best tea estates in the region with the most up-to-date and best-equipped factory in Sri Lanka. Mark's inventiveness was responsible for introducing a number of machinery innovations and manufacturing ideas to the factory and, with his great knowledge of tea-tasting and manufacture, the best prices were obtained for the tea. Some of these ideas have since become standard in many factories in Sri Lanka and India.

By this time A.J. Wickwar had died and the family took over Malwatte, his home. They enjoyed staying in the quaint old place. It was built of wattle and daub and became the setting of many happy holidays with the children. There was a ravine at the bottom of the garden which created a wonderful habitat for many species of birds. One of the traditions which the children enjoyed was to have their own version of a traditional Sri Lankan festival of '*pera hera*'. This festival 'The Festival of the Tooth' is a very grand affair and takes place in Kandy during July or August, it is a Buddhist festival consisting of dances and processions. There are fire-dances, whip-dances, Kandian dances and various other cultural dances. The elephants which participate are usually adorned with lavish garments, with the Temple Elephant actually carrying Buddha's tooth in a richly decorated casket. The festival ends with the traditional '*diya-kepeema*'. The *perahera* at Malwatte was a rather more modest affair, but no less fun for all that. The family would dress up in fancy dress, arm themselves with bells and various musical instruments and would then process down to the boundaries of the property which abutted the road. Some among the revellers would pretend to be the elephants – the main players in any *perahera* – a role which entailed waving an arm as if it were a trunk.

But beyond all the success of Aislaby and all the fun at Malwatte the storm clouds were gathering. For months there had been talk of a 'Land Reform Bill'. In November 1973 it became a reality and the Government of Sri Lanka nationalised Aislaby. The family was only allowed to keep barely 50 acres of the 1,000-acre Estate, which ran contrary to the law covering privately-owned estates; their legal entitlement should have been 50 acres per adult member of the family, which would have resulted in the family having 450 acres (i.e. nearly half the total acreage).

Before nationalisation, Mark had been seeking to set up a scheme whereby there could have been shared ownership between Mrs. Bandaranaike's Government and the Bostock family. Mrs Bandaranaike herself was most enthusiastic, but unfortunately the Communist element in her

Government was totally against the idea, and Colvin R. de Silva – the Trotskyist Minister of Plantations – announced that "nationalisation was an avowed policy".

Heartbreakingly, under Government supervision, the Estate gradually deteriorated as there was no investment in up-keep of machinery, purchase of fertilizer, workers quarters, etc. In fact, at one time, the Bandarawela town refuse was being tipped into the tea bushes in lieu of fertilizer, while a piece of machinery from the factory was removed in order for it to be converted into an air-conditioner for a Minister.

The next chapter of Aislaby opened when Kirchhayn bungalow became a government-approved tourist bungalow, thanks to the speedy action of the Minister of Tourism who was a friend of Mark, and this saved it from requisition. Mark was finally able to face up to the pain of re-visiting his beloved Aislaby and was then determined to make his 50 acres the best area of tea in the Uva district. As he had no control over the factory, sadly he could not use his great expertise to ensure the best possible manufacture of the green leaf, although he was always prepared to offer his advice freely when asked.

All the family was relieved that Mark's father Norman had not lived to see the requisitioning of his beloved Aislaby. He always used to sit on a special bench along one of the tracks and look at the view as the estate stretched out in front of him. His ashes are scattered at the very far corner of the estate, on the Kurukudde Division, which was a very special place for him. Mark informed Colvin R. de Silva, the Communist Minister responsible for Land Reform, that he had better take good care of Aislaby or Norman's ghost would haunt him. Sinhalese people being rather superstitious, the Minister apparently took this warning seriously.

Subsequently, the Government has privatised and re-privatised estates, but Aislaby has so far not returned to its former glory.

The terms and conditions of estate nationalisation were that the previous owner was permitted to take all movable assets – in particular any form of transport. However, later on the Government changed its mind and it was decided to requisition the transport belonging to the Bostocks. Mark told the Government representatives that all the vehicles should be brought down to Colombo in order to be valued by the Automobile Association. Down they all came and Mark secreted them in various stores owned by John Keells. Only the hand tractor was housed in the garage of Mark and Lif's home in Colombo. After a few days, a posse of police came round to Sweden Bank and demanded that Lif hand over the tractor. For some reason she was sure it belonged to John Keells and after a long argument, the Police went away.

That evening when the couple attended a cocktail party, Lif related the story to a friend whose husband at that time was the Governor of the Central Bank. The friend, Norma, was horrified and quite convinced that the Police would return and that it was essential the tractor was hidden.

She went off to have a think about it and came up with the suggestion that we should hide the machine in the Cathedral grounds which were in the vicinity of the house. Mark and Lif laughed at the very idea but later in the evening at home when they were enjoying a bowl of soup, they began to think 'why not'. So at dead of night, they hitched the tractor on to the back of the car and silently drove round to the Cathedral. Mark was very friendly with the then Bishop's Chaplain who lived on the spot and so rang his bell and asked if he could house the tractor. A very sleepy Kenneth asked if Mark was doing anything illegal and on assurance from Mark, he summoned a young 'podian' to open his garage door and in went in the tractor. It was housed there for many years and proved very useful when the newly-developed area surrounding the Cathedral was landscaped.

Tony Whitham also remembered that time. 'I arrived in Colombo to hear the news that the takeover would be on the following day. Having heard that these takeovers were fairly boisterous affairs, Nola and I drove back immediately and spent the night and early hours of the morning sending away as much as we could of the ornaments and furniture in Malwatte and Kirchhayn, especially items of sentimental value.

'I also tried to move out the new lathe from the workshop, but by then the word was out and the Police arrived in full force and put a stop to any more moving.

'I stayed on for two months as a Government Servant and was able to keep an eye on the assets. I then told the State Plantations Corporation that I was leaving and was promptly ordered to see the Minister of Plantations, Dr Colvin R. De Silva, a strong leftist. He asked me why I was not prepared to "take the Queen's shilling" and work for the Government. I told him the terms the Government was offering were poor and, in any case, I was emigrating to Australia. He was very understanding.

'Meanwhile, Mark was getting increasingly annoyed by the fact that the Government was using his machines, vehicles, type writers etc etc and hadn't paid him a cent. A plan was hatched and when I left Aislaby finally, I was to take with me all the vehicles on the pretext that I needed them all to transport my belongings. When the vehicles arrived in Colombo Mark arranged for them to disappear, and all hell broke loose. Finally the Government recovered all the vehicles and it has to be said that the authorities were definitely not amused.

'Mark had invested a great deal of money in his time in charge, building new worker accommodation, a hospital and maternity ward for the workers. We also had a sports club with a fairly decent cricket team, which took part in the local league. Our tea-makers, clerks and field staff used to double up as batsmen and bowlers in the evenings, and net practices were a regular feature.

'The Aislaby we knew is no more. While it had originally been a commercial venture, in fact it turned into much more, it had been a dream, an ideal – in short, a Camelot.'

The first Manager of the nationalised Aislaby estate was Ralph de Run. He had once been a Christian but had subsequently converted to Buddhism. Using his influence he persuaded the Japanese to build a Peace Pagoda, similar to the one in Milton Keynes on the estate. This was situated on the hill above the factory and a young Buddhist monk was put in charge. He was upset on hearing that the Bostock family had lost the estate, so much so that every day on his way to and from Bandarawela he would beat some sort of gong and intone prayers, asking for the estate to be returned to its rightful owners.

There existed a good relationship between Ralph and the Bostock family and he was very helpful in getting the 'short cut' road re-surfaced, again using his influence with a government official to access Kirchhayn bungalow.

Lif recalled: 'For many years Mark could not bear to go up to Aislaby until some dear friends, the Burleys, persuaded Mark and myself to join them at the Kirchhayn bungalow which they had booked for a weekend. One lasting memory is of a fiercely contested game of volley ball between the '40 acres' and the main estate workers in the rain and under a rather inadequate shelter made up of cotton saris. Anyway, this visit broke the ice and Mark became a regular visitor after his retirement in 1986 during his six-monthly stay on the island.

'After a series of assorted managers for the Aislaby Estate & Farm (as it became known), in 1987 Mark secured the services of Paul Manickam. Formerly a Head Clerk, Paul had previously been offered a training in tea planting in India in order to become an Assistant Superintendent. Paul was a most meticulous manager of the small property and continued to learn from the expertise of Mark. Moreover, he did all the jobs of a Head Clerk with no assistance.

'Mark continued to introduce many innovative ideas, including new folia spray for the tea bushes, composting, planting out new plants in a triangular pattern and soon the estate achieved the highest yield in the Uva District and subsequently received the 'Best Small Holding' award in 1991. The estate was visited by many Government officials, including the Minister of Plantations (Colvin R. de Silva) and the Chairman of Small Holdings Development Authority (The Sri Lankans have always loved complicated names for the various Government offices). Thereafter a flood of visitors came to see this 'wonder' property and Paul spent much time taking them round and explaining the many procedures that were done differently from other small holdings.

'On one occasion, Mark attended a meeting of The Ceylon Planters' Association. If anyone wanted to raise a question, they had to stand up and identify themselves by name and involvement in the tea industry. Mark stood up and proclaimed himself as a bought leaf supplier. It took some time for this to sink in to the audience and then there was a roar of laughter. After the Government takeover of course the family also lost our tea factory and thus we were obliged to sell the leaf to a neighbouring factory.

'Returning from a visit to India, Mark had filled his pockets with some very special coffee seeds and these were planted out in the 'nursery' and then at the right time transplanted in to the 'field'. This was a very special type of coffee, originally propagated in Portugal and thence smuggled in to India and later to Sri Lanka. This dwarf variety of coffee, known as Cattimore is a prolific bearer and has been a great addition to the estate.'

Mark and Tony were to be reunited in 1991 when Tony returned to his native Sri Lanka and joined Mark in his Victoria Golf Club scheme, becoming the Project Manager, and he was responsible for overseeing the development of the first truly international golf course in Sri Lanka.

The requisitioning of Bostock property and land did not stop with Aislaby. Mark tried to keep the Malwatte bungalow, not only for sentimental reasons, but because of the fact that it was surrounded by some of the best tea, but the Government allotted the Kirchhayn bungalow, and the area surrounding that, to the Bostocks. However, cruelly, after a few years it emerged that the Government also had its eye on the Kirchhayn bungalow and one day a junior cabinet minister who happened to be a friend of Mark's, came to him and said 'Sign this', to which Mark responded by saying that he never signed anything without reading the contents carefully. The Minister said there was no time to lose as he was about to go in to a Cabinet Meeting. As Minister for Tourism, he assured Mark that if he agreed to use Kirchhayn as a Government approved guest house, its future would be guaranteed. Thus it appeared that Kirchhayn's future was secured.

The family did manage to run Kirchhayn as a guest house, and quite successfully as well, however, despite many improvements and modernisations, there was no profit to be made; crucially there were never sufficient funds to support an overseas manager capable of running the place and keeping it up to international standards. By then all members of the family were either in the UK or Australia, and they soon learned that managing such a project from a distance of 5,000 miles was not practicable. So, with much regret, the family decided to sell their beloved Aislaby and this took place in 2008, fortunately that was eight years after Mark's untimely death.

Just prior to the sale of Kirchhayn an unusual visitor in the person of His Holiness Syedra Mohamed Berhanuddin – leader of the Dawdo Dawood Borah Community came to stay. This community originated in Egypt, then spread to Yemen, Pakistan and Sri Lanka. There are only about 550 families in Sri Lanka who are part of this community so it was seen as a great honour to have him visit the island. The head servant of Kirchhayn, Mohamed, was particularly thrilled with this unusual guest. His Holiness had specifically requested to stay at the Kirchhayn Bungalow but he had very exacting requirements which involved a major "make over" of the property. The whole house had to be re-carpeted in a rather ghastly electric blue; a temporary kitchen had to be built in the old chicken sheds; the Bostock Suite bathroom had to be totally altered to suit His Holiness as he was not permitted to bathe where an "infidel" had been.

Evidently his arrival at the Bandarawela railway station was more than a bit chaotic as a special dais had been set up to coincide with his carriage and the train driver specifically instructed to stop a few yards short of his normal halting place. Of course, he stopped at his usual place and all the "welcomers" had to make a mad dash along the platform to greet him.

Mark had, however, mentioned to his older sister, Eve, that he could foresee the day when it might be necessary to sell up. Despite many set-backs and many take-overs of property and business, Mark retained his enormous love of Sri Lanka and definitely regarded it as HIS country. He was determined and single-minded in all he did and his mind was full of new ideas and projects to the very end of his life.

18

FROM
TEA TO TEE

Owning one's own tennis court or swimming pool is a dream of many people, but Alex Poulson, a colleague and friend of Mark's, came up with a far more outrageous idea. It was the occasion of Mark's retirement from the Board of John Keells. Poulson, a Dane, had purchased Mark's shareholding in the company in accordance with the set of rules that he laid down, which is to say, all directors on retiring from the Board had to sell their shares in the Company. This was in 1986, and sometime after acquiring Mark's holding Poulson said, "Wouldn't it be marvellous to have our own private golf course?"

The thought appealed greatly to Mark, and he was given an even greater incentive when Poulson added, "You find the land and I will put up the cash and a further £100,000 'finders' fee!"

It just so happened that Mark already knew of the perfect site for a golf course, because during his days of visiting estates as the John Keells' manufacture expert he had ear-marked a particular plot of land as the perfect place on which to build a hotel for John Keells. He knew instinctively that the plot had great potential to be turned into a wonderful golf course. The land he had in mind had previously been a mixed farm, which he had visited on behalf of John Keells before nationalisation. Mark used to tell the manager at that time that it was a pretty rotten farm and that it would be much better served as a golf course.

When the Victoria Reservoir was eventually constructed, it entailed the damming of two rivers, in order to create the vast expanse of water. The resulting spit of land between the two rivers meanwhile had formed a peninsular which projected in to the Victoria Reservoir. Thus the land between two rivers was largely surrounded by water, while beyond there was nothing to be seen but the Knuckles range of hills.

Mark had already approached the Minister of Lands and Mahaweli Development, Gamini Dissanayake, and asked that if ever the land were ever to come up for private development, could he have first refusal on it. Needless to say, there were protracted negotiations with the Government in order to obtain a renewable 99-year lease.

This was finally achieved in December 1996, due to the tireless efforts of Tony Whitham, who had taken early retirement from his job in Australia in order to work with Mark. During these long years of heartbreaking negotiations with the Government authorities Mark would frequently repeat his dog Latin mantra to Tony Whitham of not letting the bastards grind you down.

By this time of course Mark himself was spending six months in UK and six months in Sri Lanka and so he could only advise from afar. The Central Environmental Agency caused the most delay with ridiculous objections such as if a golf ball were to be hit in the wrong direction, the dam might be damaged. Another objection put forward was that if wind surfing was permitted on the reservoir, the waves created might eat in to the sides of the reservoir. Now, float planes regularly land on the reservoir.

Despite the frustrations and endless trips that had to be made between Kandy and Colombo, Tony persevered. However, it was not until January 1997 that work could finally be started. And that, sadly, was too late for Alex Poulson, who had run out of money, so Mark was then left to try to sort out finance.

He duly managed to persuade several friends, and John Keells, to invest in the project; there was also a large contribution from Mark himself as well as from Aislaby Estates Ltd. A holding company was then formed under the name of Rajawella Holdings Ltd. All major share-holders in the Company were invited to have a seat on the Board.

But there were other ways to raise funding as well. The sharp-eyed Mark had studied the land extremely carefully and he had noted that there were areas in the 517 acres allotted which were unsuitable for the creation of golf holes, the terrain just not lending itself to tees, greens and fairways.

As a result Mark had these areas surveyed, and then they were divided up into building plots for residential housing. Mark's original vision anyway had been that Victoria would be an ideal retirement location, since there were no similar-sized areas that were ideally suited to conversion to a golf course-cum-retirement complex anywhere else on the island.

Fortunately the retirement homes idea caught the imagination of people and the Bostocks' good friends Derek and Vivi Samarasinghe were among the first to buy in to this arm of the Victoria project, together with Tissa Attapattu, Sohli Captain, Ken Balendra, Helmut Suchy and the Kailasapillais. The Samarasinghes purchased two blocks of the land, Tissa Attapattu three, this last on the basis of one phone call inquiring into the viability of the project. Then came another boost when John Keells took a sub-lease on a further 20 acres, with a view to possibly putting up a hotel on the land.

Initially Mark had been deeply worried about the shortage of funds before any outside interest had been shown in the project, so Lif had suggested that they should pray for financial help. Mark's response was typical of the man; he said that he had never thought it was good to ask God for help in personal matters. Lif disagreed, prayed, and then, a few days later, came the Samarasinghes' offer, naturally Lif claimed that it was in answer to her prayer.

Government permission sorted, cash in place, although it has to be said that cash flow, was, and still is to a lesser extent, a problem with Victoria, it was time to address the practical side of things, the construction of an international standard golf course. Again Fortune favoured the project, because Tiru Fernando, the younger daughter of Ceylon's most famous golfing family, Pinsiripala and Pam Fernando, had put forward the name of Donald Steel, the golf writer, to design the course.

Steel, in addition to having been the Golf Correspondent of The Daily Telegraph in the UK, is an acclaimed international golf course architect, and, having visited the area and fallen in love with the place, he readily agreed to undertake the design of Victoria golf course. So Mark, Tony, Tiru and Lif accompanied Donald and his young assistant, Martin Ebert, on a helicopter ride to view the land from the air. It should be mentioned here that Martin, although half Sri Lankan, had never previously visited the country of his birth.

The following day Donald announced he wanted to walk the proposed course. As he set off into the totally overgrown area, all that could be seen of him was his hat moving through the undergrowth. But once back in the hotel that evening Donald clearly had the whole lay-out of the course in his mind already. Lif recalled him saying, "You know that area where I said the 10th tee might be, well, I now think it should be moved slightly."

At that time Donald and Martin were working on creating a golf course at Horsted Keynes in Sussex for a Hong Kong Chinese millionaire, who had bought Harold Macmillan's property. Donald kindly invited Mark and Lif to play on this course to celebrate his 60th birthday. Lif accepted, but Mark preferred to travel round the course helping with the drinks' buggy. Previously Donald had suggested that Mark came and saw the work in progress and to see the 'shaper' of the greens at work. This expert (Mark Ely) subsequently flew out to Sri Lanka to initiate the shaping of the greens at Victoria. He was amazed at the dexterity of the local plant operators, but they had begun by having no idea of how to read a green plan or to follow Martin's very precise instructions on how fairways, greens and tees were to be contoured. So Martin would draw the plan and then would give instructions on the design to Tony, who would interpret them, before passing on these detailed day-to-day instructions to the machine operators, and setting the levels for them.

All the greens were planned in detail by Martin with changes in elevation measured in centimetres. Later, Martin would say that he had never had his plans so closely followed.

At a certain stage, Martin thought it would be fun to name the individual holes. The very tricky Par 3 at the fourth was named 'Tiru's Terror'. Lif was then invited to choose her favourite hole, which she did, but later cancelled her idea when she learned the hole was to be named "Old Bones". The reason behind this rather macabre name was that an area in the middle of the fairway had been used to bury some bodies, although this was not common knowledge locally and in fact it was only when a bulldozer uncovered a whole lot of bones that it became obvious that this was not a solitary human skeleton. The bones were quickly and discreetly re-buried in order to avoid an uproar over the apparent desecration of a burial site.

Meticulous work had to be done in order to bring the course up to USPGA standards. This included the purchase and importing from Australia of, not one, but *five* types of Bermuda grass – three of these were selected, one was for the greens, one was for the tees, while a third was used to create the fairways. These stolons had to be quarantined at the Peradeniya Botanical Gardens, Kandy, before they could be used. Different shapes of sand had to be scrupulously examined abroad in order to provide good drainage on the greens as well was retaining water.

The sieving of the sand to the required USGA size spectrum was a major undertaking. Each green required around 50 tractor loads of sieved sand which was brought in from Mahiyangana, about 60 km away. It arrived wet and the sieve meshes clogged up within seconds. There was no question of drying the sand in those volumes. Finally, in desperation Tony tried washing the sand through the sieve. Thankfully this worked, and by the finish more than 9,000 tractor loads of sand had been washed through the sieves, with the workers, standing knee deep in water, going flat out in shifts for 24 hours a day.

The grasses proved to be a good investment as the stolons could be transplanted to form new blades of grass and so they were self-perpetuating. The process of transplanting was very akin to tea-planting and the army of workers, the majority of whom were women from the tea estates, were therefore very adept at the job.

Years later, the Victoria Turf Management section of Victoria company has proved to be a good source of income, since many schools, sports grounds and Government organizations are keen to have this grass. The company was even asked to re-turf the Galle Face Green in Colombo which has exceptional wear due to it being the general evening venue for walkers and kit flyers. Tony Whitham explained: 'That original imported load of 10 bushels of stolons has now been multiplied thousands of times, and very profitable sales have resulted. Victoria can justly claim to have introduced modern turf varieties to the island.'

Before the course work had really started in earnest, Mark and Tony thought it would be a good idea to attend a golf convention in Singapore in order to promote Victoria. A friend, Reggie Candappa had a design company and he quickly assembled a brochure. Interestingly, the logo he designed is almost identical to the present one. Of course, a photograph was necessary, but unfortunately at that point Victoria had nothing to show off, so Mark, Tony, Tiru and Lif went to the Royal Colombo Golf Club and searched around to find a spot with no houses in view. There, under a tree beside the 14th green Lif took a photo of the three, Mark, Tony and Tiru.

The original plan for the course had been to construct 36 holes, but 80 acres had to be set aside in order to re-house the displaced farm workers, since their current homes were situated on an essential area of the course. Mark was pretty wily about all this, since he knew as soon as the workers got wind of housing being offered, there would rapidly be many hurried marriages of sons and daughters, who would also expect to be housed, so a census was quickly taken.

In the end a superb model village was created, and the residents were very proud of their new homes, and quickly built on their own kitchens, painted their front door and had plants at the entrances.

A short while before the inaugural tournament in 1999, it was realised that there were no facilities whatsoever for the players, not even to change their shoes, or wash their hands. However, on site, just above the current 17th tee, there was a truly dilapidated 'shack', which had previously been lived in, but was, at the time, inhabited mainly by goats and chickens. Thanks to the talent and untiring efforts of Nola Whitham, this was miraculously transformed in to a respectable clubhouse, complete with changing facilities. Nothing much has altered and the original plan of having a 'state of the art' clubhouse remains a dream for the future.

The inaugural tournament was held in 1999 and an impressive number, around 100 players, took part, mainly from the Royal Colombo and Nuwara Golf Clubs as well as members of Victoria. Tony Whitham remembered: 'Mark opened the course with a very respectable drive down the first fairway, and then went on to act as starter, frequently encouraging sluggards in his booming voice to "Get on with it."

Donald Steel and Martin Ebert also competed and Donald generously offered to sponsor the tournament in 2000. Thus the Donald Steel Tournament was established and later Martin donated the 'Ebert Pot' for the player with the best net score. Martin was somewhat taken aback when he asked his playing partner, who was a Nuwara Eliya Golf Club Member, what he thought of the greens compared with those constructed elsewhere to the exacting USPGA standards, and the reply came back, "I think our greens are better'. As Tony was to remark wryly: 'So much for the discernment of the Nuwara Eliya golfer.'

Victoria subsequently came to be regarded as the best golf course in South-East Asia, and there have been many sponsored tournaments held there since. In 2012 the first Professional golfers played there, competing in a Pro Am tournament for the Seniors; more than forty professionals took part, and the Winner was Mike Harwood from Australia. The local hero – Nandasena – came in a very creditable seventh. How proud Mark would have been to have seen that; and what a wonderful, and lasting, legacy it is, from him for the country of his birth.

19

THE END
OF
THE LINE

The beach house at Chilaw provided many happy hours for Mark, Lif and the rest of the family, not to mention their many friends. Mark was once more able to relax, enjoy his surroundings, and rid himself of any and all stress, but sadly these wonderful occasions were to be tragically cut short. It was in 2000 and Mark and Lif were anticipating a quiet weekend on their own, apart from Poomani, the Watcher (caretaker for the house). It was the Easter Weekend which happened to coincide with the Sinhalese and Tamil New Year.

The Bostocks were preparing for bed, and Lif had just gone to the bathroom to clean her teeth, leaving Mark sitting on the verandah, enjoying his last whisky and soda of the day. Lif then remembered hearing the familiar groans as Mark tried to lever himself out of his cane chair, but then she heard a thump and a splitting and cracking of wood. She rushed out to find Mark was no longer on the verandah, he had fallen to the ground below, cracking his head on a block of concrete. He was still conscious and very puzzled as to what had happened to him, but when Lif told him he had had a fall and that she was trying to get him to hospital, he said to her "Thank God you are here". Those were virtually his last words, apart from when Lif had finally managed, with help, to get him on to the deck of the boat, at which point Mark said to his wife, "I am tired".

Lif said: 'Once on the other side of the river, we enlisted the help of Robinson from the ice factory to get Mark to the car. We eventually reached the hospital, but he was pronounced dead from a ruptured spleen. I then had to go through the ordeal of informing the Coroner, going to the local Police Station and making a statement – all of which had to be gone through again the following morning. The faithful Poomani was an enormous support and he organised a coffin and transport to take Mark down to Colombo. Things were made much more difficult on account of all the public holidays. The driver later admitted he had been nervous from the moment he had dropped us off and left us on the island on our own, since he had heard a gecko calling a certain number of times, which apparently boded ill luck.

'How one is given the strength to go through such an ordeal is beyond belief and the full impact of what has happened strikes home later. I was even able to smile at the Coroner's obvious delight in pronouncing the name – Mark Cresswell Bostock.'

When Tony Oxlade revisited the island later he found a number of odd coincidences, the first was that the cane chair on which Mark had been sitting was the only one with a 'dodgy' leg; the second thing was that the wooden strut of the verandah, the one which had given way, with the result that Mark was sent tumbling backwards to the ground 12 feet below, was the only one that had been loose; the third element of the accident was that the block of concrete on which Mark had hit his head was the only one to be found on that particular spot, the rest of the ground under and around the verandah consisted of sand, on which the whole verandah had been constructed originally.

Lif adopted a fatalistic attitude to the whole tragedy in the light of the 'conspiracy of coincidences' uncovered by Tony Oxlade. 'It almost seemed that the accident was meant to happen,' she said. 'And anyway, it would not have been like Mark to go to his Maker in a normal way. Everything he did always seemed to require a touch of the dramatic. But in retrospect, the family has always been grateful that Mark never grew old with all the attendant problems of the aging process, instead he can be remembered for the vital man he always was.'

The funeral arrangements were made and the family began to gather in Sri Lanka, with Claire arriving from Australia within 24 hours of her father's death; she was closely followed by Gillian, Jenny and Chris (Holloway family) and Chris Thornton. Not long after that Lif's two sisters-in-law arrived together, "So I had wonderful family support," she said.

Having eventually obtained clearance to have Mark cremated, (the authorities normally not allowing cremation if the person has died under unusual circumstances) the family held a private service at the Crematorium (where Mark's grandfather and brother were buried) which was then followed by a memorial service in the Cathedral which despite the short notice and the fact that it was a holiday period was packed with people who had been associated with Mark, even going back to his early rugby playing days.

Gillian has recently reminded Lif of the amazing love and loyalty shown to Mark by those who came to honour him. Ken Balendra who later became Chairman of John Keells, insisted at the Crematorium of walking round the building three times, according to Hindu practice and he also ignited the flame as he didn't trust the crematorium staff. This is normally the duty of the son of the deceased and shows admirably the wonderful relationship between the two men.

Further loyalty was shown by the staff of Kirchhayn who hired a mini bus to come down to Colombo and went to pay their respects at the funeral parlour. The driver of the mini bus also asked the family if they would like him to sit with Mark 'as he looked so lonely'. It is the practice in Sri Lanka for the body of the deceased to be embalmed and dressed in their "best" in their open coffin so that the mourners can see them and pay their last respects. Kalimuttu, the long-term head servant to the Bostock family came down from Nuwara Eliya with his wife Mary and even hired a three-wheeler to complete the journey from Kandy onwards, a journey of many hours. Finally, but by no means least, the family spied a tiny little lady standing shyly by a pillar of the Cathedral and she turned out to be the girls' much loved nanny, affectionately known as 'Little Theresa'. She was greeted by Lif and the girls with much love and hugs.

Gillian was entrusted to take Mark's ashes back to England and he would have been amused to find that the chosen receptacle was an earthenware cooking pot or "chatty pot" which was taken through customs as hand luggage. Gillian was asked if she had any souvenirs and didn't dare admit she was transporting her father's ashes as a very special souvenir. He was subsequently buried in the cemetery of the delightful little church at Aislaby in Yorkshire with a grand view of the River Esk in the distinguished company of many Pymans.

Prior to Mark's death Lif had been planning to return to the UK in early May and she decided to keep to this schedule. Before that her brother, Ken, kindly flew out to Colombo especially in order to accompany her home and was also able to help her with, among other things, the emotionally difficult task of dealing with some of Mark's personal effects.

Lif said: 'I had no idea how tiring grieving can be. Doing absolutely nothing all day, I still felt tired. My level of concentration on reading did not extend beyond the first

Harry Potter book which the grand-daughters had lent me. However, life had to go on, and quite quickly I was able to pick up the threads of mine again.'

Once back in Crowborough, life began in earnest and Lif recalled one small incident: 'I remember going in to town down a little short-cut where I passed an elderly lady and I thought to myself, "I suppose I am now one of them."'

All Saints Church came to Lif's support and even gave her a job in the church office. Lif remembered meeting one lovely lady, whom she did not know at all, crossing the street and offering her sympathies and any help that Lif might need. Something Lif would never forget.

In many ways she considered herself blessed having been separated from Mark frequently throughout their marriage, due to the nature of their lives out in Sri Lanka coupled with the trips back to the UK, so, to a certain extent, she had grown used to organising her life on her own.

Also Lif loved living in England. The large and beautiful garden at Tree Tops was a great solace. She was quickly absorbed into the life of All Saints Church, and over the years took on more and more responsibilities, commencing with assisting Jim Wheeler who at that time was the part-time Administrator. Lif assisted archiving the church's paperwork prior to moving into the newly extended church. Through her involvement with the church she has over the years managed to build up a large group of the most amazing loving friends and supporters.

She was also very actively involved in what started as the Cancer Research Campaign. When she first became involved in early 1988, her brother Ken Mills was working for the Cancer Research Campaign as Director of Volunteer Fund Raising and kindly "volunteered" his sister to start a local committee in Crowborough. In all innocence, Lif fondly imagined at the time that this would be easy. She would invite her doctor, the bank manager and maybe members of the local Council to join. However, in the end none of these people accepted the challenge, so Mark and Lif had put an advertisement in the local Courier newspaper, to which quite a few people responded, including Phil Ronan and their long-term Treasurer, Les Bray who had also been "volunteered" by a friend.

Lif remembers that their first very modest fund-raising occasion was a Christmas card sale in the local Red Cross Hall and a coffee morning which raised £1,000. Things progressed rapidly and included a most successful sponsored assault course at the Army Camp in 1991. This was not only successful in being a good money raiser, but shortly thereafter Gwen Young joined the committee and has since proved to be a great stalwart. Another popular event was the staging of an art show – the brainchild of Gillian Nassau, Crowborough's second Mayor.

Between 2006/2008 the Cancer Research Campaign amalgamated with the Imperial Cancer Research Fund to become the main cancer charity under the title of Cancer Research UK. In all the activities, Lif continued to act as Chairman and chief organiser until in 2013 she finally retired, having served Cancer Research UK for 25 years. However, the Local Committee provided Lif with an extra dimension to her life after Mark's death and to the time of her retirement they had raised over £270,000.

The family also proved a marvellous support to Lif, and with annual visits to Sydney she was able to keep in touch with Claire and her family. Lif always loved these visits and many of Claire's good friends welcomed her in to their circle. Lif was also a Director of the Board which is responsible for the running of Mark's golf course project, and this role entailed regular visits to Sri Lanka, and so links with that island were maintained and were good occasions for catching up with old friends out there, as well as inspecting what property remained in family hands.

One of those trips back to Sri Lanka took place in February 2006 when Lif was clearly impressed with how things were, most notably at Kirchhayn, where the bungalow had been transformed into a desirable holiday destination. It was by now luxuriously appointed and was attracting plenty of bookings. Lif marvelled at what had been done and credited Rob and Ronnie Antill (Australian friends of the family) with a great deal of the hard work and thought that had gone into it. 'Ronnie had been doing great things in clearing and cleaning up all the staff quarters, old chicken processing room, etc *and* getting paid for old scrap metal which needed throwing away. Tony Oxlade had started the modernisation of the Kirchhayn bungalow, creating five suites which were named Bostock, Lushington, Wickwar, Pyman and Taylor. These were completely re-furbished by the Antills who stood in as managers for a period of six months.

'The swimming pool is a popular addition. The new grass for the tennis court and golf holes looks wonderful, and a dear old lady keeps it in excellent condition with daily weeding by hand.'

But it was still far from perfect. Rob pointed out to Lif that maintenance of the lawn tennis courts and the greens for the golf were too labour intensive for the staff presently employed, so he and Lif arrived at a pragmatic solution. 'So we both decided that the tennis court area could be used for general games such as croquet, badminton etc, and the greens as tees, with one's golf shot being aimed at an area just behind the bunker or on to the tennis court.'

Then there was the question of the lake, or rather its absence. Lif explained: 'The lake area was not filled with water as apparently the black plastic is not sufficiently strong and tears easily. We had an idea of concreting the bottom and then putting a rock wall up to a certain level with, possibly, rocks at random on the bottom of the pool so that at least it would not look unsightly, even if it was not over full of water.'

For all that, Kirchhayn was still able to attract guests, and by an odd coincidence, those emanating from the United Kingdom, used a booking agent based in Horsmonden, a village in the Weald of Kent and not all that far from Benenden, the Bostock girls' *alma mater,* it was also no distance from Crowborough, which made it conveniently placed for Lif, as she remarked.

'Two couples were there at the same time as me and all agreed that Kirchhayn was the highlight of their holiday and one of them tried to prolong their stay but would have had to pay a cancellation fee for their next stay-over. Both couples came through the same Agency in UK which is called Kerala Connections, and since it is based in Horsmonden, in Kent, I thought I might pay them a courtesy call.'

There was a memorable visit to Sri Lanka some five years later, when, to celebrate Lif's 80th birthday she, her daughters Gillian and Claire, and Gillian's two girls Catherine and Alexandra, took a trip down memory lane.

'It was a wonderful holiday', recalled Lif, 'We called ourselves the Famous Five and we all had a ball and were wonderfully hosted and feasted for two memorable weeks.

'Gillian was not at all impressed with Colombo's modernised airport, and much preferred the old higgledy-piggledy airport that she remembered from her schooldays. However, she was determined to 'party' from the very start, so the evening of the first day of our arrival we had the first celebration of many, generously hosted by Susantha Ratnayake the Chairman of John Keells at Keell Hall.' Catherine and Alexandra have always been rather dismissive when Gillian has told stories of Sri Lankan days, considering them too impossible to be plausible but the celebration that night was to be a turning point. Amongst the guests were many who had played active parts in these stories and to the amazement of the girls the events were repeated, most often with further embellishments by the participants so their truth could not be disputed. They were also extremely touched by memories involving Mark recounted by the people who had worked with him and the love they expressed for him.

Susantha also ensured that the family received VIP treatment, and that same evening they were all accommodated in the best hotel in Colombo.

The following day being May Day and a national holiday, the family did not want to be on the road anywhere so they all spent the day searching out the various homes where Mark and Lif had stayed for the first few years of their marriage. The first was difficult to locate since the surrounding area had been developed over the years but the second was to prove fascinating. As the group loitered outside the gates, a delightful Chinese gentleman and his wife came to the door and when it was explained to them why the group was there, they were invited in to the front room of what was now the reception of a Chinese medicine surgery. The lady of the house was a doctor of Chinese medicine and gave the family a "taster" of the cupping technique using sections of bamboo. Mr Chen not to be outdone by his wife asked if anyone played a musical instrument and then enquired if they would like to hear him playing the saw! It was a bizarre situation, sitting surrounded by Chinese herbs, listening to Sinhala songs and a Christmas carol being played on a saw.

The family home in Bullers Lane was hard to see as it had been surrounded by a great high wall and a raised security post. This was because the family had sold the house to Lakshman Kadirgama who was at the time the Foreign Minister. He had built a large swimming pool in the garden and used to take a regular evening swim. Sadly, on the last occasion, he was assassinated from an upstairs flat next-door by an unknown person. We learned that his widow still lives in the house.

Lif said: '*En route* to Habarana where my birthday was actually due to be celebrated, we visited our island hideaway just north of Chilaw. We managed to obtain the Certificate of Registration in my name and then proceeded to the island. We were horrified by the state of the house as all the roofing, guttering and wood-work had been removed leaving only the bare concrete central structure.

'However, we were exceedingly surprised when we went round to the back of the house to find the kitchen block intact and a photo of Mark on the kitchen slab with flowers and a sort of votive offering beside it.

'We also discovered a tin trunk with a small brass plaque with the name of N.S. Bostock and Mark Bostock painted in large white letters. We chatted to the couple acting as 'watchers' or caretakers, and we obtained various mobile numbers which had been painted on the kitchen wall. Clearly the family regarded the place as theirs, even though they were actually little more than squatters in our eyes.'

The "Famous Five" proceeded to Habarana, which was Lif's favourite place on the island and where they were to spend her birthday. The five of them were joined by the son of their very good friends, the Curchods, Jean-Michel and his wife Marie Paule who had come over especially from Switzerland for the occasion and another good friend Andy

Simpkin (who had earlier experienced curfew times in Colombo with the Bostocks and had competed with Mark in showing off his knitting skills) from Australia.

Lif admitted: 'I was thoroughly spoilt and reckoned I was at least 85 after the many celebrations we enjoyed.' She seemed to receive a special birthday cake at each stop. They were also able to take part in the Mark Bostock Memorial Trophy golf competition held at the Victoria Golf and Country Resort, with Lif handing out the various prizes.

The final celebration was in June back in Crowborough where they were joined by many friends and family members for a magnificent lunch – all the food for which had been cooked by Gillian for her mother. As one guest commented, it was wonderful to hear so many lovely things being said about Lif in her presence rather than as normally happens with eulogies being given at a funeral.

Lif continues to enjoy a happy and busy life in Crowborough and is ever grateful for all the support and love she receives. She became more stoical as she sailed into her eighties and said: 'I have learned that it is no good having regrets and allowing myself to fret at the 'take-over' of various family assets by different Governments.

'It is far more important to have the wonderful and happy memories of the 'golden days' spent in Ceylon/Sri Lanka, which are to be treasured. And there remain many opportunities to renew and maintain friendships with old 'Ceylon' friends at various get-togethers in London.'